PAKISTAN'S ISLAMIST FRONTIER

Islamic Politics and U.S. Policy in Pakistan's North-West Frontier

BY JOSHUA T. WHITE

PAKISTAN'S ISLAMIST FRONTIER

Joshua T. White, *Pakistan's Islamist Frontier: Islamic Politics and U.S. Policy in Pakistan's North-West Frontier*, Religion & Security Monograph Series, no. 1 (Arlington, VA: Center on Faith & International Affairs, 2008).

Copyright © 2008 by the Center on Faith & International Affairs at the Institute for Global Engagement.

Printed in the United States of America.

First published November 2008 by the Center on Faith & International Affairs at the Institute for Global Engagement.

This monograph may not be reproduced in whole or in part (beyond copying allowed under Sections 107 and 108 of U.S. Copyright Law and excerpts by reviewers for the public press) without the written permission of the publisher.

Please direct correspondence to CFIA,
P.O. Box 12205, Arlington, VA 22219-2205.
Email: jwhite@cfia.org.

Report available at: http://www.cfia.org/go/frontier/

ISBN: 978-0-615-22586-9
ISSN: 1945-3256

RELIGION & SECURITY MONOGRAPH SERIES
NUMBER ONE

PAKISTAN'S ISLAMIST FRONTIER

Islamic Politics and U.S. Policy in Pakistan's North-West Frontier

BY JOSHUA T. WHITE

CFIA | Center on Faith & International Affairs

ABOUT THE AUTHOR

Joshua T. White is a Research Fellow at the Center on Faith & International Affairs and a Ph.D. candidate at The Johns Hopkins University School of Advanced International Studies (SAIS) in Washington. His research focuses on Islamic politics and political stability in South Asia. He has been on staff with the Institute for Global Engagement since 2001, and spent nearly a year living in Peshawar, Pakistan in 2005/6. He returned to Pakistan in the summers of 2007 and 2008 as a Visiting Research Associate at the Lahore University of Management Sciences. He has presented his findings in various academic and policy fora; has been interviewed on BBC, Voice of America, and Geo News; and in February 2008 participated in the U.S.-sponsored election observer delegation to Pakistan.

Mr. White graduated *magna cum laude*, Phi Beta Kappa from Williams College with a double major in History and Mathematics. He received his M.A. in International Relations from Johns Hopkins SAIS, where he concentrated in South Asia Studies and International Economics. Upon graduating from SAIS, he received the 2008 Christian A. Herter Award, the school's highest academic honor. He has co-authored a chapter in *Religion and Security: The New Nexus in International Relations*; and has written for *The Nation* (Pakistan), *The Review of Faith & International Affairs, Christianity Today, The Wall Street Journal Asia, Current Trends in Islamist Ideology*, and the journal *Asian Security*. He has also been active in promoting Christian-Muslim dialogue, and participates in interfaith events in both the United States and Pakistan.

ACKNOWLEDGEMENTS

For their encouragement, assistance, and criticism, I would like to thank Walter Andersen, Qibla Ayaz, Patrick Bean, Jonah Blank, Stephen Cohen, Christine Fair, Thomas Farr, Asif Gul, Lakhan Gusain, Mary Habeck, Rebecca Haines, Theodore Hamilton, Dennis Hoover, Adnan Sarwar Khan, Sunil Khilnani, Daniel Markey, Kimberly Marten, Mariam Mufti, Anit Mukherjee, Rani Mullen, Haider Mullick, Shuja Nawaz, Philip Oldenburg, Rasul Bakhsh Rais, Philip Reiner, Hasan-Askari Rizvi, Mano Rumalshah, Naeem Salik, Matthew Scott, Niloufer Siddiqui, Daniel Simons, Allyson Slater, Brian Smith, Chris and Priscilla Smith, Mohammad Waseem, Marvin Weinbaum, Anita Weiss, the staff of the American Institute of Pakistan Studies, and many others who wish to remain anonymous. The conclusions which follow are, needless to say, entirely my own.

I am also deeply grateful to my parents in Oregon, who have modeled for me the religious life; my sister in Mongolia, who is more adventurous than I will ever be; my dear *nana* and *nani* in California, who introduced me to international relations; my mentors Bob, Margaret Ann, and Chris Seiple, who continue to inspire; and my friends at the Church of the Resurrection, who are fellow sojourners in the truest sense.

Finally, I would like to say a word of thanks to my many friends in the Frontier — students, journalists, bureaucrats, politicians, businessmen, activists, clerics, and scholars — who showed me the very finest in Pashtun hospitality and pushed me, time and again, to see past sensationalism and stereotypes. *Main ap ka shukr guzar hun.*

— *Joshua White*

CONTENTS

ABOUT THE AUTHOR

ACKNOWLEDGEMENTS

CONTENTS

PREFACE 1

EXECUTIVE SUMMARY 3
    Islamic Politics, Counterinsurgency, and the State
    The Frontier, 2001–2008: Evaluating Islamic Politics
    The Present Crisis: U.S. Policy Recommendations

INTRODUCTION 11
    The Changing Frontier
    Key Questions
    Project Scope
    Research Methodology
    A Note on Geography and Governance

GLOSSARY OF KEY TERMS 17
    Map of Pakistan's NWFP and FATA

THE RISE AND SCOPE OF ISLAMIC POLITICAL INFLUENCE 23
    Pre-1947: Religio-political Movements
    Pre-1947: The Emergence of Islamist Parties
    1947–69: State Formation and Islamic Identity
    1970–77: Islamists and Electoral Politics

1977–88: Zia ul-Haq and Islamization
1988–2002: Fragmented Politics
Patterns of Islamic Politics

THE MMA'S ISLAMIST GOVERNANCE 47
The Rise of the Muttahida Majlis-e-Amal
The Islamization Program: Ambitions and Realities
Islam as Din: *The Islamization Agenda Writ Large*
Constraints on Islamization
In Summary: The Limits and Lessons of Islamist 'Moderation'

NEW ISLAMISTS AND THE RETURN OF PASHTUN NATIONALISM 85
The Rise of the Neo-Taliban
The Return of Pashtun Nationalism

U.S. POLICY TOWARD THE FRONTIER 101
Pre-2002 Historical Context
Political Engagement
U.S. Assistance to the Frontier

POLICY RECOMMENDATIONS 117
Strategic Context
Political Engagement
Public Diplomacy
Security and Counterinsurgency
Governance Reform in the NWFP
Governance Reform in the FATA
Aid and Development
Conclusion: Toward Political Mainstreaming

EPILOGUE: FRONTIER 2010 157
Addressing the NWFP: New Security Cooperation
Addressing the FATA: Counterinsurgency and MRZs

PREFACE

This monograph is the first in a series by the Center on Faith & International Affairs (CFIA) that will examine the intersection of religion and security issues in a global context. The Center has for several years been at the forefront of this topic. In 2003 it sponsored a conference which examined the role of religion and religion policy in political and social stability — an event which formed the basis of a book, *Religion and Security: The New Nexus in International Relations*.[1] The Center's Religion & Security Research Program builds on this initial work and, by way of international conferences, special reports, and CFIA's journal *The Review of Faith & International Affairs*,[2] has taken the lead in examining this critical issue from various regional and religious perspectives.[3]

A multi-faith initiative, the Center conducts this research with the conviction that the free exercise of religion, practiced peacefully, can contribute in profoundly positive ways to a stable social and political order; but also that states must take seriously, and deal intelligently, with the social and security implications of religious extremism. The Center exists, in part, to help scholars, policymakers, and practitioners strike this critical balance, and encourage discussion about the changing role of religion in global affairs.

The Center operates as an education and research program of the Institute for Global Engagement (IGE), a faith-based global affairs think tank which since 2000 has worked to promote sustainable environments for religious freedom and sponsor innovative international programs that focus on the intersection of religion, law, and security issues. It was an IGE initiative which invited NWFP Chief Minister Akram Khan Durrani to Washington in 2005 for discussions regarding political Islam in the Frontier; and which resulted in Joshua White's reciprocal trip to Peshawar as part of a small delegation. Joshua's subsequent stay in Peshawar, and his extended interaction with religious and political elites throughout the Frontier, formed the inspiration for this research project. Many of the themes and recommendations which appear below were first outlined by the author at a presentation in Washington in November 2007, which was jointly sponsored by CFIA and the South Asia Studies program of The Johns Hopkins University School for Advanced International Studies.

It is our hope that this monograph proves to be a valuable resource to both scholars and policymakers as they seek to understand the changing nature of Islamic politics in Pakistan's Frontier.

— *Dennis R. Hoover, D.Phil., and Chris Seiple, Ph.D., series editors*

NOTES:

1   Robert A. Seiple and Dennis R. Hoover, *Religion and Security: The New Nexus in International Relations* (Lanham, MD: Rowman & Littlefield, 2004).
2   For more information on the Review, see http://www.cfia.org/.
3   In 2007 the Center also sponsored, in partnership with the Carnegie Endowment for International Peace and the Institute for Public Policy in Bishkek, a conference in Kyrgyzstan on religion and security in the Central Asian context.

EXECUTIVE SUMMARY

ISLAMIC POLITICS, COUNTERINSURGENCY, AND THE STATE

Pakistan's western Frontier has been a geographic and ideological focal point for "religious" extremism for nearly thirty years. It served as a staging ground for *mujahidin* operations against the Russians in Afghanistan throughout the 1980s. It was the birthplace of al Qaeda in 1988, and the Taliban movement in 1994. More recently, over the last several years, **a "neo-Taliban" insurgency has emerged in the Pak-Afghan border areas which has grown into a complex religio-political movement with three distinct but overlapping objectives.** One is focused westward on fueling the Afghan conflict and overturning the Karzai government. A second is oriented globally toward providing a safe haven for al Qaeda and its affiliates to plan attacks against Western interests. And a third is focused on Pakistan itself — on carving out a sphere of influence within the "tribal" agencies of the Federally Administered Tribal Areas (FATA) and the nearby "settled" districts of the North-West Frontier Province (NWFP) for the establishment of Islamist rule, and on destabilizing the Pakistani state so as to disrupt its cooperation with the U.S. and Western allies.

Focusing on this third objective of the neo-Taliban movement, **this monograph examines in historical perspective the interaction between Islamic politics and the state in the Frontier,** paying particular attention to the NWFP proper and the nearby settled-tribal border regions. Although the analysis largely brackets a number of important bilateral and regional issues — such as the challenge of strengthening counterterrorism cooperation; improving Pak-Afghan interaction on border issues and larger regional questions; dealing with concerns over Pakistan's lack of strategic commitment to rooting out militant groups; and interacting with a fragile civilian government in Islamabad — it seeks to provide a framework for understanding the religious and political dynamics which are critical to the development of any successful U.S. strategy in the Frontier.

The narrative begins with an historical review of Islamism in the Frontier, highlighting several recurring patterns which shed light on contemporary trends. Against this backdrop, the monograph goes on to analyze the five-year tenure (2002–2007) of the Muttahida Majlis-e-Amal (MMA) Islamist government in NWFP — which represented the first extended attempt at actual governance by religious parties in Pakistan's history — and review the ways in which it shaped the current political environment. This analysis is followed by a discussion of the MMA's decline over the last year, the rise of the neo-Taliban insurgency, and the return of Pashtun nationalist politics. **The concluding chapters examine the history of American interaction in the Frontier, and recommend policies by which the U.S. might work with the government of Pakistan** to implement programs which deny insurgents a foothold in the settled areas of the Frontier; buttress the legitimacy of the state in dealing with religious and militant groups; increase the political utility and long-term sustainability of American development assistance; and address the "governance deficit" in both the settled and tribal areas in such a way as to lay the groundwork for more robust state influence and counterinsurgency planning.

Given the upsurge in attention devoted to the hard-core Tehrik-e-Taliban-e-Pakistan (TTP) militancy in places such as Waziristan and Bajaur, an analysis which focuses on Islamic political behavior in the NWFP might at first seem to be out of step with current crises. But this could not be further from the truth: **religio-political dynamics in the Frontier are arguably more important than ever before.** While Pakistan and the United States may increasingly resort to military action against TTP and other insurgent groups, military efforts alone will ultimately prove insufficient in producing a stable political order that satisfies the strategic objectives of either country.

Ultimately, counterinsurgency is about incentivizing political endgames. In the Frontier, this requires a much more robust and comprehensive policy focus on local governance, politics, and even religion. Many U.S. officials have come to adopt a jaundiced view of "political solutions" in the Frontier — believing that they too often serve to empower religious parties, militants, or both. In this the U.S. is often correct, but also complicit: American patronage has heavily privileged the Pakistani military, and done little to strengthen the kinds of civilian institutions that are necessary to provide a counterweight to both religious politics and insurgent mobilization.

A focus on the settled areas of the Frontier is also long overdue. While the neo-Taliban insurgency remains heavily dependent upon bases deep in the FATA, **the movement's center of gravity is gradually becoming more diffuse, blurring the distinction between settled and tribal regions.** The NWFP has been rocked by a steep rise in militant activity over the last two years, and increasingly resembles the "ungoverned" tribal areas. Political reforms in the FATA, on the other hand, are likely to make the tribal areas look more like the settled regions by introducing regular forms of political activity. This convergence makes the case for the development of counterinsurgency programs which operate across settled and tribal lines, and which deny political space to new "religious" insurgent movements.

THE FRONTIER, 2001–2008: EVALUATING ISLAMIC POLITICS

The limits and lessons of Islamist 'moderation'

The religious parties' five year tenure leading the NWFP government, from 2002 to 2007, represents a valuable case study of the ways in which involvement in the political process can serve to shape — and ultimately moderate — Islamic political behavior. Rather than serving as the vanguard of Taliban-like rule in the Frontier, as many observers had feared, the MMA instead became relatively pragmatic and found its Islamist agenda limited by both internal and external pressures. **The lessons of the MMA's transformation remain deeply relevant in the Frontier, even following the alliance's defeat in February 2008.** Religious parties will continue to play a significant role in NWFP politics, particularly if and when their right-of-center patrons among the PML-N return to power in Islamabad. The United States, which has generally avoided engagement with the religious parties, also has lessons to learn from the constructive role that the international community played in shaping the MMA's Islamist experiment.

Understanding the mainstream-militant divide

The rise of the neo-Taliban insurgency since 2005 has deeply complicated the relationship between mainstream religious parties of the MMA, such as the Jamaat-e-Islami (JI) and the Jamiat Ulema-e-Islam (Fazl) (JUI-F), and more militant organizations such as the TTP. While these two kinds of Islamists often share a common political discourse (e.g., regarding the West and the *shariah*) and retain many informal linkages, **the religious parties are increasingly ambivalent about the goals of the neo-Taliban, and threatened both directly and indirectly by the movement's expansion** into areas which were traditionally dominated by "democratic Islamist" groups. This realignment has reduced the influence of parties such as the JUI-F over the younger generation of *madrassah* graduates (many of whom are now easily recruited to militant groups), but has also created new common interests between the religious parties and the state in channeling discontent into the formal political process.

Insurgency as local politics

Just as analysts in 2002 made the mistake of reading the MMA through the lens of the Afghan Taliban, and thus underestimating the degree to which religious parties would be shaped by local political interests, so today observers often make the mistake of reading the neo-Taliban insurgency narrowly through the lens of al Qaeda and the Waziri militant networks. In doing so they again tend to underestimate the ways in which **these insurgent groups and their agendas are woven deeply into the fabric of both local and regional politics.** Neo-Taliban organizations operating in places such as Swat, Khyber, Darra Adam Khel, and South Waziristan — while all linked — are also quite distinct and require unique strategies on the part of the government. While there is clearly a unifying ideological dimension to the insurgency, it nonetheless remains highly fragmented and dependent upon local grievances.

Legitimacy and 'peace deals'

The Waziristan accords in 2006, signed by the Pakistan army and local militants, demonstrated that "successful" negotiations with neo-Taliban groups can easily end up as strategic failures. American policymakers, however, have been slow to recognize that the converse can be equally true. The "failed" peace deals in Swat in the spring of 2008 were in many ways effective, in that they demonstrated the government's good faith and created political space for the state to undertake strong action when the militants reneged on their commitments. **While some agreements with militants are clearly counterproductive, not all peace deals are created equal.** Negotiations can contribute to a larger strategy of delegitimizing Islamist insurgent activity.

The false 'secularism vs shariah' debate

The MMA's defeat in the February 2008 elections sparked optimism that secular nationalism would replace religious politics in the Frontier. The Awami National Party (ANP) took advantage of public disillusionment with the Islamists' governance and with their inability or unwillingness to stem the rising tide of militancy. **The nationalists' victory, however, says more about cyclical politics and anti-incumbency sentiment than it does about political Islam.** The ANP-PPP coalition government, vulnerable to criticism from the right-of-center parties, has in fact adopted a religious rhetoric of its own, and promulgated new *shariah* regulations in an attempt to undercut public support for Islamist insurgent groups.

Local governance and Islamism

The rise of a new, militant Islamism in the Frontier is rightly attributed to political, ideological, and demographic factors. But comparatively less attention has been paid to the internal and structural weaknesses of the state which opened the door to insurgent influence. **Musharraf's 2002 governance reforms inadvertently facilitated the rise of new insurgents by crippling the state's ability to respond to threats at the local level,** and by further bifurcating administration of settled and tribal regions. The government's consistent failure to follow through with basic governance reforms in the FATA has also weakened its hand against groups which have established a "religious" basis of legitimacy in the tribal areas.

THE PRESENT CRISIS: U.S. POLICY RECOMMENDATIONS

American policy toward the Frontier has focused heavily on counterterrorism objectives in the FATA. The spreading insurgency, however, calls for a more integrated and creative agenda designed to bolster the state's political legitimacy and improve its capacity to respond to new threats. This means **crafting policies which encourage local communities to side with the state and against Islamist insurgents.** These policies, which may take distinct forms in the FATA and the NWFP, must integrate political engagement, public diplomacy, security programming, and development assistance.

Broadening political engagement

Throughout the Musharraf era, American political engagement was tentative and overly focused on a few elites. Although this is slowly beginning to change, it is important that the U.S. continues to find practical ways to signal its commitment to civilian governance, institutionalize indirect support to moderate parties in the Frontier such as the ANP, and retool its bureaucracy for long-term engagement with Pakistan. **American diplomats also need to make greater efforts to engage with right-of-center and religious parties.** Regular, consistent interaction with parties such as the PML-N and JUI-F would, ironically, help to normalize and depoliticize the interaction, and allow the U.S. to be better prepared for political realignments which may bring these parties back into power.

Refocusing public diplomacy

America's public diplomacy strategy is often overly focused on trying to reduce anti-Americanism. **The focal objective of U.S. public diplomacy in Pakistan should be to encourage Pakistanis to see cooperation against militancy and extremism as being in their own interest.** This requires that U.S. politicians — and not just diplomats — adopt a language of common interests and common threats; avoid framing the neo-Taliban insurgency in religious language; and find ways to highlight the bleak realities of insurgent "governance" in both the settled and tribal areas. There are also opportunities for the U.S. to promote track-two dialogues on issues of religion and on the role of religious leaders in fostering social and political stability. And rather than interacting with those Muslim leaders who are moderate by the standards of American liberalism, the U.S. must instead seek out interlocutors who are both moderate and influential in their *own* contexts.

Planning for counterinsurgency in the NWFP

Communities in the settled areas of the Frontier increasingly view local neo-Taliban groups as criminal enterprises rather than legitimate religious movements, and have in some areas begun pushing back against insurgent advances. The U.S. should work with the provincial government to take advantage of this trend by **funding and equipping rapid-response police forces which could supplement and support community-based *lashkars*; as well as programs which address local discontent over the judicial system** — discontent which the insurgents often use to their advantage. American policymakers should also encourage reform of provincial and local governance frameworks in the NWFP which might improve the state's capacity to respond to militancy, particularly across complex settled-tribal boundaries.

Planning for counterinsurgency in the FATA

U.S. support for counterinsurgency efforts in the FATA has been focused largely on the provision of equipment and training to the Frontier Corps. This support is worthwhile, but it should not be confused with promotion of actual counterinsurgency, which turns on political contestation over government legitimacy. **Absent institution-oriented governance reform in the FATA, successful and sustainable counterinsurgency activities are effectively impossible.** The United States should take the lead in organizing an expanded and more robust Friends of Pakistan consortium which could serve as an umbrella organization for multilateral development efforts in the FATA. This consortium should then work with the government of Pakistan to promote the establishment of Model Reform Zones (MRZs) in the tribal areas which would integrate critical governance reforms (e.g., elected councils and judicial access), highly concentrated and visible development programming, stepped-up security presence, and political incentives in such a way as to incrementally build the legitimacy of the state and create a demonstration effect throughout the FATA.*

Leveraging fragmentation

The Pakistani government has a long history of taking advantage of cleavages within and among tribal structures. **In the wake of the "Anbar Awakening" in Iraq, American policymakers have discussed whether similar strategies might be successful in Pakistan.** Carrying out a tribe-oriented Anbar model in and around the FATA would pose real challenges on account of the internally fragmented, egalitarian, and increasingly entrepreneurial nature of the Pashtun tribal system. Although tribal *lashkars* may prove to be useful in pushing back neo-Taliban advances in some areas, and should be supported by the state when they do so, these *ad hoc* alliances are likely to disintegrate quickly or even turn against the government. Any effort to take advantage of fragmentation in the Frontier must integrate political strategy with tactical approaches *from the outset* and, as argued above, should be oriented around a concerted program to incentivize tribal communities and relatively moderate Islamist groups to integrate into the political mainstream.

Increasing the effectiveness of development

Just as successful counterinsurgency campaigns require institutional frameworks, so U.S. development programs in the tribal areas need to come to terms with the massive "governance gap" in the FATA. **Much of the USAID programming in the FATA is innovative, but is unlikely to be sustainable or politically effective.** Given the scope of the American aid commitment in the FATA, policymakers should insist that broader governance issues are concurrently put on the table. The U.S. government should also develop plans to direct more aid to the NWFP proper,

---

*For more on the MRZ concept, see "Epilogue: Frontier 2010."

especially the border areas adjacent to the FATA; and explore skills training programs in partnership with moderate *madrassah* networks and local universities situated in the southern part of the province.

CONCLUSION

As the United States looks toward formulating a more comprehensive strategy in the region, it would do well to recognize that Islamism in the Frontier remains highly fragmented — not only between those groups which participate in the democratic process and those which contest the legitimacy of the state, but also between those which have ideological or transnational agendas and those which simply operate in the realm of local politics. **Solutions to the problems posed by illiberal or insurgent Islamism ultimately require political mainstreaming.** This, in turn, calls for legitimate and capable state institutions — both civilian and military — which can set the political boundaries for Islamist participation, and respond effectively to new and unexpected forms of "religious" insurgency.

INTRODUCTION

THE CHANGING FRONTIER

Pakistan's North-West Frontier Province (NWFP) is increasingly a geographic and ideological focal point for "religious" extremism. Bordering Afghanistan and the troubled Federally Administered Tribal Areas (FATA), the NWFP has experienced a social and political shift over the last two decades toward conservative, and sometimes militant, Islam. The overwhelming success of the Muttahida Majlis-e-Amal (MMA) Islamist alliance in the 2002 NWFP provincial elections — an alliance dominated by conservative religious leaders who espoused anti-American rhetoric and shared an ideological affinity with the Taliban — appeared to many to signal a shift toward a "Talibanized" Frontier inimical to both Pakistani and U.S. long-term interests in the region.

That narrative, however, turned out to be far too simple. The reality which has unfolded over the last six years has instead been unexpectedly complex. Rather than acting in the radical mold of the Afghan Taliban, the MMA bent to the exigencies of governance and moderated on a host of key policies. Rather than forging a qualitatively new political form in the Frontier, the Islamist alliance succumbed to the cyclical nature of local politics, losing spectacularly to Pashtun nationalist parties in the 2008 general elections. And rather than maintaining their hold on right-of-center religious politics, the MMA constituent parties were outflanked by a new class of "religious" actors operating on the blurred boundary between formal politics and insurgent militancy.

How dramatically has the Frontier changed in six short years? In 2002, the preeminent concern of policymakers was that a coalition of anti-American and pro-*shariah* religious parties would establish an electoral foothold in the Frontier, and would use their political position to enact an array of discriminatory laws in the mold of the Afghan Taliban. Less than six years later, the preoccupations of policymakers are both more profound and more complex. Today the concerns — to list only a few — are that al Qaeda has reconstituted its operations in the FATA, and is planning international operations against the West; that regional strongmen such as Baitullah Mehsud are facilitating cross-border militancy against coalition forces in Afghanistan, and internal disorder in cities such as Islamabad and Lahore; that local Taliban-like insurgencies, often in collaboration with Punjabi or Waziri groups, are gaining ground in the settled areas of the NWFP, threatening the writ of the state and the long-term viability of civilian governance; and that religious parties, once feared as the vanguard of Talibanization, are now losing even the ability to draw religiously-minded young people away from insurgent activity and into the political mainstream.[1]

In light of these dramatic changes, the key objectives of this monograph are twofold. First, to examine through a political lens the overlapping Islamist narratives of the last six years — the rise and fall of the MMA, and the concomitant rise of new insurgent actors. And second, to propose a set of policies by which the United States, in close cooperation with the people and government of Pakistan, might constructively respond to the prevailing situation in the Frontier.

The first objective is important for the simple reason that much of the analysis of religious politics in the Frontier tends to focus on militant capabilities and outcomes (access to resources, organizational structures, number of attacks, etc.) rather than political and social drivers (objectives, rivalries, partnerships, leverage, etc.). In doing so, it is easy to miss the fundamentally political nature of the conflicts in today's Frontier. In and around 2002, for example, observers often made the mistake of reading the MMA through the lens of the Afghan Taliban; in doing so they underestimated the degree to which the Pakistani Islamists would be shaped by (even *entrapped* by) local political interests. Similarly, observers today often make the mistake of reading the new class of neo-Taliban insurgent groups narrowly through the lens of al Qaeda and the Waziri militant networks; in doing so they again tend to underestimate the ways in which these insurgents and their agendas are woven deeply into the fabric of both local and regional politics.

The second objective is equally critical. In the years since 2001, the United States has unfortunately not adequately come to terms with the implications of this changing Islamic political activity for America's core interests. U.S. policy toward the Frontier has been politically cautious, generally uncreative, largely driven by counterterrorism objectives, and poorly coordinated with the Pakistani government. Although the Frontier has historically been a recruiting ground for militant groups, U.S. political engagement, public diplomacy, and aid initiatives in the region are only beginning to focus in a coherent way on countering ideological support for extremism. Both the U.S. and Pakistan have also been slow to recognize the importance of good governance and access to justice in co-opting local support for Islamist insurgent groups.

KEY QUESTIONS

The work which follows does not purport to be a study of terrorism, extremism, or militancy as such. Neither does it purport to delve deeply into the macro political environment in South Asia, or the transnational character of Pakistan's current security dilemmas. It is, rather, a focused attempt to trace the dynamics of political

Islam in the Frontier in the post-9/11 era. In particular, it seeks to provide insight into several fundamental questions about religious dynamics and political stability in the Frontier, the answers to which may have resonance beyond simply the scope of U.S. policy toward Pakistan:

i) What can we learn from the MMA's experience about the moderating effects of governance on Islamic political behavior? What were the enabling and constraining factors which acted upon the alliance's ability to carry out the illiberal aspects of its agenda? What are the legacies of the MMA's Islamist experiment?

ii) What are the advantages and disadvantages of Islamist participation in the formal political process? That is, how do we weigh, on the one hand, the risks of illiberal political behavior by Islamists against, on the other hand, the mitigating advantages of Islamist participation in politics — namely, the co-opting of potentially radical religio-political impulses?

iii) What are the patterns of relationship and the lines of contestation between religious parties and groups which engage in vigilantism or militancy? Are there cleavages between and among these groups that Pakistan can leverage in the pursuit of regional stability?

iv) How can the U.S. craft a forward-looking policy toward the Frontier that, in cooperation with the government of Pakistan, engages the full range of political actors in such a way as to buttress moderate, democratic, and politically accommodationist elements over the long-term?

v) How can the U.S. partner with Pakistan to address the underlying weaknesses of the state, especially in those areas which are most prone to the advance of an Islamist insurgency? And what does the recent history of Islamist governance in the NWFP tell us about the trade-offs inherent in undertaking structural and governance reforms in the Frontier?

PROJECT SCOPE

This study is bounded in two significant ways. First, the narrative covers six years, from September 2002 through September 2008. Given that nearly five of these years fell under the governance of the MMA alliance in the NFWP, the history and politics of the religious parties in the Frontier forms a large part of the analytical discussion. More recent developments, including the rise of new insurgent groups and the victory of the ANP, are also dealt with, although it is still too early to draw conclusions about many of the broad trends which underlie these more recent events.

Second, rather than presuming to discuss the entire Frontier region comprehensively, this analysis focuses predominantly on the NWFP proper, that is, the areas under the control of the provincial government. One cannot, of course, discuss the NWFP without seriously accounting for the FATA, and issues of tribal governance and the state's management of the settled-tribal border areas will indeed be examined below. That being said, what follows is not a detailed review of the situation in the FATA itself.[2] The history, analysis, and recommendations seek instead to fill an analytical gap by focusing in large part on the settled areas, and the implications of recent Frontier developments for policymakers in the U.S. and Pakistan.

RESEARCH METHODOLOGY

This analysis is for the most part descriptive, and is drawn largely from the author's own experiences in the Frontier, as well as formal interviews and background research.

The bulk of the fieldwork was conducted in the spring and summer of 2007, during which time the author was a Visiting Research Associate at the Lahore University of Management Sciences (LUMS). During that period, he conducted over a hundred semi-structured interviews in Peshawar, Islamabad, and Lahore with leaders from the major religious parties; senior officials in the provincial and federal governments; local experts and civil society groups; representatives of international organizations; and officials from the military and security services.

The author also drew upon his experience of living in Peshawar as a CFIA fellow from the fall of 2005 through the summer of 2006, during which time he had extensive interaction with the MMA leadership and traveled widely in the NWFP; his participation in the U.S.-sponsored election observer delegation to the February 2008 general elections; a review of existing literature, including English and Urdu newspaper archives; a research trip to Pakistan in August 2008; and interviews in Washington conducted during 2007–8.

A NOTE ON GEOGRAPHY AND GOVERNANCE

Pakistan's Frontier is managed under a complex and sometimes baffling patchwork of governance systems, many of which were inherited and adapted from British times.[3] For the purpose of this monograph, the term "Frontier" is taken to include both the North-West Frontier Province (NWFP), which is governed by an elected provincial government in Peshawar; and the Federally Administered Tribal Areas (FATA), which operates under the oversight of the federal government through the office of the governor in Peshawar.

The NWFP is subdivided into both "settled" and "tribal" areas. The settled areas are those in which all or most of Pakistani civil law, regulations, and taxation apply.[4] The Provincially Administered Tribal Areas (PATA), on the other hand, are those in which some or all aspects of regular Pakistani law have been withheld (or in some cases, rescinded) in favor of tribal or *shariah* systems of governance. Of the 24 administrative districts in the NWFP, 17 are settled areas and 7 are tribal. Each district, whether settled or tribal, is managed by a district coordination officer (DCO). The PATA districts often operate as a hybrid between settled forms of governance and autonomous tribal rule. Malakand district in northern NWFP, for example, is a PATA region which in many respects operates like a settled district (with local elections, courts, etc.), but is also exempt from taxation and other regulations, and has a hybrid system of governance which, *inter alia,* draws on levied rather than professional police forces.[5] All told, the NWFP covers an area of about 29,000 square miles and has a population of about 21 million, which constitutes 13% of Pakistan's total. Its economy is heavily oriented around services and agriculture (although only 30% of the land is cultivable), and it ranks third out of Pakistan's four provinces with respect to most health and development indicators.[6]

The FATA, for its part, is subdivided into tribal agencies and frontier regions (FRs). Each of the seven tribal agencies is administered by a political agent (PA) who reports to the governor of NWFP. Under the framework established by the Frontier Crimes Regulation of 1901, the PA negotiates principally with tribal leaders who have been appointed by the state as *maliks*. The six FR areas, which are considerably smaller than the agencies, are each attached to a nearby settled district (Bannu, Dera Ismail Khan, Kohat, Lakki Marwat, Peshawar, and Tank), and are managed by an assistant political agent (APA) who reports to the DCO of that district. Although the FR areas are federally administered, the provincial government also at times plays a role in the frontier regions on account of their proximity to the settled areas, and their oversight by DCOs who operate in the settled districts. The FATA covers an area of about 10,500 square miles, and has a population of about 3.5 million. Male and female literacy are approximately 30% and 3%, respectively, and the area suffers from a profound lack of infrastructure and basic services.[7]

NOTES:

[1] Examining these and other challenges, a bipartisan group concluded in September 2008 that "we find U.S. interests in Pakistan are more threatened now than at any time since the Taliban was driven from Afghanistan in 2001." Pakistan Policy Working Group, *The Next Chapter: The United States and Pakistan*, September 2008, 1.

[2] For a more comprehensive, regional policy perspective on the current challenges of the Frontier, see Daniel Markey, *Securing Pakistan's Tribal Belt* (New York: Council on Foreign Relations, August 2008); as well as forthcoming reports on Pakistan by the Center for Strategic and International Studies (CSIS) and the Center for American Progress (CAP). (Note that the author participated in advisory groups for these publications.)

[3] For a detailed background on these systems, see Markey, *Securing Pakistan's Tribal Belt*, 3–10; Joshua T. White, "The Shape of Frontier Rule: Governance and Transition, from the Raj to the Modern Pakistani Frontier," *Asian Security* 4, no. 3 (Autumn 2008); and Naveed Ahmad Shinwari, *Understanding FATA: Attitudes Towards Governance, Religion & Society in Pakistan's Federally Administered Tribal Areas*, (Peshawar: Community Appraisal & Motivation Programme, 2008).

[4] The concept of "settled" areas under the British Raj referred primarily to the presence of normal systems of taxation. In today's context, "settled" refers more broadly to the presence of Pakistani law and regulations.

[5] Some officials refer to Malakand and other PATA regions as "agencies," but for all intents and purposes they are treated as districts of the NWFP.

[6] For comparison with other provinces, see United Nations Development Programme, *Pakistan National Human Development Report: Poverty, Growth and Governance*, 2003. The most comprehensive analysis of the NWFP's economic situation is World Bank and Government of NWFP, *Accelerating Growth and Improving Public Service Delivery in the NWFP: The Way Forward*, Pakistan North West Frontier Province Economic Report, December 8, 2005.

[7] Civil Secretariat (FATA), Government of Pakistan, *FATA Sustainable Development Plan (2006-2015)*, 2006.

GLOSSARY OF KEY TERMS

This glossary is provided as a basic reference for the narrative and analysis which follow.[1]

Agency — an administrative unit within the FATA, further subdivided into tehsils; overseen by a political agent.

Alim — a religious scholar.

Amir — a title referring to the leader of a party or group.

ANP — Awami National Party, a left-of-center Pashtun nationalist party.

Barelvism — a Sunni Sufist Islamic movement with roots in British India.

Chief Minister — the senior elected official of a province, chosen by the leading party of the governing coalition.

Counterinsurgency — a form of warfare that has as its objective the credibility and/or legitimacy of the relevant political authority with the goal of undermining or supporting that authority.[2]

Counterterrorism — the tactics and strategy of detecting and deterring potential terrorist acts.

DCO — District Coordination Officer, a civil official who oversees a district; reports to the chief minister of the province.

Deobandism — a Sunni Islamic revivalist movement with roots in British India.

District — an administrative unit within the NWFP local government system, further subdivided into tehsils.

Division — an obsolete administrative unit within the NWFP which aggregated several districts.

Durand Line — a term for the border between Afghanistan and Pakistan, delimited in 1893 by Sir Mortimer Durand; the Line is not accepted by Afghanistan.

FATA — Federally Administered Tribal Areas, comprising seven tribal agencies and six frontier regions.

Fatawa — religious opinions issued by an Islamic scholar (plural of fatwa).

Fatwa — a religious opinion issued by an Islamic scholar.

FC — Frontier Corps, a paramilitary force recruited from the Pashtun tribal areas of Pakistan, and led by Pakistan army officers.

FCR — Frontier Crimes Regulation, the legal framework which governs the FATA, and which last underwent major revision in 1901.

Frontier — Pakistan's north-west territories, encompassing both the NWFP and the FATA.

Frontier Region — an administrative unit within the FATA, overseen by the DCO of an adjacent district of the NWFP.

Governor — the head of government of a province, appointed by the president.

ISI — Inter-Services Intelligence Directorate, the largest and most powerful intelligence agency in Pakistan.

Islamism — an ideology which advocates a political agenda based on Islamic principles.[3]

JI — Jamaat-e-Islami, an Islamist party founded by Maulana Mawdudi; also referred to as the Jamaat.

Jihad — struggle, defined as internal (e.g., spiritual purification) or external (e.g., the legitimate defense of Islam); also commonly used as a shorthand to refer to the campaign against the Soviets in Afghanistan in the 1980s.

Jirga — an assembly of tribal leaders which reaches decisions on a consensus basis; may be convened *ad hoc* or at the request of a political agent or other government official.

JUI — Jamiat Ulema-e-Islam, a Deobandi Islamist movement whose antecedent was the Indian Jamiat Ulema-e-Hind (JUH).[4]

JUI-F — Jamiat Ulema-e-Islam, Fazlur Rehman faction.

JUI-S — Jamiat Ulema-e-Islam, Sami ul-Haq faction.

Khassadar force — a tribal police force tasked with protecting roads and other state interests.

Lashkar — a tribal militia; often raised in an *ad hoc* manner to implement the decisions of a jirga.

Madaris — Islamic schools or seminaries (plural of madrassah).

Madrassah — an Islamic school or seminary.

Mainstream parties — the PPP, PPP-S, PML-N, and PML-Q.

Malik — a tribal leader, appointed by the tribe or by the state.

Maulana — a title for a Muslim religious leader or scholar.

Maulvi — a title for a Muslim religious leader or scholar.

MMA — Muttahida Majlis-e-Amal (United Action Council), an alliance of six Islamist parties, of which the JI and the JUI-F were the dominant members.

MPA — Member of the Provincial Assembly.

MNA — Member of the National Assembly.

Mohajir — a Muslim immigrant from India who settled in Pakistan; refers particularly to those who settled in Karachi following the 1947 Partition of India and Pakistan.

Mufti — a title for an Islamic judge qualified to rule according to the shariah.

Mujahidin — those who engage in jihad.

Mullah — title for a Muslim religious leader or scholar.

Nationalist parties — the ANP, Mohajir-focused Muttahida Qaumi Movement (MQM), and the Baloch parties.[5]

Neo-Taliban — a term used for a loose movement of self-described Taliban groups which emerged in Pakistan's Frontier after September 11, 2001; many of these groups have tenuous connections, or none at all, to the original Taliban movement.

NWFP — North-West Frontier Province, one of the four provinces of Pakistan; the others are Punjab, Sindh, and Balochistan.

Pashto — an Indo-Iranian language spoken by ethnic Pashtuns; pronounced "Pashto" in southern areas of the Pak-Afghan border areas, and "Pakhto" in northern areas.

PATA — Provincially Administered Tribal Areas, comprising seven tribal districts/agencies which fall under the governance of the NWFP.

Pashtun — an ethno-linguistic tribal group based in northwest Pakistan and southern and eastern Afghanistan.

PML — Pakistan Muslim League, a right-of-center party founded by Pakistan's first leader Muhammad Ali Jinnah.

Pashtunwali — an unwritten code of Pashtun tradition and values.

PML-N — Pakistan Muslim League, Nawaz Sharif faction; a party founded by former Pakistani Prime Minister Nawaz Sharif.

PML-Q — Pakistan Muslim League, Quaid-e-Azam faction; a party which supported President Musharraf.

Political agent — an administrative office in the tribal areas through which the governor exercises authority on behalf of the state.

PPP — Pakistan People's Party, a left-of-center party founded by Zulfikar Ali Bhutto in 1967.

PPP-S — Pakistan People's Party, Sherpao faction; a splinter party from the PPP, led by NWFP politician Aftab Sherpao.

Qazi — title for an Islamic judge qualified to rule according to the shariah.

Qazi court — an Islamic court presided over by a qazi; these courts are found in various forms throughout the Muslim world (including India) and traditionally rule on matters of family law, operating parallel to the civil legal system.

RCO — Regional Coordination Officer, a civil official who oversees several adjacent districts and tribal agencies; reports to the chief minister of the province.

Religious parties — political parties which take an explicitly Islamist agenda; the most prominent examples are the JI and the various parties of the JUI.

Settled areas — those regions in which all or most of Pakistani civil law, regulations, and taxation apply.

Shariah — the body of Islamic religious law, as derived from the Quran and Sunnah (practices of Muhammad).

Talib — a student.

Taliban — a religio-political movement, largely Deobandi in orientation, which emerged in 1994 in the Frontier and ruled much of Afghanistan from 1996–2001.

Tehsil — an administrative unit within the NWFP local government system, made up of union councils.

Tribal areas — those regions which are not settled areas, that is, in which civil law, regulations, or taxation do not apply.

TNSM — Tehrik-e-Nafaz-e-Shariat-e-Muhammadi (Movement for the Enforcement of the Islamic Law of Muhammad), a movement founded by Maulana Sufi Muhammad in 1992; it has been particularly active in and around Swat.

TTP — Tehrik-e-Taliban-e-Pakistan (Movement of the Pakistani Taliban), a loose umbrella organization of neo-Taliban groups, formed in 2007.

Ulema — religious scholars (plural of alim).

Ummah — the worldwide community of Muslim believers.

Union council — the lowest administrative unit in the NWFP local government system.

NOTES:

1. This glossary does not presume to put forward comprehensive or rigorous social science definitions. Note also that transliterations of Urdu, Arabic, and Pashto words have been simplified in this monograph. In general, common spellings have been retained; letters such as the *'ayin* have been removed; plurals are occasionally formed according to English convention (e.g., *lashkars*); and short and long vowels are not distinguished (with the occasional exception of *aa* for *ā*).

2. This definition is adapted from the working definition of "irregular warfare" approved by the U.S. Deputy Secretary of Defense on April 17, 2006. The U.S. army's new counterinsurgency manual also provides a helpful description of this form of warfare: "Political power is the central issue in insurgencies and counterinsurgencies; each side aims to get the people to accept its governance or authority as legitimate. Insurgents use all available tools — political (including diplomatic), informational (including appeals to religious, ethnic, or ideological beliefs), military, and economic — to overthrow the existing authority. This authority may be an established government or an interim governing body. Counterinsurgents, in turn, use all instruments of national power to sustain the established or emerging government and reduce the likelihood of another crisis emerging." U.S. Department of the Army, *Field Manual 3-24: Counterinsurgency* (Washington, DC: Headquarters, Department of the Army, December 15, 2006), §1–3.

3. There are many definitions of Islamism. In the context of this monograph, it is used to refer to political Islam, as a concept which is distinct from Islam as a religion, or Islamic religious practice.

4. Unless otherwise specified, JUI refers to the Jamiat Ulema-e-Islam party as it existed before its split into JUI-F and JUI-S factions following Mufti Mahmud's death in 1980. When used in a post-1980 context, JUI refers generally to both factions of the movement.

5. Note that the party was originally known as the Mohajir Qaumi Movement.

Map of Pakistan's NWFP and FATA | 21

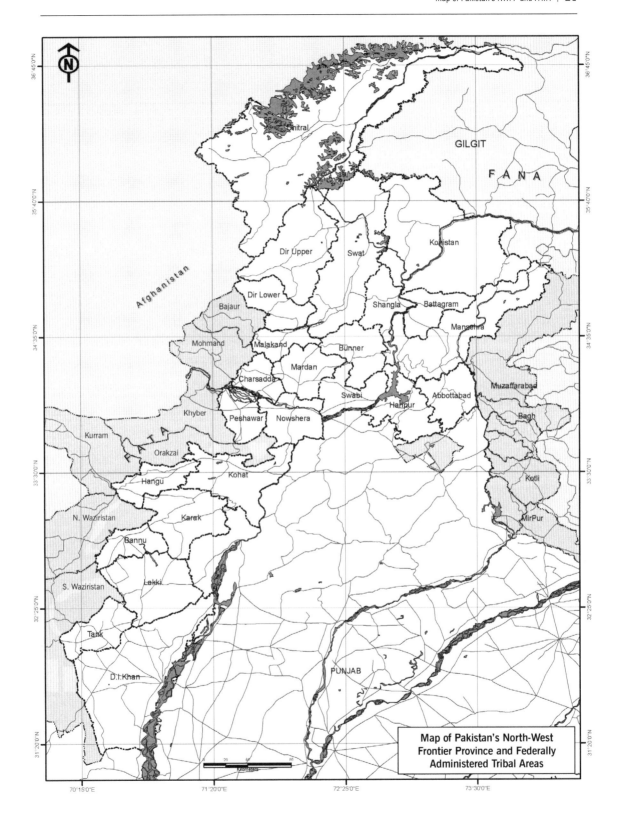

Map of Pakistan's North-West Frontier Province and Federally Administered Tribal Areas

I
THE RISE AND SCOPE OF ISLAMIC POLITICAL INFLUENCE

The history of Islamist influence in the Pakistani political process has been extensively documented and debated. The historical review which follows is simply a capsule summary of major trends which have shaped the Islamism of the modern Frontier, as well as a discussion of several key patterns of Islamic politics which help to frame the contemporary situation. As the focus on this work is on the changing dynamics of political Islam, this narrative focuses in large part on the origins and development of Pakistan's major Islamist parties, their interaction with the state and with external actors, and the politics which lie behind their agitation. This history is essential for framing a proper evaluation of the post-2001 Frontier, in which the religious parties — and their insurgent affiliates on the political fringe — played a central role in reshaping the region's political and security environment.

PRE-1947: RELIGIO-POLITICAL MOVEMENTS

The ninety years between the failed uprising of 1857 and the partition of 1947 laid the groundwork for Islamic political expression in independent Pakistan. The history of this period is multifaceted and deeply complex, and has received excellent scholarly treatment in several recent works.[1] A number of important movements arose during this period — particularly in the North-West Frontier Province and the Indo-Afghan borderlands — which are worth noting insofar as they set into relief the contemporary political context of the Frontier.

The first of these was the uprising of 1858, which arose in the areas dominated by the Yusufzai clan — the region now roughly constituting districts Buner, Malakand, Mardan, Swabi, and Swat. This region has a centuries-long history of alliances-of-convenience between charismatic spiritual leaders and their tribal supporters. What began as an internecine struggle between two such power blocs eventually coalesced into overt opposition to the British.[2] Akhund Abdul Ghaffur, a Sufi *pir* (saint) who succeeded Sayyid Akbar Shah as leader of the Swat kingdom, cultivated a network of *mujahidin* who were known to the British as the "Hindustani Fanatics," as well as a line of *murids* (disciples) who would come to have enormous influence in the religious and political development of the adjacent tribal areas.[3] A confrontation unfolded in 1863 between these *mujahidin* and the British, and following a pattern which would continue well into the modern era, the conflict was eventually resolved along essentially political lines. The Akhund, fearful of the prospect of British armies advancing into an area which had resisted foreign rule for nearly three hundred years, turned on his Sayyid allies and assisted the British in expelling the *mujahidin*. By assisting the British with their tactical objectives, he assured his own continued role in the northern frontier areas, and at the same time leveraged the British action to decapitate his leading religio-political rival.

The three decades which followed the Swat uprising were by no means uneventful for British administrators on the frontier: they were forced to confront widespread criminal activity in the Indo-Afghan border areas (leading to the enactment of the first Frontier Crimes Regulation in 1873), and engaged in full-scale armed conflict in Afghanistan in the second Afghan War, beginning in 1878. This was, significantly, a period marked by the gradual expansion of British influence: in 1881 the railroad reached Peshawar; in 1893 the border with Afghanistan was finally settled; and in 1895 British administrators demarcated Malakand agency, which included the princely states of Chitral, Dir, and Swat.[4] What looked to the British like a simple plan of rationalizing a once-chaotic frontier policy looked to the tribesmen like a scheme designed to encircle, co-opt, and control regions which had for centuries remained autonomous. As a result, the tribes rose up in 1897 against this British expansionism, first in Malakand, and then throughout nearly all the frontier regions.[5] The resistance was led in large part by the Hadda Mullah, a *murid* in the line of the late Akhund, and the Hadda Mullah's own disciple, Sartor Faqir, who was dubbed the "Mad Mullah" by the British.[6] The resistance of 1897 did not last long in the face of large-scale British military operations, and by 1898 the British had restored peace, and effectively extended their writ to the boundaries of what is today the modern frontier.

The creation of the NWFP as a formal political space in 1901 by Lord Curzon not only influenced the ways in which the British conceived of their project of frontier governance. It also, by the second decade of the twentieth century, began to influence local conceptions of ethnic Pashtun identity, and create pressures for Pashtun participation in the rising tide of pan-Islamism that was creating linkages among Muslims in India, Afghanistan, and the Arab states. In the Silk Letter Conspiracy of 1914–16, British intelligence uncovered a wildly ambitious plot by leading clerics in the United Provinces (modern-day Uttar Pradesh, India) to raise an Islamic army of Pashtun tribesmen in support of the Turkish sultan against the British.[7] And on the far western front, the British became embroiled in a third Anglo-Afghan war in which the new Afghan *amir* rallied the "Hindustani fanatics" from the tribal areas to Afghanistan for *jihad*.[8] (All of this was in addition to the regular British expeditions against the fiercely independent Mehsud tribes in Waziristan.)

Important changes in mass politics were also taking shape in the Frontier. Alongside Gandhi's noncooperation movement, designed to pressure the British to honor their pre-war rhetoric of "self-determination," Muslims launched the Khilafat movement in 1919, which agitated against the proposed abolition of the Ottoman caliphate.[9] One of the stranger sub-narratives of the Khilafat story was the attempted *hijrat* (migration) of tens of thousands of Muslims from India into Afghanistan in 1920, seeking to cross the Durand Line into the *dar ul-Islam* (abode of Islam). While both the Khilafat movement and the *hijrat* were spectacular failures, these movements marked the first attempt to mobilize pan-Islamic sentiment across the subcontinent, and presented the religious clerics of the Frontier with an opportunity to rally the Pashtun in opposition to the British, build networks with other organizers, and try their hand at activist politics.[10]

The locus of Islamic agitation in the Frontier shifted somewhat in the 1930s and '40s, away from Swat, the Peshawar valley, and Afghanistan proper and toward the tribal agencies. In 1930, the government mobilized its largest frontier operations since the war of 1919, in response to *lashkars* raised by local *mullahs* and Khilafat committees.[11] The British were also forced to confront quite regularly the specter of *ad hoc* tribal militias led by charismatic leaders in Waziristan. Often these leaders used pan-Islamic language in order to provide a veneer of legitimacy for their project of aggregating self-interested tribal factions against a larger neighbor or an external power. The Faqir of Ipi was one famous exemplar of charismatic leadership in Waziristan, bringing together in 1936 a *lashkar* of Mehsuds, Wazirs, and assorted *mullahs* to conduct raids against the British military.[12] His influence would continue well through independence a decade later.

PRE-1947: THE EMERGENCE OF ISLAMIST PARTIES

The two major Islamic political movements operating in Pakistan today both have their antecedents in pre-1947 India. The first of these are the Deobandis. This movement traces its roots to modern-day Uttar Pradesh, where a group of clerics founded the Dar ul-Ulum Deoband in 1866. Established in the wake of the failed uprising in 1857, this *madrassah* became the focal point of a wider religious revivalist movement which sought to reconsolidate and refocus the religious and cultural life of the Muslim *ummah* on the subcontinent. Far from being political, the early Deobandis were for the most part "inward-looking and primarily concerned with the Islamic quality of individual lives."[13]

Through the First World War, most Deobandi clerics remained apolitical. Some, however, came to believe that the revivalist message which began at Deoband had to be broadened beyond its pietistic vision so as to include a political restoration of the Muslim community. Several of the clerics, such as Maulana Mahmud ul-Hasan and other faculty at the Dar ul-Ulum implicated in the Silk Letter Conspiracy, sought a military response to the dual problems of British rule and Muslim disenfranchisement. Others — perhaps the majority of the politically-minded Deobandis — entered the political realm by means of the Khilafat movement. Of these clerics, a great number eventually formalized their political participation by joining the Jamiat Ulema-e-Hind (Assembly of Indian Clerics, JUH), a party established in 1919.

Throughout the 1920s, the JUH clerics struggled to define their political agenda, and their role in the anti-British agitation. The party's activist energy, however, could not be sustained after the failure of the Khilafat movement, and from the end of the 1920s to the middle of the 1940s, the JUH again turned inward, focused (as in the early days of the Dar ul-Ulum) on aggressive cultural renewal and improving the conditions of the Muslim minority.

By the mid-1940s, however, the majority of the Deobandi *ulema* were no longer debating whether or not they ought to engage in politics; the question before them was, "politics toward what end?" While they shared a common opposition to British rule, deep fault lines began to emerge surrounding the "two-nation theory" proposed by Muhammad Ali Jinnah and the Muslim League, and its call for Pakistan as a homeland for Muslims of the Indian subcontinent. In 1945, the JUH split over this issue: the pro-Muslim League faction became the Jamiat Ulema-e-Islam (JUI), and the JUH maintained its affiliation with the Indian National Congress Party, arguing that the creation of Pakistan would divide and dangerously weaken the Muslims of India.[14]

Despite support from the British, who sought to blunt the influence of pro-Congress politics in the Frontier, the JUI performed poorly in the 1946 NWFP elections. The results in any case were short-lived. In 1947 India was partitioned, and NWFP joined the new Pakistani state. In spite of competition between the JUH and the JUI, which continued right up until the Partition, neither side was able to gain overwhelming support among the Muslims living in the frontier areas. There was a wide diversity of opinion among the Pashtuns as to whether the establishment of Pakistan was truly in their interest, and if it was, whether Muhammad Ali Jinnah and the Muslim League represented legitimate Islamic principles.[15] The JUI began in the new state with limited influence in the Frontier, but would in time emerge as one of Pakistan's leading Islamist movements, and play a major role in post-2001 Frontier politics.

The second important movement to emerge out of the pre-Partition milieu was the Jamaat-e-Islami (JI). The Jamaat, as it is known, was founded by a Deobandi cleric, Maulana Abul Ala Mawdudi in 1941. Unlike the JUI, which drew largely from a rural support base and recruited the clerical classes, the JI sought to recruit technocrats and activists, and drew its support predominantly from the "devout middle classes" of Pakistan's urban centers.[16] Opposed to the Muslim League, the JI was Mawdudi's attempt to institutionalize a movement of Islamic renewal among Muslims in India.

The Jamaat's Islamist vision was somewhat different from that of the Deobandi clerical class. Mawdudi's ideology emphasized the importance of reforming the state and the legal apparatus, and his focus on political transformation influenced the writings of Arab Islamist intellectuals such as Hassan al-Banna and Sayyid Qutb.[17] As Vali Nasr has argued in his excellent treatment of Mawdudi's life and ideology,

> In traditional Islam there had been a balance between religion as individual piety and religion as social order. It was the piety of men that created and sustained a religious order. In Mawdudi's formula, although individual piety featured prominently, in the final analysis, it was the society and the political order that guaranteed the piety of the individual: "a very large part of the Islamic system of law, however, needs for its enforcement in all its details the coercive power and authority of the state."[18]

This ideological bias toward reform of the state (in contrast to the original Deobandi focus on reforming the individual and society) did not emerge fully formed when the Jamaat was founded in the early 1940s. It was, as we will see below, shaped profoundly by the creation of Pakistan.

1947–69: STATE FORMATION AND ISLAMIC IDENTITY

The opening years of Pakistan's history were a formative period for the country's two major Islamist movements — the JUI and the JI — each of which were wrestling with their role in the first modern "Islamic state." In the first place, key leaders in both movements had chosen to support the "wrong" side in the years leading up to 1947: members of the pro-Congress JUH who ended up in Pakistan after Partition had to pivot to join the JUI, which adopted a more state-centric view of Islamization; and Maulana Mawdudi of the Jamaat, who had outright opposed not only the creation of Pakistan (believing that "he should be the one to found and lead the Muslim state of Pakistan if there had to be one"[19]) but also the Kashmiri *jihad* in 1948, was forced to compensate for these decisions by becoming the leading advocate for an Islamist Pakistan.

Once the religious parties came to terms, politically speaking, with the creation of the state of Pakistan, they set out to influence its early development as an Islamic institution. The Jamaat, though small numerically, was particularly influential in this regard in the first two decades of Pakistan's history. In the early years after Partition, the party put forward a vision of the ideal state as an Islamic institution, with the *shariah* as its legal code. The Jamaat's ideology was, and remains, a synthesis of revivalist Islam — with an emphasis on preserving the *ummah* in the face of colonial and neo-colonial pressures — and a modern, institutionalist, quasi-technocratic Islamic vision not unlike that of the Muslim Brotherhood.

Particularly after the establishment of Pakistan, Mawdudi became convinced that the state was the proper and indeed indispensible vehicle for Islamic revival. In contrast to the philosophy of the early Deobandis, the Tablighi Jamaat, and other revivalist movements of the subcontinent, Mawdudi argued that individual and social reformation was not possible in the absence of an Islamic state structure.[20] Islam must work from the outside-in.[21] This fundamentally state-centric logic of the Jamaat was brought to bear on Mawdudi's efforts to influence the framing of the Objectives Resolution, a statement of principles that was eventually adopted as an annex to Pakistan's first constitution in 1956.[22]

Early attempts by the JI and the JUI to give the new state a substantive Islamist character were, on the whole, unsuccessful. Many of their failed efforts, however, set the pattern for future Islamist strategies of political agitation. For example the Tehrik-e-Khatam-e-Nabuwat (Movement for the Finality of the Prophethood), which pressed for the government to declare the Ahmadiyya sect as non-Muslim, was harshly suppressed by the government in 1953; but by 1974, after significant public pressure by Islamist groups, its main objectives had been accommodated in the form of a constitutional amendment.[23]

The Jamaat's early experiences of confrontation with the martial state would also anticipate its future interaction with the military and bureaucratic elite. When Governor-General Iskander Mirza declared martial law in October 1958 and appointed General Ayub Khan as Chief Martial Law Administrator, he did so in part to thwart the designs of the Jamaat and its growing involvement in the political process.[24] And when Ayub Khan took control from Mirza later that same month and inaugurated his own martial law government, the result was the banning of political parties. Although Mawdudi chose to follow a pragmatic path that avoided direct confrontation with the military regime — perhaps because he was aware of the fate of the Muslim Brotherhood in Egypt — the Jamaat remained one of the fiercest opponents of Ayub's martial rule.

The basic political orientation of the Jamaat during the Ayub era was pro-democracy, anti-militarist, and above all, anti-secularist. It resented Ayub's modernist experimentation, which ran almost directly counter to its vision of the ideal Islamic state. Its popular slogan in the 1960s, *"Tajaddud Band Karo!"* (Stop the innovations!), expressed the spirit of its protest and its fear of a polity modeled increasingly along Western lines.[25] The party's antipathy toward secularism in the Ayub era was part and parcel of its antipathy toward the West. Mawdudi saw the secularizing trends in the Arab and Persian world, and feared that, with America's help, the Ayub regime was charting a similar course. In language which very much foreshadowed the Jamaat's rhetoric four decades later, he claimed in 1960 that America "[does] not want Muslim nations to remain Muslim;" that the Americans "most unscrupulously … support dictatorships against democracy;" and that their policies are "possessed by the devil called Jewry." In spite of his strident opposition to the atheism of the communist bloc, he concluded that the Western countries "loom upon Islam as a greater menace than communism."[26]

On the whole, Ayub's tenure was an era of vociferous rhetoric by the religious parties, but minimal Islamist influence. The 1965 war with India brought the Jamaat and Ayub onto the same page for a short while, but it was only a temporary convergence of interests.[27] The Islamists' influence would begin to change in the decade which followed.

1970–77: ISLAMISTS AND ELECTORAL POLITICS

The late 1960s and early 1970s saw the rise of leftist politics in Pakistan, led by Zulfikar Ali Bhutto and his Pakistan People's Party (PPP). The religious parties, forced to confront the emergence of a new mass politics, split on the question of socialism: the more politically-minded (Madani faction) Deobandis insisted that socialist thought was basically in resonance with the populism and anti-imperialism of the pre-Partition Jamiat Ulema movements, while the less politically-active (Thanwi faction) Deobandis and, especially, the Jamaat-e-Islami claimed that socialism amounted to *kufr* (infidelity).[28] The Madani Deobandis were ultimately more adept at aligning their politics with the leftism of the time, and did so in a way that established patterns of JUI politics which continue to the present day.

Few expected that it would be Mufti Mahmud who would take up the mantle of leftist Deobandi politics in Pakistan. Born in the southern NWFP district of Dera Ismail Khan in 1919, he studied at a Deobandi seminary in Muradabad in the United

Provinces, where he became involved in the JUH before returning north to teach at a *madrassah* in Mianwali, a Pashtun-dominated district adjacent to Dera Ismail Khan.[29] During the 1940s, the Mufti formed close ties with the pro-Congress Maulana Husain Ahmad Madani (traveling with him in NWFP in 1943) and began building a political base in his home district. By the late 1960s, the Mufti had inherited the socialist-leaning Madani wing of the JUI, and had developed an active Pashtun constituency in the southern NWFP and the tribal agencies.[30]

When it came time for the 1970 elections, Mufti Mahmud's JUI did not fare particularly well, with one notable exception: the Mufti himself managed an upset victory over Zulfikar Ali Bhutto, chairman of the PPP, in the hotly contested national assembly seat from Dera Ismail Khan. The Mufti's political stature and influence among the JUI *ulema,* particularly in the Frontier, paid off once Bhutto came to power as President in late 1971 following the war which saw the defeat of Pakistan and the creation of Bangladesh. Seeking to form a government, Bhutto, Mufti Mahmud, and Wali Khan (son of the great Red Shirt movement leader Khan Abdul Ghaffar Khan) of the National Awami Party (NAP) signed a Tripartite Agreement in 1972 that set up a joint JUI-NAP government in NWFP.[31] On May 1, 1972, Mufti Mahmud was sworn in as chief minister.

The JUI-NAP government was not to last for more than ten months.[32] It was, however, the first instance of a religious party coming to power in Pakistan, and it served as a high water mark for Deobandi influence in the political arena. Mufti Mahmud's agenda as chief minister would set the tone for the next 30 years of JUI politics. He began a vigorous Islamization program; banned alcohol; introduced an Islamic reform of the inheritance law; and mandated the observance of Ramadan. He further (though unsuccessfully) set out to grant interest-free loans; establish an *ulema* advisory board; make reading of the Quran and study of Arabic compulsory for university admission; require women to be veiled in public; insist that the *shalwar-kamiz* tunic to be mandatory for government servants; ban dowry; and prohibit gambling.[33]

The Mufti's tenure was brief and unsuccessful, but once his government fell he seemed not dissuaded in the least. His politics in the final years of Bhutto's democratic era involved the proposal of increasingly sweeping and stringent Islamic-oriented legislation, including anti-blasphemy amendments to the constitution. In 1974, he took the lead with Maulana Yusuf Binori of the famous Madani-influenced Binori *madrassah* in Karachi to once again raise — this time successfully — legislation that would declare Ahmadis as non-Muslims.[34] (Zulfikar Bhutto went along with these Islamist initiatives in the latter years of his tenure in an effort to strengthen his increasingly tenuous political position.)

By the time Zia ul-Haq took power in 1977, the JUI of Mufti Mahmud had grown into a serious and vociferous political voice in Pakistan. Its association with the socialist PPP and its simultaneous use of Islamist rhetoric and promotion of a *shariah* agenda led many to dismiss it as hypocritical, expedient, and cynically pragmatic — a movement that "was only committed to keeping itself alive, and not an ideological organization fighting for a given cause."[35] The early reticence by Madani Deobandis to create an Islamic society "from above" had been washed away by the opportunities that Partition presented them to redefine their politics and make themselves newly relevant to state and society.

1977–88: ZIA UL-HAQ AND ISLAMIZATION

Zia and the Jamaat

General Zia ul-Haq seized power in a coup d'état in July 1977, and quickly declared martial law. His tenure marked a period of tremendous expansion of Islamist influence in Pakistani politics, the contours of which are now well known. Zia began a drive to Islamize Pakistan's institutions, from the army to the courts to the bureaucracy. He propagated the Hudood Ordinance, revised the penal code to make blasphemy a capital crime, and promulgated a number of token Islamic reforms which nonetheless sent a powerful message about the ideological character of the state.[36] It was a program that he would continue for 11 years, until his death in 1988.[37]

The Jamaat's domestic policy during this era was consumed with the question of whether to give precedence to Zia's program of Islamization, or to hold to the party's democratic principles and insist on civilian governance. After much internal disagreement, Mawdudi's successor Mian Tufail decided that the opportunity to do away with Bhutto and institutionalize the *shariah* program of the Jamaat was too appealing to pass up: the party became a partner with Zia and contributed several cabinet members to his government.[38]

The Jamaat's governance experience during the early years of the Zia regime was, on the whole, disappointing. Aside from Khurshid Ahmad — who promoted new policies for *zakat* and banking — the ministers were unable to stir the federal bureaucracy into implementing their *shariah* agenda.[39] Their influence was more pronounced, however, in the Council of Islamic Ideology, where Jamaat nominees helped to formulate a new package of Islamic penal reforms; and, most of all, in the military, where they were given unprecedented access to the senior officer ranks. This became most evident during the Afghan *jihad*, where the JI was mobilized to take on a major role.

The years of the Afghan *jihad* under Zia are often characterized as the heyday of the Jamaat, and in a sense they did represent the apex of the party's influence in official circles. But the narrative linking military rule and Islamic politics is not as clean cut as some observers would make it. Just as there was sporadic and symbiotic manipulation between the military and the religious parties during the Ayub era — punctuated by periods of outright hostility — so the relationship between Zia and the Jamaat played out in complex and ambivalent ways.

Even in the heady, early days of the *jihad*, some elements within the party were less than enthusiastic about the martial government; they considered the opportunities that came from partnership with Zia to be a distraction from the real political vision of the movement. It was, therefore, only a matter of time before the Jamaat became disillusioned with its step-child role in the Zia government and in the *jihad* operations.[40] By 1982, the relationship had begun to sour. Zia was feeling more confident in his support from the United States and from the *ulema*, and at the same time more concerned about the potential for the Jamaat to mobilize its well-organized student base against him.[41] After the 1985 non-party elections, in which Jamaat-affiliated candidates performed poorly, the split was complete. The results demonstrated to Zia that the Jamaat had lost its influence, and he turned to other parties for popular support.[42]

The Deobandis and the Afghan jihad

The JUI had a much more limited interaction than the Jamaat with Zia's government as such; by the early 1980s, the JUI, like the JI, was disillusioned with Zia's reforms and began agitating for a return to civilian rule. But the Deobandis were ultimately shaped in profound ways during the Zia era through their participation in the Afghan *jihad,* and by the patronage they received from the state. The *jihadi* campaign against Soviet forces in Afghanistan, funded by the Americans and Saudis and operated by the Pakistani intelligence services, resulted in the establishment of hundreds of *madaris* throughout the Frontier.

Not only did the *madaris* proliferate, but their quality deteriorated markedly throughout the 1980s. The *jihadi* ideology became more important than mastery of traditional scholarly subjects. The careful and comprehensive curriculum designed by the founders at Dar ul-Ulum gave way to mass education that was decidedly more ideological in character. In one respect, the education system itself changed, from a model which valued extended study under a learned *alim,* to one that promoted something of a freelance, franchise model. These changes did not take place in a vacuum. They were part and parcel of the *jihad* in Afghanistan — a conflict which fundamentally altered the face of Deobandism, particularly in the Frontier. Many of the *mujahidin* were trained in NWFP, either by or with Deobandi compatriots. And leading Deobandi *ulema* including Mufti Mahmud in Dera Ismail Khan and Mufti Yusuf Binori in Karachi issued *fatawa* encouraging *jihad* against the Soviet infidels. These new legitimating ideologies of *jihad* that had previously not held a significant place in Deobandi religious thought, combined with a newly decentralized educational infrastructure, facilitated the rapid spread of radical ideologies in the Frontier.

The *jihad* also began to change, in basic ways, the role of the *ulema* in Pashtun society. Traditionally, the village *mullah* did not have a separate political role outside the scope of his religious duties.[43] The *ulema* were able to operate in a political role only if they managed to leverage their religious credibility in the pursuit of power politics. Akbar Ahmed's account of how Maulvi Nur Muhammad — a disciple of Mufti Mahmud — played this game beginning in the 1950s in South Waziristan is an example of the ways in which some leading clerics learned to "control Islam rather than be controlled by it," that is, to impose "a religious frame on a secular [issue]" so as to wield religious language for non-religious ends.[44] In this way the *mullah* functioned opportunistically as a political mobilizer, sparring for influence with tribal elders and government officials.[45]

Such figures are still prominent in Pashtun society today; indeed, one could argue that the current generation of JUI leadership largely operates in this mold, leveraging the symbolism of Islam in order to mobilize what is essentially a political base. The real legacy of the Afghan *jihad,* however, is to be found not only in the proliferation of the *madrassah*-as-franchise culture of the 1980s, but in the *alim*-as-entrepreneur culture which followed it. Lower-level *ulema* benefited only indirectly from state patronage during the *jihad*; following the end of the war and the withdrawal of foreign involvement, these poorly trained clerics — a product of the theologically shallow *madaris* that had proliferated throughout the province

— found themselves unemployable, or at least discouraged by the bleak prospects available outside of the *jihadi* line of work.[46] These *ulema,* Vali Nasr argues, "began to stake out their own claim to power and wealth — satiating appetites for power, status and wealth that Islamization had whetted but left unsatiated."[47]

The second-order effects of the emergence of this new class were also, in retrospect, of great import. Both the prestige and the external financing which came with the *jihadi* vocation began to upend the traditional social order, particularly in the tribal areas. Tribal elders, including those *maliks* who served as paid liaisons between the tribes and the state's political agent, found their standing undermined by new groups of entrepreneurial youth. This trend dovetailed with the explosion of remittance income from the Gulf states in the 1970s, which further reshaped in dramatic ways the political economy of the tribal areas.[48] The systems of indirect rule which the state had relied upon for over a century began to deteriorate in the face of new regional and economic realities.

The Afghan *jihad,* and the political-economic shifts which it occasioned, opened the door to new forms of Islamism in the Frontier. It brought to the forefront a new clerical class, largely Deobandi in orientation, which was both more diffuse and more ideologically entrepreneurial than its antecedents. It was these "petty *ulema*" — many of whom, to be clear, had only loose connections to the scholarly Deobandi establishment — who in part carried on the most destructive aspects of the *jihad* into the post-Zia era: the proliferation of small arms and the development of the so-called "Kalashnikov culture;" the entrenchment of sectarian movements and their ideologies-of-difference;[49] and, perhaps most dangerously, the creation of a vast cadre of both ideological and opportunistic veteran *jihadis* beholden in only the most tenuous fashion to the state system.

The *jihad* also fundamentally reshaped the demographic profile of the Frontier. The influx of refugees from Afghanistan, beginning in the early 1980s, eventually reached staggering figures; many estimates put the number above 3 million.[50] Peshawar, once dominated by speakers of Hindko (a Punjabi dialect) was soon filled with Pashto-speaking Afghans who quickly overwhelmed the education and social service capacity of the provincial government, and came to dominate the transportation sector and important routes of the smuggling trade. The sprawling refugee camps near Peshawar and the tribal belt became, over time, *mujahidin* recruitment centers — even long after the end of the *jihad* and the Soviet withdrawal from Afghanistan.

This "Afghanization" of the Pakistani Frontier was complemented by the constant stream of foreigners who passed through Peshawar during the 1980s, seeking to stoke the *jihad* and serve as facilitators for pan-Islamist cadres in their own countries. These foreigners hailed from the Arab world, Chechnya, and the Horn of Africa. Among their ranks were, most infamously, Abdullah Azzam, founder of the Maktab al-Khidmat (the precursor to al Qaeda), and Osama bin Laden. The broad international participation in *jihadi* activity in the Frontier in the 1980s foreshadowed the post-9/11 environment, in which the Frontier would once again become a proving ground for young "religious" militants from the far-flung corners of the Muslim world.

1988–2001: FRAGMENTED POLITICS

Political realignments (1988–93)

The first two civilian governments which came to power in Islamabad after more than a decade of martial rule faced a host of problems in asserting civilian dominance over an entrenched military-bureaucratic complex. This was a period of relatively minimal political involvement for the Deobandi clerics, and one of indecision for the Jamaat, which was torn between its anti-martial idealism and the pressures of political expediency.

Benazir Bhutto's PPP garnered a plurality of votes in the elections held after Zia's death in 1988, and managed to form a government in the face of a rival electoral alliance orchestrated by the ISI — the Islami Jamhuri Ittihad (IJI) — which included the Jamaat and pro-military mainstream parties. The IJI leveraged Islamist rhetoric, played on fears of a female prime minister, and argued for the necessity of continuing the *jihad* in Afghanistan.

Even in defeat, the IJI parties continued to be a thorn in Bhutto's side: her government, which lasted less than two years, was hobbled by the awkward power-sharing arrangement with President Ghulam Ishaq Khan and Chief of Army Staff Aslam Beg, as well as local competition from Punjab Chief Minister Nawaz Sharif.

The Jamaat, though it had played a major role in the IJI's election campaign, was never entirely comfortable with its place in the pro-military alliance. In 1987 Qazi Hussain Ahmad had taken over leadership of the Jamaat from Mawdudi's successor, Mian Tufail. As an ethnic Pashtun, Qazi Hussain was the first non-Mohajir to lead the party since it inception in 1941, and was more sympathetic than his predecessors to populist political mobilization.[51] Under his leadership the Jamaat retained its ideological focus on Islamization, but broadened its political agenda to include populist agitation and more rhetoric on socio-economic issues. This orientation did not always fit comfortably with the IJI's political approach.

The JI's ambivalent relationship with the pro-military block in the post-Zia era was also accelerated by domestic political realignments which were threatening its hold on its traditional base of support among the Mohajir community. The rise of the Mohajir Qaumi Movement (MQM) in Karachi in the late 1980s — a rise engineered in part by Zia and the army to weaken the Jamaat — left the party casting about for new constituencies. Qazi Hussain's ethnic background and Islamic-themed populism allowed the Jamaat to broaden its base of support among the non-Mohajir middle classes in Punjab and — perhaps most importantly — into the Pashtun frontier areas.

As a result of these shifts, the Jamaat played a very vocal but relatively insignificant role in the five years following the return to democratic rule. Its politics were almost consistently contrarian. During the 1988 campaign it joined the pro-military IJI reluctantly. In March 1990, upset at the IJI's pressure on the army to overthrow the PPP government, the Jamaat looked for an excuse to back away from the alliance. It found it, as it so often did, by pivoting around a foreign policy issue and announcing its "principled" intention to stand with Benazir Bhutto in her support of the Kashmiri independence movement.[52] When it became clear several months later that the IJI was on track to win the new elections, the JI, in a shrewd act of bandwagoning, at last decided to re-join, and again used an international issue to pivot domestically — in this case, opposition to the U.S. decertification of Pakistan under the Pressler Amendment.

But once again the Jamaat would chart its own way. Dissatisfied with the IJI's failure to carry out Islamic reforms, the party once again became disillusioned, and one again turned to foreign policy in order to provide a convenient cover for its pivot with respect to domestic politics. When the IJI government decided to accept a settlement to the conflict in Afghanistan, the Jamaat crowed that it was selling out the *mujahidin* and betraying the path of *jihad*. It quit the IJI in May 1992 and began agitation against the Nawaz government that lasted until its fall in April 1993.

New Islamist movements (1993-99)

The final six years of democratic governance in the late 1990s saw second terms for Benazir Bhutto (1993–96) and Nawaz Sharif (1996–99). This was a period full of significant developments, including a financial crisis; Pakistan's first nuclear test; the rise of the Taliban in Afghanistan; and a war over Kashmir. From the perspective of religious politics, both the Deobandis and the Jamaat played foundational roles during this era in faciliating the emergence of new Islamist movements.

The most visible of these new movements was the Taliban, led by Mullah Muhammad Omar, and seeded from the extensive network of Deobandi *madaris* which had sprung up in the Pakistani frontier areas after the Afghan *jihad*. As noted above, the *jihad* not only resulted in a proliferation of *madaris*, but spawned a new, entrepreneurial class of clerics whose ties to the Deobandi establishment were informal at best. Many of the *talibs* (students) who eventually joined the Taliban movement had studied at Sami ul-Haq's Dar ul-Haqqania *madrassah* outside of Peshawar, and many others at Madani Deobandi *madaris* in Karachi.[53] At the time, the JUI leaders went out of their way to highlight their connections with, and influence over, the burgeoning Taliban movement.

In reality, their influence on the new movement was overstated; they had been overtaken by the entrepreneurial character of Deobandi politics in the Frontier. It was the poorly educated, ideologically hardened, disenfranchised *ulema* who formed the core of the movement. Responding to this trend, the traditional leaders had gravitated toward the role of broker, trading on access, influence, and rhetoric to mediate between institutions (governments, *madaris*, political parties) and the organic movements themselves. Perhaps no political figure was so adept at this as Maulana Fazlur Rehman, son of Mufti Mahmud, who threw his support behind Benazir Bhutto during her second term, but was also, like nearly every element of the Pakistani military-political establishment — including Bhutto herself — providing rhetorical and logistical support to the Taliban.[54] The support for the Taliban among Deobandi figures in Pakistan was largely attributable to their shared history among the *madaris* and the opportunities which the Taliban movement presented to the Pakistani clerics for advancing their own political agendas. But the "Pashtunization" of the Pakistani Deobandis was also a major contributing factor. The Taliban represented a set of obscurantist (and supposedly Islamic) values — many of which would have shocked the early, scholarly Deobandis. In reality, their aims were more closely aligned with the spread of conservative Pashtun values than with any grand Islamic vision. The Deobandi experience in the Frontier had produced over time a syncretic form of Sunni Islam, and one in which, as a practical matter, Pashtunwali trumped traditional Hanafi interpretations.

Although the Jamaat was not at the forefront of the Taliban's advance into Afghanistan, it did play a role indirectly in the emergence of another Islamist movement during this period. The Tehrik-e-Nifaz-e-Shariat-e-Muhammadi (TNSM), or Movement for the System of the Shariah of Muhammad, was established in 1989 in district Dir, part of the Malakand administrative division in the northern, mountainous region of the Frontier province. The region which became known as Malakand division was originally constituted by princely states; these independent states acceded to Pakistan in 1969.[55] But by the mid-1970s, there was agitation in district Dir over the rights of local merchants to timber royalties, and a local movement formed which demanded a return to the more favorable legal *status quo* which was operative before 1969.[56]

In response to the demands from Malakand division, Zulfikar Ali Bhutto imposed a new system of tribal law in the area. This system, in turn, was challenged in the Peshawar High Court by lawyers from Malakand during the first prime ministership of Benazir Bhutto, and was eventually overturned. The legal wrangling over the tribal law created an opening into which Maulana Sufi Muhammad, the first *amir* of the TNSM, rallied members of the movement to demand *shariah* as the proper successor to the system of tribal law. The movement was also, not surprisingly, able to rally local smugglers and timber merchants to the cause.[57] The Maulana and his followers were not highly educated ideologues in the traditional mold of the Jamaat (they drew, for example, on anti-modernist Wahhabi influences as well), but they did have linkages to the JI, and their focused insistence on the implementation of the *shariah* was resonant with the party's political approach.[58]

Eventually the state relented to the TNSM's demands, and in May 1994 promulgated a *shariah* ordinance for Malakand which was to remain in effect for four months.[59] The ordinance instituted *qazi* courts which were to be enforced by the provincial government.[60] The TNSM conducted further protests after the ordinance expired, and the conflict turned violent. Eventually, an agreement was reached between the TNSM and the government, in which the state adopted a hands-off approach to the areas around Malakand. The new *shariah* system resulted in few *de facto* changes to the structure of governance, and the state avoided intrusive taxation policies which might inflame local "religious" sentiment.[61] The policy was effective in muting the impact of the TNSM for seven years. Only following the U.S. attacks in Afghanistan after 9/11 was the movement again able to mobilize the masses around a cause.

A return to military rule (1999–2001)

Pervez Musharraf's coup in October 1999 brought a return of military rule. One of the most notable aspects of the two years which followed was Musharraf's policy of supporting an "enlightened moderation" with respect to domestic affairs, while continuing vigorous state support for Kashmiri militant groups and for the Taliban. Shortly before the coup, Nawaz Sharif had been under pressure by the United States to reverse course on Pakistan's policy toward the Taliban, and the army coup was at least in part an attempt to forestall that change.[62]

The government's support for the Pashtun Taliban was extensive, and the state intelligence services also provided a protective cover over al Qaeda members operating in Pakistan, including the North-West Frontier.[63] In May 2000, Musharraf publicly attested to his support for the Taliban:

> I just want to say that there is a difference of understanding on who is a terrorist. The perceptions are different in the United States and in Pakistan, in the West and what we understand is terrorism.… Afghanistan's majority ethnic Pashtuns have to be on our side. This is our national interest.… The Taliban cannot be alienated by Pakistan. We have a national security interest there.[64]

The state's support of the Taliban, much of which was covert, was facilitated in part by the Pakistani religious parties, most notably the Deobandi JUI. In July 2001 Human Rights Watch reported that a "retired senior Pakistani military officer claimed in an interview with Human Rights Watch that up to 30 percent of Taliban fighting strength is made up of Pakistanis serving in units organized by [Pakistani] political parties."[65] On account of the extensive links which had been established in the 1980s between the Deobandi political establishment and the Pakistani intelligence services, the JUI by and large had only a muted response to the military coup in 1999; the party's investment in the Taliban precluded it from taking a more confrontational approach to the return of military rule.

The Jamaat, by contrast, had considerably less political investment in the Taliban movement and realized that, for all of the state's support for Taliban and Kashmiri Islamist proxies, Musharraf would be unlikely to make even half-hearted attempts at expanding the reach of Islamist legal or political influence. The party thus conducted protests following the coup; Qazi Hussain was temporarily banned from the NWFP, and party activities were closely monitored by the government to prevent domestic unrest.[66]

PATTERNS OF ISLAMIC POLITICS

There are several recurring themes which emerge from the brief narrative above regarding the ways in which Islamic politics — and religious parties in particular — have developed in the Pakistani context. These patterns form an important contextual backdrop to understanding the rise of the MMA in 2002, and the subsequent fragmentation of Islamism in the Frontier.

Mutual manipulation

Much has been made of the Pakistan army's use of the Islamists. This nexus, commonly known as the "mullah-military alliance," is seen to be at the heart of the state's duplicity with respect to Islamic militancy — i.e., its history of selectively empowering and undercutting Islamist actors in the pursuit of political ends.[67] This story contains a great deal of truth. The military's cultivation of Islamist fighters during the Afghan *jihad,* and subsequently during the Kashmiri infiltrations, established deep linkages between the military-bureaucratic complex and the web of Islamist parties and militant groups.

The "mullah-military" nexus is, however, a more complicated story than is commonly portrayed. It is a relationship anchored in mutual manipulation, and one which has produced at least as much antagonism as cooperation. The military often used the Islamists for domestic or foreign policy ends: to distract from the unpopularity of a martial government, or antagonize India, or extend its sphere of influence into Afghanistan. But it is also evident that the Islamists were not infrequently at odds with Pakistan's martial regimes. The religious parties bitterly opposed Ayub Khan. Even during Zia ul-Haq's martial government, as the mutual manipulation reached its zenith with the army's instrumentalization of the religious parties for the *jihad* and the Islamists' attempts to garner state funds and press for Islamist reforms, the partnership was short-lived. By the mid-1980s the relationship had soured and groups like the Jamaat were again deeply disillusioned with the martial state.

Leveraging external events

Second, as might be expected from any political movement, the Islamists have a long history of leveraging external events in order to advance their political standing at home. This was true for both the Deobandis and for the Jamaat, though they tended to focus on different regions and issues. For the modern JUI, Afghanistan was always the dominant external issue around which the party would pivot politically. The JUI's predominantly Pashtun base felt a strong connection to the Pashtuns in Afghanistan, and as a consequence of its historical ties to Deoband, was often ambivalent about the fierce anti-Indian rhetoric of the martial governments.[68]

The Jamaat adopted a considerably more pan-Islamic perspective, drawing on events in the wider Islamic world to incrementally advance its standing at home. It was particularly adept at fomenting public outrage over foreign events for the purpose of forcing the sitting government in Islamabad to make a show of its Islamic credentials. It vigorously criticized Pakistan's early pro-Western orientation; became deeply involved in supporting the Kashmir insurgencies in the 1990s; vocally opposed the American war to oust Saddam Hussain from Kuwait; and stoked the violent protests against Salman Rushdie in 1988. This broader, internationalist outlook reflected the Jamaat's loose ties to the Muslim Brotherhood, and its historical pan-Islamism which saw the Islamization of Pakistan as an important catalyzing event for a wider, global Islamist movement.

Shifting constituencies

Third, Islamist movements have been forced to respond to the shifting character of their own constituencies. This is especially true for Islamist parties which depend on electoral support from particular demographic blocs. The early Deobandis, for example, had a long history of interaction with *madaris* in Afghanistan and the tribal areas, but the movement did not begin as one dominated by ethnic Pashtuns. The Afghan *jihad* accelerated the process of "Pashtunization" among the Deobandi parties in Pakistan — a process which has resulted in the emergence of JUI factions which often put greater emphasis on ethnic and regional issues than on the broader implementation of Islamic revivalism throughout Pakistan.[69]

The Jamaat too has seen dramatic changes to its constituent base since Partition. Founded on an appeal to Punjabi and Mohajir urban religiosity, the party was weakened by the rise of the MQM in Karachi in the 1980s, which cut into its voter base. The selection of Qazi Hussain as *amir* in 1987 and the party's efforts to broaden its appeal to a Pashtun constituency subsequently realigned the Jamaat's approach to mobilizing its political base. Most notably, it increased its focus on issues relating to foreign influence in Afghanistan, and played off of gender issues (e.g., condemning gender-integrated events) in a way that was likely to appeal to the socially conservative Pashtun population.

Limited electoral influence

Prior to 2002, Pakistan's Islamists had put forward a very poor showing in electoral politics. At the most, they were fringe players in parliament, garnering no more than 12% of national assembly seats.[70] Even their parliamentary high water marks were not especially substantive: the 1970 Mufti Mahmud government in NWFP in 1970 collapsed after less than a year; the Jamaat received cabinet positions in the early years of the Zia ul-Haq regime, but made little headway outside of some reforms in Islamic banking; and Maulana Fazlur Rehman was given the chairmanship of the Foreign Affairs committee during the second Benazir Bhutto government, but implemented no significant policy changes.

In spite of this limited success in the electoral arena, the Islamist parties have exerted an influence disproportionate to their electoral strength. This has come about in large part because of their effectiveness at mobilizing their political bases, and their skill at using Islamic identity and Islamist goals as "wedge issues" by which to pressure the mainstream and martial governments into adopting aspects of an Islamic platform.

Divergent Islamisms

Islamism in Pakistan is frequently portrayed as something of a monolith — as an organized and disciplined group of activists pressing for a coherent vision of an Islamic state. The reality is more multifaceted. Even the two major Islamic political blocs, the Jamaat and the JUI-F, have distinctly different visions of an Islamic state and society, and have often been at odds with one another. The parties, for example, had notably different views on the Taliban.[71] The JI's outlook is deeply ideological, modernist, and pan-Islamic. Its urban middle-class constituents are primarily concerned with restructuring the legal and political order. The JUI-F, by contrast, is a relatively pragmatic party with a rural, clerical constituency whose objectives are to protect the *madrassah* system from state interference and promote a conservative interpretation of Pashtun social values which they defend as Islamic. It should come as no surprise that these two movements have often found themselves on different sides of the political space in Pakistan and, prior to 2002, did not join together in any meaningful way to advance a common agenda.

The parties' organizational structures also reflect and shape the ways in which they approach their Islamist agendas. The Jamaat leadership runs the party like a modern corporation, with a well-staffed headquarters outside Lahore, a wide range of publications, relatively meritocratic policies of promotion, strong party discipline, an array of affiliations with international Islamist organizations, and a focus on ideological training. The JUI parties operate more loosely, with much of their political activity taking place outside of formal party committees. Key decisions by the JUI-F are routinely made by Fazlur Rehman and a traveling coterie of personal advisors, and the party has only recently invested in a well-equipped headquarters.[72] The combination of charismatic leadership and decentralized party structure has led to nearly constant dissention within the JUI-F, most of which is dealt with informally in Pashtun-style *shuras* and quiet deals.

These two major Islamist parties are often considered "mainstream," not because they meet the standards of Western liberalism, but because they participate in electoral politics and generally eschew violence. Aside from these parties, Pakistan is also home to a great number of smaller Islamist groups, including militant *jihadi* organizations, sectarian militias, and vigilante Islamist movements. These groups tend to be more localized in nature, and operate outside of the formal political space. Their Islamist objectives vary wildly — some, like the TNSM, make their appeals to the state much as would the Jamaat; others, like the Waziri movements in the early twentieth century and again today, confront the state and fundamentally question its writ; and others, like the sectarian Sipah-e-Sahaba, for the most part ignore the state, focusing their attention on cleansing Pakistan of "infidels" who take the name of Islam.

Balancing and bandwagoning

Islamist groups, having consistently been minority players in Pakistani politics, have employed various strategies to obtain political advantage vis-à-vis the state and their local opponents. As an ideological and politically revisionist movement, the Jamaat has typically chosen to balance against the state by allying itself with opposition movements; those cases in which it partnered with the state, such as during the Zia era, were relatively short-lived. The Deobandi political leadership, by contrast, has proven to be relatively less driven by ideological motivations, and more attuned to patronage incentives from the state. Its strategy, for the most part, has been to bandwagon with the ruling party so as to ensure that it retains access to state resources.

These general patterns change somewhat at the local level, particularly in areas which have a history of tribal governance, such as the FATA and present-day Swat. In these regions, Islamist political behavior is often less related to ideology or patronage concerns than it is to established patterns of group conflict which appear in segmentary lineage tribal systems. These are patterns in which small tribes or factions partner with the state or with other small factions to take on a dominant faction in their own area. This kind of perpetual balancing, and the highly provisional alliances which make it possible, are regular features of religious politics in the tribal areas, and ones which are integral to understanding Islamism in the contemporary Frontier. It is important, for example, to realize that when Islamist groups in the tribal areas ally with the state, they usually do so in the pursuit of political advantage vis-à-vis local rivals rather than in allegiance to state authority or shared political ends.

Splinter groups and 'market segmentation'

The Pakistani Islamist scene is replete with splinter groups and political rivalries. This tendency toward factionalization occurs primarily in three ways. In the first case, splinter groups are formed as a result of political rivalries grounded in personality politics. This is not to suggest that ideology does not play a role; often it does. It is, rather, that factional leaders leverage minor ideological differences in order to bring about a political fragmentation which results in a new faction under their leadership. In other instances, the factionalization is simply a result of patronage considerations, i.e., contests over which leader can bring more resources to the community.

In the second case, Islamist groups splinter because of real ideological differences. Some of the early Deobandi disputes, for example, centered around basic questions of the proper role of the clerical class in the political sphere. Most ideological splits, upon close examination, actually implicate personality politics to a considerable degree.

The third case is the most complex and arguably the most important. In this scenario, Islamist groups splinter as a result of methodological differences. These disputes center around questions such as, "What do we do if the state does not accept our demand for Islamization?" and "What forms of protest are appropriate?" Sometimes these splits are the result of real disputes regarding the proper limits of Islamization, in which a hard-core faction — frustrated with the political vacillations of a mainstream, politically-oriented body — splits off and starts a new movement.

Other times, these splits are ones of convenience, in which Islamist groups implement a form of "market segmentation" whereby they spin off politically unpalatable but strategically useful Islamist agitation into a separate entity with which they retain no formal affiliation. This approach offers several advantages to a given movement. Most essentially, it allows the movement to retain its place in the political center as a respected Islamist entity operating within the bounds of legality. At the same time, it facilitates the creation of hard-core factions which can perform specific tasks (e.g., sectarian agitation) without damaging the reputation of the movement as a whole. And finally, it establishes informal linkages between political and militant factions — linkages which can be used as channels for recruitment or the provision of resources, or as vehicles through which to extend political protections to militants who may run afoul of the law.

Deobandi politics is replete with these kind of linkages. Parties such as the JUI have historically been careful to remain in the political mainstream and act in accordance with democratic and constitutional norms, but have also cultivated links with movements such as the Taliban (and, today, the neo-Taliban), sectarian groups such as Sipah-e-Sahaba, and Kashmiri militant organizations such as Harkat ul-Mujahidin.[73] Not entirely unlike the bifurcation of political and militant wings of the Irish Republican Army or Hamas, the Deobandi establishment has produced a network of segmented organizations which together advance an overarching political or social agenda. This segmentation model, as will be explored below, can present challenges to Islamist groups, most notably in that political factions can rarely rely on militant factions to remain pliable and subservient to the movement's broadly *political* agenda.

Segmentation also, however, provides a secondary advantage to the religious parties: both the JUI and the Jamaat have learned to leverage their positions as political organizations in order to serve as middlemen between the state and the various militant factions to which they are linked. In this respect, the Deobandi parties have focused their efforts on the western (Afghan) front, positioning themselves as occasional brokers between the government and Taliban groups in the tribal areas. The Jamaat's linkages, by contrast, have proven particularly useful to the state in support of anti-Indian incursions on the eastern (Kashmiri) front.[74] Often these parties are asked to serve as interlocutors in secret negotiations; but just as often, they take up the cause of militant groups in public fora, either to rally their own political base or to express by proxy certain strategic interests of the state which cannot be expressed on an official basis.[75]

NOTES:

1. See especially Sana Haroon, *Frontier of Faith: Islam in the Indo-Afghan Borderland* (New York: Columbia University Press, 2007); and Ayesha Jalal, *Partisans of Allah: Jihad in South Asia* (Cambridge, MA: Harvard University Press, 2008).

2. See Olaf Caroe, *The Pathans: 550 B.C.–A.D. 1957* (Karachi: Oxford University Press, 2006 [1958]), 364–9.

3. For a detailed look at the lasting influence of the Akhund's *pirimuridi* line, see Haroon, *Frontier of Faith*, 43ff.

4. Caroe, *The Pathans*, 383–9. For a discussion of the development of the FCR system, and British efforts to manage the Pashtun populations in the Frontier, see Christian Tripodi, "Peacemaking Through Bribes or Cultural Empathy? The Political Officer and Britain's Strategy Towards the North-West Frontier, 1901–1945," *Journal of Strategic Studies* 31, no. 1 (February 2008): 123–51.

5. Caroe, *The Pathans*, 387.

6. Haroon, *Frontier of Faith*, 48ff.

7. See Dietrich Reetz, *Islam in the Public Sphere: Religious Groups in India, 1900–1947* (New Delhi; New York: Oxford University Press, 2006), 252.

8. Haroon, *Frontier of Faith*, 106ff.

9. The Muslims sought to persuade Britain to protect the defeated Ottoman Empire, and thus the sultan who also held the title of caliph. In an extraordinary show of solidarity, Mahatma Gandhi also advocated on behalf of the Khilafat movement.

10 Dietrich Reetz notes that Maulana Azad, who went on to be a leader in the Congress Party, and Abdul Ghaffar Khan, who went on to lead the Red Shirt movement, both participated in the *hijrat*. Reetz, *Islam in the Public Sphere*, 254.

11 The Khilafat movement had by this time lost steam, but the committees in the frontier carried on as vehicles for resistance. Note that *khilafat* can refer to the caliphate, but is also related to the Urdu word for "resistance." Haroon, *Frontier of Faith*, 161.

12 For a detailed history of the Faqir's 1936 campaign, see Alan Warren, *Waziristan, the Faqir of Ipi, and the Indian Army: the North West Frontier Revolt of 1936–37* (Oxford: Oxford University Press, 2000).

13 Barbara D. Metcalf, *Islamic Revival in British India: Deoband, 1860–1900* (Princeton, NJ: Princeton University Press, 1982), 86.

14 See, e.g., Zia ul-Hasan Faruqi, *The Deoband School and the Demand for Pakistan* (London: Asia Publishing House, 1963), 110–11.

15 See Ayesha Jalal, *Self and Sovereignty: Individual and Community in South Asian Islam Since 1850* (London; New York: Routledge, 2000), 458ff.

16 This phrase is borrowed from Gilles Kepel. See Gilles Kepel, *Jihad: The Trail of Political Islam*, tr. Anthony F. Roberts (Cambridge, MA: Belknap Press of Harvard University Press, 2002).

17 It was through Sayyid Qutb that many of Mawdudi's ideas eventually made their way to the Arab world.

18 Seyyed Vali Reza Nasr, *Mawdudi and the Making of Islamic Revivalism* (Oxford: Oxford University Press, 1996), 57. The quotation is from a work by Mawdudi in 1955.

19 Seyyed Vali Reza Nasr, *The Vanguard of the Islamic Revolution: The Jama'at-i Islami of Pakistan* (Berkeley: University of California Press, 1994), available at http://ark.cdlib.org/ark:/13030/ft9j49p32d/ (accessed October 1, 2008), chapter 1.

20 For a comparison of the Jamaat-e-Islami and the Tablighi Jamaat, see Mumtaz Ahmad, "Islamic Fundamentalism in South Asia: The Jamaat-i-Islami and the Tablighi Jamaat of South Asia," in *Fundamentalisms Observed*, ed. Martin E. Marty and R. Scott Appleby (Chicago: University of Chicago Press, 1991).

21 When asked about how the Jamaat's "outside-in" approach to Islamization works, a party spokesman explained it thus: "Many people believe but don't practice. Changing their philosophy doesn't matter. They are Muslim. But when they have an Islamic government as a role model, then it will influence the character of the people." Author interview with Ameer-ul-Azim, Jamaat-e-Islami spokesman, June 2007, Lahore.

22 The Resolution, passed in March 1949, put forward eight principles. The most important of these, at least for the Jamaat, were "Sovereignty belongs to Allah alone but He has delegated it to the State of Pakistan through its people for being exercised within the limits prescribed by Him as a sacred trust;" "The principles of democracy, freedom, equality, tolerance and social justice, as enunciated by Islam, shall be fully observed;" and "Muslims shall be enabled to order their lives in the individual and collective spheres in accordance with the teachings of Islam as set out in the Qur'an and Sunnah." Leonard Binder, *Religion and Politics in Pakistan* (Berkeley and Los Angeles: University of California Press, 1961), 142ff.

23 The Ahmadis, contra Sunni and Shia Muslims, believe in the continuation of divine revelation and are adherents of Mirza Ghulam Ahmad (1835–1908).

24 Nasr, *Vanguard*, chapter 7.

25 Ahmad, "Islamic Fundamentalism in South Asia," 474.

26 Interview with Chiragh-e-Rah, Karachi, December 1960, in Sayyid Abul 'Ala Maududi, *Selected Speeches & Writings of Maulana Maududi,* vol. 2, trans. S. Zakir Aijaz (Karachi: International Islamic Publishers, 1982), 62–4.

27 Interview with *The Asia,* Lahore, September 6, 1966, in Maududi, *Selected Speeches,* 145. (According to Mawdudi it was now "the religious duty of the Muslims to wage a holy war or *jihad* against the enemy.")

28 Seyyed Vali Reza Nasr, "The Rise of Sunni Militancy in Pakistan: The Changing Role of Islamism and the Ulama in Society and Politics," *Modern Asian Studies* 34, no. 1 (February 2000), 173. For the history of this split, see Sayyid A.S. Pirzada, *The Politics of the Jamiat-i-Ulema-i-Islam Pakistan 1971–1977* (Karachi; New York: Oxford University Press, 2000), 52ff. This conflict between the viewpoints of the clerical and the non-clerical Islamists became unusually bitter: Mufti Mahmud claimed that the real threat to Pakistan was "Maududiyyat" (a reference to Maulana Mawdudi) which was "worse than socialism," and insisted — in a claim that today seems rather bizarre — that JI was secretly working for the Americans. The amount of propaganda put out by JUI to reinforce this notion, according to one hyperbolic observer at the time, "is so huge that if put together, even without a commentary, it could make a book running into thousands of pages." Ibid., 222 (note).

29 Mianwali is situated just east of present-day Lakki Marwat district.

30 For a lively history of Deobandism in the Frontier, and the role of Mufti Mahmud, see Sana Haroon, "The Rise of Deobandi Islam in the North-West Frontier Province and its Implications in Colonial India and Pakistan 1914–1996," *Journal of the Royal Asiatic Society* 18, no. 1 (2008).

31 For more on the Red Shirts, see chapter III, "New Islamists and the Return of Pashtun Nationalism."

32 It resigned in protest over Z.A. Bhutto's dismissal of the JUI-NAP government in Balochistan following accusations over its involvement in the "London Plan" to break up Pakistan. Pirzada, *Jamiat-i-Ulema-i-Islam,* 73. See also Shuja Nawaz, *Crossed Swords: Pakistan, its Army, and the Wars Within* (Oxford: Oxford University Press, 2008), 331ff.

33 This is a partial list. See Pirzada, *Jamiat-i-Ulema-i-Islam,* 67.

34 See http://www.khyber.org/people/ulema/MuftiMehmood.shtml (accessed December 1, 2006).

35 Pirzada, *Jamiat-i-Ulema-i-Islam,* 232.

36 The Hudood ordinance makes it difficult for a woman to prove an allegation of rape, requiring four adult male witnesses. If the woman cannot prove rape, she is open to the charge of adultery, which carries a lower standard of evidence.

37 For an examination of Zia's Islamization, see Seyyed Vali Reza Nasr, *Islamic Leviathan: Islam and the Making of State Power* (Oxford: Oxford University Press, 2001), 130–57.

38 Ahmad, "Islamic Fundamentalism in South Asia," 480.

39 Ibid.

40 Nasr, *Vanguard,* chapter 9.

41 Ahmad, "Islamic Fundamentalism in South Asia," 483.

42 Nasr, *Vanguard,* chapter 9.

43 Erland Jansson, *India, Pakistan or Pakhtunistan: The Nationalist Movements in the North-West Frontier Province, 1937–47* (Uppsala; Stockholm: University of Uppsala, 1981), 59.

44 Akbar S. Ahmed, *Resistance and Control in Pakistan,* rev. ed. (London; New York: Routledge, 2004), 84.

45 Ahmed observed the way in which the prominent *ulema* began to imitate the behaviors and formalities associated with the political agents. This author also observed the same dynamic among leading JUI-F *ulema* in NWFP in 2006, who fused *jirga*-like customs with

more bureaucratic trappings (such as formal meeting procedures, flamboyant security, and layers of "handlers" and minor clerics who served as functionaries). In this respect, the JUI-F *ulema* during the MMA period became brokers between their conservative Pashtun constituency and the government apparatus, blending the traditions of the former with the affect of the latter.

46   Many of them, of course, never changed vocations. Following the end of the Afghan *jihad*, the ISI helpfully redirected them to the proxy war being waged in Kashmir.

47   Nasr, "The Rise of Sunni Militancy," 150.

48   For a discussion of Pashtun migration, see Robert Nichols, *A History of Pashtun Migration, 1775–2006* (Oxford University Press, 2008).

49   See, e.g., Nasr, "The Rise of Sunni Militancy," 144ff.

50   For a discussion of refugee numbers, see Daniel A. Kronenfeld, "Afghan Refugees in Pakistan: Not All Refugees, Not Always in Pakistan, Not Necessarily Afghan?" *Journal of Refugee Studies* 21, no. 1 (March 2008).

51   The term Mohajirs refers to Urdu-speaking refugees from India who settled in Pakistan after 1947.

52   Nasr, *Vanguard*, chapter 10. The Jamaat had extensive involvement with the Kashmir insurgency during this period, and the struggle in Kashmir became one of the most effective means for rallying the party's Mohajir and Punjabi constituencies.

53   Sami ul-Haq was the leader of what had been the Darkhawasti faction in early Deobandi politics.

54   Fazlur Rehman was given the Chairmanship of the Standing Committee on Foreign Affairs in the National Assembly, from which he was able to promote the Taliban and build contacts in the Gulf. For background on the Taliban's connection with the Deobandis and in particular the JUI-S, see Ahmed Rashid, *Taliban: Militant Islam, Oil, and Fundamentalism in Central Asia* (New Haven: Yale University Press, 2000), 88–94. For Bhutto's role in supporting the Taliban, see Steve Coll, *Ghost Wars: The Secret History of the CIA, Afghanistan, and Bin Laden, from the Soviet Invasion to September 10, 2001* (New York: Penguin Press, 2004), 298ff.

55   The princely states were those of Chitral, Dir, and Swat. These became the erstwhile Malakand division, which includes the present-day districts of Buner, Chitral, Upper and Lower Dir, Malakand, and Swat.

56   See Pakistan Institute for Peace Studies, "TNSM: A Taliban like Movement," August 15, 2007; and Muhammad Amir Rana, "Backgrounder: Shariah Movement in Malakand," Pakistan Institute for Peace Studies, April 29, 2008.

57   The TNSM reportedly had deep linkages with the gray economy in Malakand. See Pakistan Institute for Peace Studies, "TNSM: A Taliban like Movement."

58   Although the TNSM has generally opposed electoral politics, it lent support to the MMA in 2002. Links between the movement and the JI continue, particularly in Dir. Author interviews, July 2007, Peshawar. See also "Activists of TNSM reorganizing," *Dawn*, June 26, 2003.

59   "After Sufi Muhammad's release," *Daily Times*, April 23, 2008.

60   Muhammad Amir Rana, "A Court of One's Own," *Herald*, May 2007, 57.

61   Malakand district, along with Battagram, Chitral, Lower Dir, Upper Dir, and Kohistan continue to this day to be exempt from taxation. World Bank and Government of NWFP, *Accelerating Growth*, 92.

62   Douglas Frantz, "Supplying the Taliban: Pakistan Ended Aid to Taliban Only Hesitantly," *New York Times*, December 8, 2001.

63   See Ahmed Rashid, *Descent into Chaos* (New York: Penguin, 2008), 48ff.

64   Quoted in Ibid., 50–51.

65 Human Rights Watch, "Afghanistan: Crisis of Impunity: The Role of Pakistan, Russia, and Iran in Fueling the Civil War," July 2001, available at http://www.hrw.org/reports/2001/afghan2 (accessed October 1, 2008).

66 "Qazi's entry in NWFP banned," *Dawn*, October 24, 1999.

67 For writing on this subject see, e.g., Husain Haqqani, *Pakistan: Between Mosque and Military* (Washington, DC: Carnegie Endowment for International Peace, 2005); International Crisis Group, *Pakistan: The Mullahs and the Military*, March 20, 2003; Hassan Abbas, *Pakistan's Drift into Extremism: Allah, the Army, and America's War on Terror* (London: M. E. Sharpe, 2005); and Zahid Hussain, *Frontline Pakistan: The Struggle with Militant Islam* (New York: Columbia University Press, 2007).

68 The JUI-F retains close ties with Dar ul-Ulum in Deoband, and occasionally invites Indian clerics to visit Peshawar and Islamabad. The party has also been a relatively consistent advocate of Indo-Pakistani peace efforts.

69 JUI groups also exist in the Punjab, but are less politically active than those in the Frontier.

70 Frédéric Grare makes this point forcefully in his paper, "Pakistan: The Myth of an Islamist Peril," Carnegie Endowment for International Peace, February 2006.

71 While the ideology of the Taliban and the boldness of its advance in Afghanistan appealed to the Jamaat, it did not represent for them a viable model of Islamization: aside from the naming of an *amir,* the Taliban demonstrated little interest in systematized frameworks of law, or the grand Mawdudian designs of state that the Jamaat associated with Islamic progress. Speaking in October 2000, Qazi Hussain was careful to say, "I did not oppose Taliban during any session. Though I said that we do not want Taliban-like system in Pakistan. In Pakistan, we want implementation on our Constitution that includes the Objectives Resolution and Islamic provisions." Qazi Hussain Ahmad, "The US Visit: Objectives, Benefits, Apprehensions and Objections," *Tarjumanul Quran* (October 2000), available http://jamaat.org/Isharat/2000/ish102000.html (accessed May 1, 2007).

72 The JUI-F Markaz (headquarters) is located on the ring road outside of Peshawar.

73 See Office of the Coordinator for Counterterrorism, "Country Reports on Terrorism," U.S. Department of State, April 30, 2008, chapter 6; B. Raman, "Beware the Maulana!" *Rediff* News, July 23, 2003, available at http://www.rediff.com/news/2003/jul/23raman.htm (accessed October 1, 2008); Owais Tohid, "And the Jihad Goes On," *Newsline*, December 2003; and Rashid, *Descent into Chaos*, 249–50. For a discussion on the use of cover names by militant groups, see Muhammad Amir Rana, "Marriott Blast: How to Single out Culprit Group from a Pool of Terrorists?" Pakistan Institute for Peace Studies, September 24, 2008.

74 Following the decline of the *jihad* in Afghanistan in 1989, the Pakistani intelligence services, in collaboration with the Jamaat, relocated many of the *mujahidin* from the Afghan front to serve as irregulars in Kashmir. Even after direct ISI support for the insurgents was relaxed in 1993, the government continued to work closely through the Jamaat-e-Islami of Jammu and Kashmir (JIJK) to mobilize Kashmiri militants. See Yoginder Sikand, "The Emergence and Development of the Jama'at-i-Islami of Jammu and Kashmir (1940s–1990)," *Modern Asian Studies* 36, no. 3 (2002), 705–51.

75 Maulana Fazlur Rehman's harsh rebuke of military action in the tribal areas, and of Pakistan's strategic posture toward Afghanistan, can be seen as a mix of these two impulses. Such language reinforces his credibility among Pashtuns in the tribal areas, and indirectly serves to reinforce the army's case for the need to pursue negotiated settlements with "moderate" Taliban in both the tribal areas and Afghanistan. See Irfan Ghauri and Muhammad Bilal, "JUI-F chief opposes use of force in Tribal Areas: Fazl emerges as 'Taliban spokesman' in parliament," *Daily Times*, October 17, 2008.

II
THE MMA'S ISLAMIST GOVERNANCE

The Frontier today faces a new and troubling array of insurgent threats. Religious parties like the JUI-F and the Jamaat appear to have been eclipsed by new movements, and no longer set the tone for Islamist discourse. Why then is a narrative of the MMA's tenure still relevant in the contemporary context? It matters for two reasons.

First, even though the religious parties are no longer in a governing role, and no longer command the influence they did even several years ago, the relationship between mainstream "democratic Islamists" and the new insurgent movements is a critical dynamic in understanding Islamism in the Frontier. The promises and demands of groups such as Tehrik-e-Taliban-e-Pakistan (TTP), the TNSM in Swat, and the Lashkar-e-Islami (LI) in Khyber are not very far removed from those of the MMA six years ago. The tactics and organization of such groups, to be sure, differ in profound ways from those of the MMA. But the continuities are equally important. Absent the historical backdrop of the MMA's tenure, it would be easy to miss the quasi-political nature of groups like the TNSM and LI. It would also be easy to misconstrue the complex relationships between the "democratic Islamists" and the new insurgent groups — relationships which may figure prominently in the ability of the state to eventually bring insurgents into the political mainstream.

Second, taking a longer view, the MMA constitutes a worthwhile case study of Islamist governance in practice. There are few instances in South Asia in which Islamists have moved from an oppositional and agitational role to one of actual governance. The dynamics of this shift can reveal important clues about the ways in which Islamist leaders change — rhetorically, politically, and organizationally — when they are forced to interact with domestic and foreign interlocutors. In this respect, the experience of the MMA may be able to shed light on both the promises and the limits of the political process in bounding the more problematic aspects of Islamism, particularly in a Pakistani context.[1]

THE RISE OF THE MUTTAHIDA MAJLIS-E-AMAL

Regional context

The rise of the Islamist alliance in 2002 cannot be understood apart from the American invasion of Afghanistan in late 2001, which immediately became the *cause célèbre* of the religious parties, and gave them an electoral issue with strong regional, ethnic, and religious appeal. Not surprisingly, it was Pashtun religious politicians such as Maulana Fazlur Rehman of the JUI-F, Maulana Sami ul-Haq of the JUI-S, and Qazi Hussain Ahmad of the JI who were best positioned to make use of "Islamic rage" in the wake of American operations against the Pashtun Taliban in Afghanistan.[2]

In retrospect it appears natural that these politicians and their respective religious parties would coalesce into an alliance opposing the American war in Afghanistan. But in fact, the parties had a long history of dysfunctional interaction, and had never before formed a broad-based Islamist alliance.[3] In the year preceding 9/11 there were signs that such an alliance was increasingly possible; but it seems to have taken prodding from former ISI chief Hamid Gul to coalesce the Islamists into a Pak-Afghan Defense Council, which in 2002 became the basis for the Muttahida Majlis-e-Amal (MMA) electoral alliance.[4] The six-party alliance brought together the Pashtun-dominated JUI-F and JUI-S; the Jamaat-e-Islami; the Jamiat Ulema-e-Pakistan (JUP), a Barelvi party led by Maulana Shah Ahmed Noorani; the Jamiat Ahl-e-Hadith (JAH), a Saudi-influenced Wahhabi party led by Sajid Mir; and the Islami Tehrik-e-Pakistan (ITP), a Shia party formerly known as Tehrik-e-Jafaria Pakistan (TJP), and led by Allama Sajid Naqvi.[5] The formation of this broad-based alliance served the interests of the Pakistani state by stoking pro-Taliban sentiment in the Pak-Afghan border areas, but also by fostering the perception (to the Americans in particular) that Islamism was on the rise in the Frontier, and that only a strong military-executive power in Islamabad could properly check this emergent danger.

Domestic context

The domestic situation was also unusually favorable to the Islamists. President Musharraf had instituted governor's rule in the NWFP after his 1999 coup, and the 2002 polls were to be the first general elections since 1997. Two parties which had traditionally been dominant in the Frontier — the PPP and the Pashtun nationalist ANP — were both weak, fragmented, and demoralized. The MMA found it especially easy to impugn the credibility of the nationalists, who had supported Musharraf's post-9/11 "capitulation" to the Americans.[6]

The MMA alliance also benefited from support by the state, which recognized that the Islamists could serve as a useful proxy by which the Musharraf government could decapitate its chief political rivals in the Frontier (the PPP, PML-N, and ANP). Musharraf's own PML-Q faced grim prospects outside of the non-Pashtun Hazara division in the eastern part of the province and the isolated PML bastion of Lakki Marwat in the south, and the Islamists therefore presented a second-best solution to the ruling party's political quandary in the NWFP. Particularly in those areas in which representatives of the central government and security services could not convince local power-brokers to support a weak PML-Q candidate, they often asked them to throw their weight instead behind the religious parties.[7]

The role of the Pakistani security services in the 2002 NWFP elections has been much disputed. Some commentators have suggested in retrospect that the Islamists' victory was entirely engineered by the ISI; the reality is that the manipulation was significant but subtle. Rather than engaging in large-scale electoral manipulation, the services chose instead to stifle the mainstream parties while allowing religious leaders a free hand in capitalizing on the wave of anti-American sentiment in the Frontier.[8]

The government's assistance to the religious alliance took several forms. First, the mainstream and nationalist parties were given only a narrow window of time before the elections in which to campaign and counter the MMA's electoral rhetoric. This restriction, perhaps more than anything else, played to the advantage of the Islamists, who were able to organize blatantly political "religious gatherings" in mosques and *madaris* throughout the province, beginning weeks and even months before the official start of the campaign season. The result was the creation of an organizational vacuum that the MMA was easily able to fill.

Second, the election commission further boosted the prospects of the MMA by "arbitrarily" assigning to it the official electoral symbol of the book. The alliance's leadership wasted no time in playing up the religious significance of the symbol, claiming the book to be the Quran and the MMA to be the undisputed party of learning. Third, federal electoral statutes holding that candidates must possess certain educational qualifications (typically, a bachelors degree) were interpreted by the federal government so as not to disqualify candidates who held certificates from the *madaris*. This was a great boon to the JUI, many of whose members did not have degrees from accredited institutions. And finally, some MMA candidates were reportedly aided by the quiet withdrawal of criminal cases against them in advance of their nomination papers being scrutinized. This process was well-documented in the case of MMA leaders in Balochistan, and there is good reason to believe that the same process took place in the NWFP.

By late 2002, the conflict in Afghanistan had given the MMA a potent political issue and electoral momentum. Not only did the ruling elites in Islamabad find it unnecessary to use blunt instruments of electoral manipulation in support of the MMA, but doing so would have posed special challenges: unlike the feudal politics of Punjab and Sindh, Pashtun politics in NWFP is decidedly more egalitarian, and the security services have historically found it more challenging to engage in wholesale vote-buying and intimidation in the Frontier than in the other provinces.[9] And in fact, the extent of the MMA's success proved surprising even to those agencies which were charged with facilitating its victory; many in the security services reportedly underestimated the extent of the MMA's popularity in the Peshawar valley and Malakand areas.[10]

Electoral strategy and mobilization

The MMA alliance was originally formed around a relatively narrow, Afghanistan-focused agenda. As it began campaigning in 2002, however, the MMA gradually adopted a more robust platform. Unlike the mainstream parties which relied on charismatic party leadership, or the ethno-nationalist parties which relied on a set of ethnically-charged historical grievances, the JUI and the JI brought complementary methods of mobilization to the alliance's campaign strategy. The JUI drew on its *madaris* network for mass-mobilization, and the Jamaat, under the leadership of Qazi Hussain, was able to tap a burgeoning network of Pashtun political workers in the Frontier who could leverage the party's famously disciplined bureaucracy. What began as a proto-political movement oriented against Western military action in Afghanistan became over the course of the campaign a fairly robust alliance. However vague or unrealistic its promises may have been, the MMA was arguably the electoral bloc which articulated the most forceful "pro-change" agenda of any party contesting the elections.[11]

This change agenda was not only reactive, but also sweepingly proactive. The MMA promised the institution of a true Islamic system in the Frontier, including the prohibition of "obscene" material on cable television, the provision of Islamic banking, and the conversion of the provincial assembly into an "Islamic *jirga*."[12] Other pledges were considerably more vague, such as the curtailing of un-Islamic work by NGOs and foreign elements, the enforcement of "Islamic justice," the imposition of the *shariah* into the provincial framework of law, and the promotion of policies designed to encourage the use of head coverings. Much as Mufti Mahmud had done in 1970, the MMA wove this Islamic reform agenda together with a rhetoric of populist governance, an approach which in many ways echoed the language of the PPP.[13] Drawing on its lower- and middle-class roots, the religious alliance put forward a strikingly populist campaign that equated Islamic political reforms with a pro-poor agenda.[14] The MMA's plan for its first hundred days promised the creation of a half-million new jobs, free education through the secondary level, interest-free loans for low-cost housing, cheap medications, and old-age allowances.[15]

Accounting for Islamism

It was not surprising that the JUI-F would prove successful in the conservative southern districts bordering Afghanistan, or that the Jamaat would gain solid support in outlying areas such as district Dir. What surprised analysts was the MMA's success in making inroads into areas that had previously been almost off-limits to religious politics, such as the Pashtun agricultural heartland of the Peshawar valley, regions like Malakand division in which ANP and PPP had traditionally held sway, and even PML strongholds such as Hazara division. Capturing a remarkable 48 of 99 provincial assembly seats, and 29 of 35 national assembly seats from the Frontier, the MMA's victory in 2002 was a dramatic realignment of the NWFP electoral map away from virtually all of the established parties such as the PPP, the ANP, and the PML factions, and toward a group of mostly unknown, politically inexperienced religious leaders and party operatives.[16]

Federal intervention by the security services undoubtedly explains part of the MMA's success, as does the presence of the conflict in Afghanistan. But these two factors alone are still insufficient to account for the MMA's sweep.[17] If state manipulation was enough to bring the MMA to power, then why were the security services manifestly unable to engineer anything more than token victories by the ruling party's own PML-Q? If the Afghan situation had sufficient explanatory power to describe the election results, then why did the MMA make such surprising inroads into non-Pashtun Hazara division, an area in which there is minimal concern among the electorate about Afghan issues? Or why did the MMA lose in district Tank (adjacent to Waziristan), where there is a widespread affinity for the Afghan Taliban?

The Afghan situation, along with the political interference by the ruling elites designed to capitalize upon it, were necessary but not sufficient factors to explain the ascent of political Islam in the Frontier in 2002. Acute anti-establishment feeling was a significant driver of the electoral shift, as was the success of the MMA's own populist agenda and its drive to implement a new kind of politics oriented around "Islamic values" and religio-political motifs.

THE ISLAMIZATION PROGRAM: AMBITIONS AND REALITIES

At the heart of the MMA's campaign in 2002 — and at the heart of observers' fears about its implications — was its program of Islamization. The MMA constituent parties had played on broad-based sympathies for the Taliban in their 2002 electoral success, and had an ongoing and multivalent relationship with both the Taliban and with Kashmiri militant groups. There was almost universal fear following the 2002 polls that the MMA would institute a process of "Talibanization" in the frontier areas, mimicking the abortive attempt of the Afghan Taliban to establish a *shariah* state. Human rights groups, mainstream and nationalist parties, and international observers all voiced concern about the advent of an Islamist government in NWFP.

Although the MMA made efforts to assuage the fears of the diplomatic and minority religious communities in particular, its chaotic first year in power did little to quell concerns that it represented a subversive and destabilizing force in Pakistani politics. A more complete assessment, however, accounting for the MMA's full five-year tenure, reveals a decidedly more benign outcome: while the MMA certainly introduced or reinforced several troubling socio-political trends, it did not bring about widespread change in the Frontier, and neither did it demonstrate the means or the will to carry out more than a superficial program of Islamization. The story of the MMA's gradual adaptation to the exigencies of governance begins with this first, tumultuous year in power.

A troubled start

Expectations were high when the MMA formed its government in the Frontier in October 2002. The nascent government was under public pressure to show quick results on its promises relating to Islamization, anti-corruption, and social welfare. And since most previous governments in the Frontier had lasted only a year or two, MMA politicians felt extraordinary pressure to maximize their political advantage while they had the opportunity. The Islamists' first year, however, was nothing short of chaotic, as interest groups within the Islamist fold — from MPAs, to party workers, to the Chief Minister's Secretariat, to MMA-affiliated vigilante groups — began taking action on their own in "support" of the alliance's mandate.

The result was what one official described as "rampant ad-hocism," characterized by a flurry of mostly symbolic actions: opening with the *azaan* (call to prayer) in the provincial assembly; banning alcohol, even to non-Muslim foreigners; prohibiting the playing of music in public buses; announcing a crackdown on "pubs and gambling dens" (despite the fact that there were no pubs in the province), etc.[18] Alongside these official moves came a rise in vigilante-style campaigns against "obscenity" in Peshawar and other major cities. Many of these vigilante Islamists had low-level connections to the youth organizations of the MMA parties, and while the Islamist government occasionally criticized these incidents, it did not vigorously investigate them.[19]

Thrust into the spotlight, the MMA leadership also quickly became frustrated by its inability to expeditiously roll out its Islamist agenda. The provincial bureaucracy pushed back against a number of MMA initiatives. By and large, the bureaucracy considered the MMA's early attempts at Islamization to be unrealistic, outside the jurisdiction of the provincial government, or in contravention to existing law. Many of the most outlandish proposals came from the Nifaz-e-Shariat Council, a quasi-governmental recommendatory body set up by the MMA which debated the establishment of a "vice-and-virtue ministry" within the provincial government, and issued suggestions on such matters as the proper color of the *dupatta* head coverings to be worn by schoolgirls (for the record: white).[20] Almost without exception, the Council's recommendations were announced with fanfare, featured prominently in the local press, and then promptly and studiously ignored. Even the MMA's signature Shariat bill, which was passed unanimously by the provincial assembly and signed into law by the governor, did virtually nothing to advance a substantive Islamization agenda in the province.

The chaos of the MMA's first foray into governance, combined with rampant vigilantism and the specter of new Islamization programs, had by mid-2003 led to severe strains on the Islamist alliance. Concerned about the law and order situation in the Frontier, the ruling party in Islamabad had threatened to impose governor's rule, and was pressuring the MMA to accept the Legal Framework Order (LFO) which Musharraf needed to legitimate an extension of his dual role as president and chief of army staff.[21] Moreover, the international donor community, led by the World Bank, was on the verge of pulling back support from the Frontier.[22]

Just when it looked as though the MMA's tenure would be as fleeting as that of its ideological predecessor Mufti Mahmud (who ruled for a mere 10 months) the religious alliance stepped back from the brink, and slowly began moving toward a more pragmatic tack. By late 2003, it was evident that the vigilante campaigns had lost momentum, the flurry of Islamist directives had slowed, and the provincial government seemed increasingly interested in orienting its efforts toward development work and securing international donor participation to support its concrete objectives in the sectors of health, education, and infrastructure.[23] This shift was not sudden. But it is clear in retrospect that late 2003 represented a critical inflection point at which the MMA leadership began pivoting toward an Islamism that was decidedly more populist, and more practical.

The Hisbah bill as political drama

The most visible of the MMA's Islamist legal reform initiatives came well after the passage of the mostly-symbolic Shariat Act in 2003. The Hisbah ("accountability") bill was first proposed shortly after the MMA's election victory, but was not presented in the provincial assembly for almost two and a half years. The bill, in its many iterations, came to acquire an iconic status as representing both the failures of the MMA's legislative ambitions, as well as Islamabad's intent to thwart the provincial government's push for an Islamic political order.

The Hisbah bill played on the themes of Islamic justice and accountability. Some of its less contentious provisions would have discouraged beggary and the employment of under-age children; prohibited injustices perpetrated against women in the determination of inheritance; and banned honor killings. Most of these initiatives, however, were redundant with existing legislation at the provincial or federal levels. At the heart of the bill was a more controversial initiative: the bill would establish the office of *mohtasib*, a "qualified religious scholar" serving as an ombudsman, to which citizens could refer complaints about the presence of "un-Islamic" behavior in the province.[24] The *mohtasib* would be given subpoena-like powers to requisition documents and compel witnesses and, under some early readings of the language, would have a separate police force at his disposal.

The Jamaat liked the idea of a *mohtasib* because they saw it as an avenue by which the Islamist parties could gain permanent entrée into the workings of the legal system. To the JUI-F, on the other hand, the Hisbah bill's promise to employ nearly a hundred scholars throughout the province represented an ingenious jobs-creation scheme for the party's *madrassah*-educated cadres, and an avenue by which the party could mobilize its constituents for future elections.

Much to the MMA's disappointment, the international community was deeply skeptical about the legislation. Aware of this growing concern, the Islamist leadership sought to reassure those who saw Hisbah as an attempt to re-create Mullah Omar's Afghanistan: "We are not," a provincial minister objected, "doing the kind of childish things the Taliban did."[25] The MMA, not for the first time, found itself in the awkward position of defending the importance of its Islamization agenda to its electorate, while at the same time downplaying the implications of that agenda to wider domestic and international audiences. Neither audience was particularly assuaged by the MMA's implicit suggestion that the Hisbah legislation was innocuous.[26]

In the end, the Hisbah bill was passed twice by the provincial assembly and each time was referred to the Supreme Court, where it was struck down on grounds of being "vague, overbroad, unreasonable, based on excessive delegation of jurisdiction, denying the right of access to justice to the citizens and attempting to set up a parallel judicial system."[27] Even though the bill never became law, it came to symbolize the imbalance of power between the NWFP and the ruling party in Islamabad;

the difficulty of crafting Islamic legislation that does not run afoul of existing law; and the ways in which the Islamists' own legal inexperience doomed a piece of legislation which, somewhat more narrowly tailored, might have stood a reasonable chance of implementation.[28]

Even so, many observers suspected that both the Islamists and the ruling government in Islamabad were happy to keep the Hisbah issue alive throughout the MMA's tenure. President Musharraf used the legislation to summon the specter of Talibanization in the Frontier, presenting his government of "enlightened moderation" as the only bulwark standing against an imminent Islamist onslaught. And the repeated rejection of the Hisbah bill both created and nourished the Islamists' own rhetoric, allowing the MMA to keep alive the claim that true *shariah* law was just around the corner.[29] In this way, the drawn-out dispute provided political advantages to both sides, and it is no surprise that the MMA leadership, time and time again, turned to discussion of the Hisbah bill when it found its political fortunes waning.[30]

Informal Islamization

It was clear after the MMA's tumultuous first year in office that the substance of its Islamization agenda had largely stalled. Even so, the alliance continued to promote its program through informal channels. At the most basic level, the MMA did this through its use of Islamic rhetoric, which it used to shore up its credentials among the electorate; deflect attention from local problems; and generally distinguish itself from the mainstream and nationalist opposition, both of which were afraid of appearing un-Islamic in comparison to the *ulema*. Such was the MMA's use of religious language that even political rivals in the ANP and PPP were often forced in provincial assembly sessions to show their support for "Islamicized" resolutions with which they disagreed in substance, for fear that they would be politically outmaneuvered by the MMA.[31]

Outside the bounds of formal politics, the MMA used more subtle channels for furthering its agenda. Some of the most interesting and complex socio-political dynamics of the Islamists' tenure came here at the intersection of official and informal action — where Islamization "from above" met Islamization "from below." The MMA leadership would, for example, occasionally turn a blind eye to vigilante action carried out in the name of Islam, or would quietly signal to business proprietors such as owners of wedding halls, managers of video stores, and local musicians that certain behaviors were no longer "appreciated" in the province.[32] This was usually done discreetly, but most often it did not need to be done at all: the public took its social cues from the presence of an MMA government, regardless of the Islamists' formal actions. In this way, the religious government — quite apart from the mechanism of law-making — was able to influence the behavior of the population through its use of rhetoric and social signaling.

The inherent opacity of the provincial governance process, and the weak tradition of investigative reporting among the journalistic corps, meant that most people in fact had no way of distinguishing rumor from regulation. A number of bills, for example, were introduced unsuccessfully into the provincial assembly, but only their presentation received press attention. These included measures such as the "Prohibition of

Dancing and Music Act, 2005" and the "Prohibition of Use of Women Photographs Act, 2005" (which would have outlawed the commercial use of images of women which "may amount to any incentive to sensuality or excitement of impure thoughts in the mind of an ordinary man of normal temperament").[33]

The MMA, except when speaking with foreign observers, did little in public to dispel the impression that many activities had been restricted. Often, they themselves did not know precisely what had been prohibited. Even senior bureaucrats and cabinet officials in the NWFP government often had no idea whether a given restriction — say, on dancing, or on music in public transportation, or regarding head-coverings for female students — was merely a campaign promise; a bill tabled in the assembly; a bill passed by the assembly; a non-binding recommendation of the quasi-governmental Nifaz-e-Shariat Council; a chief minister's directive; a publicly-announced cabinet directive; a cabinet directive kept under seal; an administrative regulation; or simply a rumor.[34]

The MMA's strategy of "governance by perception" — of encouraging the masses to take their cues from the religious leadership without having to be instructed through any medium so explicit as actual legislation — was, in the end, perhaps a more significant channel of Islamization than any of the alliance's formal initiatives. It speaks, moreover, to the power of "social bandwagoning" in the Frontier, and the ways in which Islamist groups — whether elected like the MMA, or unelected like the neo-Taliban — are able to actively shape social norms in the absence of formal legislative or regulatory authority.

Security, militancy, and inaction

One of the most salient criticisms of the religious government in Peshawar had less to do with its Islamization program than with the ways in which the MMA's stated agenda and constituent politics affected its ability to carry out its law enforcement obligations. Opponents claimed that the MMA leadership was often reluctant to take action against insurgent groups, or even against clerics who were causing trouble for local authorities. By and large, this was true: the Islamists frequently found themselves boxed in by their own religious rhetoric, such that they could not afford to confront any individual or group which carried out activities in the name of religion, lest they be seen as undermining their own message.

Provincial bureaucrats who worked closely with the MMA government described how the Islamists' own rhetoric made them hesitant to act against even those clerics who were not formally part of their religious alliance. This dynamic was most problematic during the first year of the MMA's rule, in which religious party cadres engaged in vigilantism; and in the last two years of the MMA's tenure, in which new insurgent groups began challenging the writ of the state. (Ironically, as described below, a number of senior MMA leaders were in fact quite upset at the bombing of girls' schools and the rise of TNSM-backed militancy in Swat, and took pains to differentiate themselves from that activity.) And though they spoke out in general terms against vigilantism and violence, they usually would not do so in *specific* cases, or against *specific* troublemakers.[35]

For most of the MMA's tenure, this remained a relatively minor problem; the law and order situation in the Frontier between mid-2003 and mid-2005 was quite good relative to the other provinces, and disturbances by religious groups were relatively few in number. But with the rise of the TNSM and neo-Taliban–linked bombings in 2006 and 2007, the MMA's hesitance in confronting religious insurgents began to have tangible and adverse implications for the province.

By the spring and early summer of 2007, the religious parties were coming under severe criticism for their indecisive response to the TNSM's militancy in Swat, and to a wave of bombings which had penetrated into the settled areas of the province.[36] Politicians from the religious parties unconvincingly blamed the federal government and its security services, rather than the Taliban groups, for fomenting instability in the Frontier to destabilize the MMA government (though in private they acknowledged the spread of dangerous militant organizations into the settled areas).[37] The situation in NWFP further deteriorated in the summer of 2007 following retaliations by militant groups after the siege of the Lal Masjid (Red Mosque) in Islamabad. The MMA government put off any kind of action against the TNSM until the final weeks of its rule, when the JUI-F chief minister quietly agreed to an expanded security presence in the Swat valley.[38] Even then, the JUI-F did so reluctantly and in the face of internal opposition by the Jamaat, and later denied that it had ever acceded to allowing military action in Swat.[39]

It is an overstatement to suggest, as some observers have, that the rise in militancy in 2006 and 2007 in NWFP was a result of the MMA provincial government; as is noted below, the religious parties were often at odds with the new insurgent movements, and upset about their expanding influence. At the same time, however, the MMA clearly played an indirect role in facilitating the spread of the insurgency by virtue of its inaction. While the alliance performed decently well in carrying out its law and order obligations under relatively peaceful conditions, the rising tide of insurgency eventually exposed the MMA's political limitations in being able to take action against other self-described "religious" movements.

ISLAM AS *DIN*: THE ISLAMIZATION AGENDA WRIT LARGE

The leadership of the MMA saw its Islamization agenda as one which extended beyond the bounds of law and formal politics. Apart from its support for an explicit *shariah* agenda, the Islamist alliance also sought to integrate religious values into other aspects of its governance, and to advocate a view of Islam as a *din* (faith) which had a bearing on all sectors of society and the state.

Patronizing the madaris

There continues to be widespread anxiety in the West about the Pakistani *madrassah* system, particularly the Deobandi institutions in Karachi, Balochistan, and the NWFP. This apprehension is not with reason: although by most accounts the vast majority of *madaris* are engaged simply in teaching the memorization of Quran, and serve an important function as a social safety net for poor families and their children, a very small percentage are used as intentional recruiting platforms — or even training camps — for extremist organizations. (Anecdotal evidence suggests that the most problematic aspect of the *madrassah* system is not its curriculum as such, but its narrow pedagogy and openness to itinerant recruiters affiliated with sectarian or militant organizations.)

One of the largely unexamined questions of the MMA's tenure in NWFP is the degree to which the Islamist parties in general, and the JUI-F in particular, leveraged their position in government to benefit the *madaris*. Not since the Afghan *jihad* had the Deobandi parties been granted such extensive access to state resources, and it was clear that for the JUI-F — as one up-and-coming party leader noted — "the *madaris* are our number-one priorities."[40] Given their important social welfare function, the flow of government resources to religious organizations is not prima facie a cause for concern. Still, there are legitimate fears that some of these *madaris* may have had linkages with the neo-Taliban movements now active in the Frontier.

It was surprising to some observers that the MMA did not use its political influence in NWFP to more forcefully institutionalize the government's role in funding the *madrassah* system. Spending for mosques and seminaries under the official Auqaf framework — a program which provides regular provincial grants to religious institutions — did in fact increase, but only modestly.[41] But the JUI (and the Fazlur Rehman faction in particular) have a long history of opposing outside interference in religious schools, and of avoiding direct government funding of their institutions lest they be co-opted by the state.[42] The MMA's tenure did little to lessen this suspicion of state encroachment.

As a result, instead of authorizing direct state funding of the *madaris*, the JUI chose to utilize development channels and other discretionary funds to provide benefits to the *madrassah* system. These grants tended to be one-off concessions rather than the sort of systematic re-structuring of the government-*madaris* relationship that would have, in the mind of the JUI, threatened the long-term independence of the religious institutions. Interviews with JUI party members and provincial bureaucrats suggest that the discretionary funds granted to the party's MPAs and MNAs (between 5 and 10 million rupees per member per year) were often channeled to the *madaris*. Occasionally these payments took the form of outright grants, but were more commonly structured as development initiatives, e.g., providing electricity, tube wells, road access, and repairs to constituent institutions.[43]

A review of provincial development documents indicates that several discretionary pools of money were tapped to provide benefit to these institutions. The District Development Funds, Chief Minister's Special Package, and the Tamir-e-Sarhad ("Building Frontier") Program all recorded significant and repeated grants to various *madaris*.[44] Not surprisingly, most of the *madaris* which received these benefits were located in the southern districts which constituted the JUI-F's political heartland: Bannu, Tank, and Dera Ismail Khan. By way of funds channeled to JI Senior Minister Siraj ul-Haq, seminaries in Dir and Swat were also patronized.[45] In comparison with the size of the provincial budget, the individual grants to the *madaris* in the southern districts were relatively small (usually less than $20,000). These grants, often made without public notification, were commonly authorized at the discretion of the chief minister, who shrewdly altered the provincial budgeting process in order to vest the ruling party with greater powers to direct discretionary funds to areas and institutions which represented its core constituency.[46]

In addition to channeling funds to the *madaris,* the JUI-F became adept at channeling funds *through* the *madrassah* system as an indirect means by which to solicit bribes. Multiple sources, including some with close links to the JUI-F, described the ways in which party workers who held government positions would request that "charitable donations" be made to their *madrassah* in exchange for contracts or other public services. Sometimes, written receipts were even issued for these transactions. The effect of this innovation was to channel monies toward the *madaris* while keeping the assets, at least on paper, out of the hands of the politicians. The JUI-F, with its extensive network of *madaris* — most of whose books were outside the scope of government oversight — used this arrangement extensively.[47]

It is impossible to reliably assess the net impact of the MMA's patronage of the *madaris*. It is clear that substantial funds were channeled to religious institutions during the Islamists' tenure; but it is also clear that many of these funds were provided in-kind, and to institutions which served important social as well as religious functions.

Education and health

The MMA's policies on education and health deserve an entire study of their own.[48] Without question, the Islamist alliance brought its religious values to the table when making policy on social development issues. But it often did so to a lesser extent than outsiders predicted, or in ways which differed markedly from public expectations.

After the MMA came to power, the international donor community anticipated a possible roll-back of educational access for women in the NWFP. Playing against expectations, the MMA leadership decided instead to focus *specifically* on increasing female primary enrollment, and to petition the World Bank for funds in that regard. Statements by MMA leaders seemed to indicate that this emphasis on female education was due in part to a desire "to quash western propaganda that Islam did not guarantee women's rights."[49] Regardless of the rationale, however, the MMA did eventually convince skeptical donors that they were serious about educating women.[50] "I do believe now," said one World Bank education advisor in 2007, "that they want women's education. I don't question that anymore."

Female enrollment figures reflected the province's investment in girls' education, with some of the most striking gains coming from the most conservative areas dominated by the MMA. Over two years, Bannu saw a 38% increase in female primary enrollment; in Dir, 22%; in Buner, 40%; and in Dera Ismail Khan, 85%.[51] Middle and secondary school female enrollments also increased, sometimes dramatically: in poor districts like Buner and Hangu, girls' enrollments were up over 50%; in Dir, 39%; and in Shangla, Mahsehra and Lakki Marwat, over 20%.[52] Overall, between 2001/02 and 2006/07, the gross female enrollment ratio in public primary schools increased from 48% to 57%.[53]

In general, the MMA's education policies at the primary and secondary levels were singled out for praise by the donor community, including its programs of providing free education and free textbooks throughout the province.[54] Other decisions, like the plan to build dozens of new post-secondary institutions, were criticized as being little more than patronage schemes for senior MMA officials. (Construction contracts provided one of the most lucrative channels of corruption for provincial officials, many of whom had informal or familial links with contractors.) What surprised many observers was that MMA party members ended up being so supportive of female education and saw it as serving their own interests as well as those of the outside community.[55] Critics were quick to point out, however, that they were much less supportive of expanding opportunities for women's employment which might absorb the newly-educated female population.

Compared to its emphasis on primary education, the MMA's higher education agenda was much more modest. The two major initiatives of the government at the higher education level were the establishment of the Khyber Girls Medical College in Peshawar, and the University of Science and Technology Bannu (USTB). The fact that the JUI-F leadership chose to open a female-only medical college in the most cosmopolitan city of the province (which some critics argued was unnecessary and redundant), while establishing a co-educational university in one of NWFP's most conservative regions (which happened to be the home of the chief minister), speaks to the complex ideological and political impulses which lay behind the MMA's thinking on gender and education issues.

The only major occasion in which the MMA pursued a formal Islamization effort with respect to the public school system was in 2005, when the federal government reduced the number of *ayats* of Quran and *hadith* in the Islamiyat and Urdu curricula.[56] The MMA objected strenuously, and after much back-and-forth the matter was resolved to the mutual satisfaction of both the province and the central government.[57] The fact that it was the gross number of *ayats* — and not the content of the curriculum as such — that the MMA took as its metric by which the reforms were to be judged indicates the *ulema's* sensitivity to perceived federal interference in local curricular issues. Seen, however, in the overall context of the alliance's Islamization agenda, it is striking that the MMA's most serious attempt to bring its religio-political agenda to bear on public school curriculum amounted to little more than a rousing defense of the *status quo*.

The MMA government's record on health and social welfare issues was much the same: the alliance, lacking a clear agenda tying health to its Islamization mandate, deferred almost entirely to the advice of the provincial bureaucracy and the international donors. Most outside experts agree that the Islamist government adopted responsible health policies which differed little from those of previous governments, and interacted in a professional manner with domestic and foreign institutions.

The more interesting story in this sector is what the MMA did not do: aside from some disputes with international donors about the priority given to condom distribution, the religious parties did very little to bring their Islamism to bear on the health sector.[58] The government generally continued with previous plans — and even increased budgets — for the population welfare department, expanded the Lady

Health Worker program, and opened new family planning centers. It also made a sustained effort to carry out polio vaccination programs in Malakand division, against the opposition of local groups like the TNSM.[59] There were hopes early in the MMA's tenure that the Islamists might be able to leverage their unique grassroots linkages at mosques and *madaris* in order to pursue social mobilization and promote health and welfare goals at the community level. By and large, however, that did not happen, as the MMA's health and welfare policy — far from advocating dramatic Islamist reforms — mostly reflected the *status quo*.

The gender agenda

It was widely expected that the rise of the MMA would lead to the imposition of strict gender norms — even by the conservative standards of the Frontier. Both major constituent parties tailored their gender discourse to appeal to conservative local values, and to fears of a loss of Pashtun honor. The appeal to Pashtunwali was often framed in Islamic terms, but there was rarely any question as to which standard was ultimately normative on questions of gender: as Anita Weiss has observed, MMA members would acknowledge that widow remarriage was condoned in Islam, but would not support it for fear of opposing Pashtun tradition.[60] On those occasions in which the religious parties did oppose local traditions, such as the practice of *swara* (honor killings), their opposition was mostly rhetorical and included little in the way of enforcement.[61]

In spite of the MMA's views on the role of women in public life, its impact on the gender policies of the province, and on the norms of the society at large, were relatively modest. Aside from a few abortive attempts to mandate the wearing of head coverings for female students, the alliance's education and health policies basically supported the *status quo* on gender issues. Any greater ambitions to institutionalize enforcement of gender norms died with the repeated failure of the Hisbah bill. On a social level, the MMA did exert informal influence (e.g., people noticed more women observing *purdah* in local markets), but even here the change was not dramatic.

Opposition to the MMA by women's advocacy groups moderated somewhat over the course of the provincial government's tenure, as the religious parties became more realistic about their policy options, and the advocacy groups calibrated their expectations accordingly. The alliance's gender policies nonetheless continued to attract criticism on two fronts. First, there were charges that the religious parties were interfering with gender-oriented programs: MMA leaders, for example, campaigned against the Aurat Foundation, which they saw as advancing a Western notion of female empowerment.[62] (They even demanded at one point that the organization, which takes its name from the Urdu word for "woman," change its name.[63]) And second, perhaps the most substantive complaint about the MMA's approach to gender issues was its consistent opposition to legal reforms on issues which affected women. The religious parties opposed any change to the notorious Hudood ordinances in 2004, and strongly resisted the Women's Protection Bill in 2006. Their strategy was to label any changes to the legal *status quo* as "un-Islamic" and a capitulation to Western values.[64]

There is no question that the MMA leadership was uncomfortable with gender reforms. "Deep down," admitted a party advisor in the Frontier, "the JUI does not want to give a free role to women. They think that free mixing is not Islamic."[65] This did not mean, however, that the religious parties tacitly supported a Taliban-like agenda on gender issues.[66] In reality, many of the most troubling and high-profile actions which set back women's rights in the NWFP, such as the forcible closing of girls' schools, were not sanctioned by the alliance's leadership, and actually ran counter to the MMA's political and institutional interests. The religious parties, for example, received a great deal of criticism for the closing of girls' schools in the northern districts of NWFP beginning in 2007, when in fact that activity was carried out almost entirely by the TNSM and affiliated neo-Taliban groups, in contravention to the MMA's own program of expanding female primary education.[67]

The religious leadership was frequently torn between its own commitment to conservative gender norms, and political realities. Faced with local constituent opposition to women's participation in politics (especially in rural areas), but also with the desire to fill the seats which were reserved for women, the Islamist leadership split the difference: MMA women were given tickets to run for seats at the district and provincial levels, while at the same time the religious parties occasionally went along with local agreements at the union council and *tehsil* levels to exclude women from voting. After a writ petition was filed following the 2001 Local Body Elections, citing written evidence of prohibitions against women voting, these sorts of arrangements tended to be oral rather than written, and conducted in such a way as to retain plausible deniability for mid- and senior-level party leadership.[68]

Religious minorities and sectarianism

The NWFP has historically experienced less conflict between Muslim and non-Muslim communities than neighboring Punjab. In part, it is suggested, this reflects egalitarian Pashtun values and traditions of local hospitality. It is also due to simple economics and demographics: the minority communities in the Frontier are either small, poor, or both.[69] Unlike parts of the Punjab, in which the Christian community has become a source of economic competition to the Sunni majority, the religious minorities in the Frontier are, by and large, economically and politically marginalized.

Nonetheless, minority groups in NWFP were uniformly concerned about the MMA's victory in 2002: Christians worried about being tarred as "Western" by the anti-American religious parties; Ahmedis about being subjected to further legal discrimination; Hindus and Sikhs about the potential for anti-Indian demagoguery; Kalash (a small non-monotheistic faith community which lives in three isolated valleys in Chitral district) about the growing tensions surrounding conversions to Islam; and Shia about the strong Deobandi character of the religious alliance and its ties to sectarian groups such as Sipah-e-Sahaba.

The MMA's impact on minority communities, as on so many other issues, proved to be mixed. Contrary to early expectations, the religious parties did not seek to further marginalize minority groups. In fact, the MMA leadership, concerned about its collective reputation and by the suggestion that it might act irresponsibly toward religious minorities, tried to overcome this negative optic by reaching out to minority leaders, particularly those from the Christian, Hindu, and Sikh communities. The Islamists' policy of minority engagement was not necessarily disingenuous, but was clearly a calculated move to bolster the alliance's electoral and reputational prospects in the Frontier.[70] These outreach efforts included a mutually awkward visit by Senior Minister Siraj ul-Haq to a Christmas service in Peshawar; regular statements by Chief Minister Akram Khan Durrani about tolerance and shared religious history, especially during times of interreligious tension; participation in interfaith events, including the Faith Friends initiative organized by several leading scholars and clerics; provision of funds for reconstruction of churches; and visible protection of churches, temples, and gurudwaras during holy days.[71]

These actions were largely symbolic, but nonetheless important in setting the overall tone of the MMA's interaction with the minority communities. The chief minister, for example, laid a foundation stone for the reconstruction of a church building on the campus of Peshawar University in late 2006, as a Christmas gift of the MMA government to the local Christian community. When students at the university later filed a writ petition with the Peshawar High Court claiming that the reconstruction of the church would "trigger sectarianism" and violate majority sentiment on the campus, the High Court pointedly referenced the chief minister's own actions in dismissing the case, adding rhetorically, "Why did the head of a religious party's government allocate funds and attend the reconstruction ceremony as a chief guest, if the church's construction were un-Islamic?" In cases such as these, outreach by the MMA leadership was helpful in signaling to other party cadres, and even the courts, the alliance's image as tolerant and democratic Islamists.[72]

These outreach efforts did not make the MMA immune from criticism. Some Christian leaders objected to the MMA's oft-repeated assertion that they would "protect" the minorities living under their rule, arguing that the language of *dhimmitude* was patronizing and cast the minorities as somehow less than full Pakistani citizens.[73] Other leaders noted that the MMA leadership often dismissed the minority groups' claims of discrimination, and did little to provide economic opportunities to the poorest communities.[74] Other minority leaders complained that the gracious words of the MMA leadership were sometimes at odds with the actions of lower-level party cadres. When, for example, an MMA cleric in Charsadda began broadcasting anti-Christian propaganda on an illegal FM station, the provincial government provided extra police to the local Christian community — along with a special provision of small arms to be used in self-defense — but for political reasons would not take action against the cleric himself.[75]

There is, remarkably, little to note about the MMA's track record on sectarian issues. On the whole, the alliance adopted a moderate rhetoric toward the Shia minority, and also did its best to stay out of the middle of intra-Sunni disputes between Deobandis and Barelvis which arose in nearby Khyber agency. Some observers noted that the participation in the MMA alliance of parties which were ideologically at odds — such as the Shia Islami Tehrik-e-Pakistan (ITP) and the Wahhabi Jamiat Ahl-e-Hadith (JAH); and the Barelvi Jamiat Ulema-e-Pakistan (JUP) and the Deobandi Jamiat Ulema-e-Islam (JUI) — helped to moderate the public statements of the senior tier of Islamist leadership, and put pressure on the parties to rein in sectarian activities which might reflect poorly on the alliance's governance.

On balance, the minority communities in the Frontier were relieved that the MMA's tenure was not as problematic as they had feared, and expressed satisfaction with the official efforts at outreach on the part of the Islamist leadership. But they also were frustrated over the actions of lower-level Islamist cadres which the leadership did not or could not control, and over the trend toward more conservative values under the MMA, which increased the social pressures on communities which did not conform to the Deobandi Sunni norm.[76]

The rise of 'Islamic populism'

Beyond the explicitly religious content of the MMA's agenda, the Islamists also brought with them a unique style of governance and a distinctive political culture. These remain important even in the post-MMA era, as they shaped the political landscape of the Frontier and helped to redefine the boundaries of Pashtun nationalist discourse. Echoes of the MMA's "Islamic populism" can be seen in the style of the ANP-led government which followed, and also in the *ad hoc* forms of Islamist governance established by the neo-Taliban in both the settled and tribal areas.

Unlike any previous ruling party in the Frontier, the MMA brought to its exercise of governance a unique lower- and middle-class sensibility. The JUI-F drew its base of support predominantly from the underdeveloped southern districts, and the Jamaat relied on support from the so-called "devout middle classes" in the Peshawar valley and the poor districts in the north. Appealing to these constituents, MMA parliamentarians often spoke at length about wanting to help small farmers, shopkeepers, transport workers, and the young *berozgar* (unemployed) class, including *madrassah* graduates. Party workers from the PML-N, ANP, and PPP, by contrast, would often begin their criticism of the MMA by critiquing the Islamists' ineffective industrial policy, or their lack of commitment to large-scale irrigation projects of the kind favored by the landed elites.[77]

The class and educational background of the MMA politicians shaped their political discourse and, more directly, their exercise of governance. Some of the provincial ministers, hailing from a *madrassah* background, were wholly unequipped to run large ministries and relate with international donors. And since most of the alliance's MPAs and MNAs were unschooled in English, the MMA government insisted that the provincial bureaucracy switch its language of everyday operation from English into Urdu.[78] The situation in the provincial assembly — in which some MPAs were not wholly conversant in Urdu, their nation's *lingua franca* — was even more complex. One advisor in the provincial assembly explained wearily, "The directives from the secretariats come to the assembly in English ... have to be translated into Urdu ... and then explained in Pashto."[79]

Ultimately, the hallmark of the MMA's populist governance style was not its use of vernacular language, but its use of vernacular Pashtun cultural motifs. Even fierce critics of the provincial government generally acknowledged that, in the words of one bureaucrat, the MMA "has been the most accessible government in Pakistan's history."[80] Drawing on the Pashtun inclination for egalitarian politics, the MMA instituted something of a "hujra culture," modeling its interaction with the people on that of the tribal elder's daily audience in the village courtyard. Compared to previous governments, the MMA made more of an effort to be accessible to lower-class petitioners seeking patronage and petty favors and took care to emphasize the relatively modest means of its own politicians.[81] The JUI-F MPAs, many of whom delivered the weekly *khutbah* at their local mosques, were particularly accessible. "The people see us every Friday," one *alim* noted, with a hint of resignation. "How can we hide?"[82]

More tangibly, the MMA's populism was reflected in the ways in which it altered the established patronage patterns of the Frontier. Whereas previous governments had directed funds largely to the Peshawar valley and the eastern Hazara division, the Islamists allocated state monies disproportionately to their own political bases — areas which had been relatively ignored for decades.[83] While a full accounting of such spending is not available, it is clear from analysis of provincial development records that several districts benefited disproportionately from the MMA government's largesse: Bannu, Buner, Dir, and Dera Ismail Khan were over-represented in almost all categories of discretionary spending.[84] These districts represented the hometowns of, respectively, the chief minister (JUI-F), the speaker of the assembly (JI), the senior minister (JI), and Maulana Fazlur Rehman (JUI-F). The MMA defended these lopsided allocations on both historical and moral grounds: "Why should we widen a road in Peshawar," argued one JUI-F advisor, "when in Bannu there is no road at all?"[85]

The MMA's realignment of patronage within the province had both negative and positive effects. The religious leadership took advantage of an already-politicized system of development planning to divert resources to its own client base. This simply reinforced the fundamentally inequitable process by which development funds were allocated at the provincial level. Taking a more positive view, however, the MMA's tenure unquestionably channeled assistance to the long-neglected southern districts and to under-developed Jamaat-dominated areas of Malakand division in the north. In the south, the chief minister directed massive development monies to Dera Ismail Khan and to Bannu, mostly in the form of infrastructure projects, but also education. Bannu was given a new access road from the Indus Highway, new road projects within the city proper, a new university, and new bridges. Districts Buner and Dir also saw a great deal of development in the health, education, and utility sectors.[86]

Even leading opposition members in parliament conceded that the MMA's focus on previously-neglected districts was not entirely without merit.[87] The infusion of funds into these districts, particularly in the south, had impact both substantively and politically. Apart from the direct effects on commerce, education and health, the realignment of clientelist politics had a politically integrative effect as well: informal interviews conducted during the MMA's tenure revealed, for example, a feeling in the southern districts that people there had been politically re-enfranchised, and that it was in their interest to take note of what happened in Peshawar. Some local experts argued that the present situation in southern districts like Bannu (as bad as it is) would be noticeably worse today had the MMA not invested there.

The MMA's style of Islamic populism was undoubtedly a form of political posturing, but it also points to the way in which the Islamists sought to articulate a vision of an Islamic welfare state which equated religious values with populist reforms likely to appeal to lower-class voters. It is, for example, remarkable to note the extent to which the MMA's published manifesto focused not on the enactment of *shariah* legislation or the curbing of un-Islamic acts, but on promises to curb corruption, ensure provision of "bread, clothes, shelter, education, jobs and marriage expenses" (an effective play on Zulfikar Ali Bhutto's famous promise of *roti, kapra aur makan*), ensure speedy justice, promote literacy through free education, and "[take] care of backward areas and classes."[88] In this sense, the language of Islamic populism was a rhetorical bridge which joined the MMA's concern for Islamization and religious symbolism with its efforts to expand a patronage base among its lower-class constituency.

One way in which the MMA did this was to blend lower-class values with a dose of popular religious wisdom. In late 2006, for example, the chief minister expressed his displeasure at the increase in crime and kidnapping in the province. In addition to issuing formal directives on the matter, he also advised that corrupt police officers be sent for four months to the Tablighi Markaz — the headquarters of the Islamic missionary group Tablighi Jamaat — so that they could learn proper Islamic values before returning to their posts. (A newspaper commentator opined that this was a fine idea, but suggested dryly that, in keeping with the chief minister's approach, perhaps the government should send the most serious offenders straight to Mecca for *hajj*.[89]) The MMA leadership also sought to link Islam with good governance, directing in 2003 that "all senior officers shall persuade their officials to attend prayers regularly… [and] encourage regular motivation sessions for their employees to enable them to become practicing Muslims. This will enable honest, transparent and humane dealings thereby ensuring good governance."[90]

Not surprisingly, the MMA's Islamic populism did not come close, in reality, to fulfilling its early promises of creating hundreds of thousands of new jobs.[91] But it had a notable effect in helping the religious parties to carve out a political space in Frontier politics which not only the Islamists, but also the other mainstream parties, would be forced to contest. Even after the ANP victory in February 2008, observers noted that the MMA had been able, in part, to co-opt the ANP's traditional rhetoric, and reframe Pashtun nationalism in religious and class terms.[92] This shift, though subtle, is consistent with a broader post-9/11 trend-line in Frontier politics in which historic, trans-Durand Line notions of Pashtun nationalism have slowly been displaced by a nationalism that is both more focused on affiliation to the Pakistani state, and to religious identity. As the MMA was in many ways a very Pashtun phenomenon, it was able to tap into an ethnic nationalist counter-narrative and align it with its own religious and political agenda.

CONSTRAINTS ON ISLAMIZATION

The portrait which emerges above is that of the MMA as a right-of-center but essentially *status quo* political force. And indeed, as early as 2004 it had become obvious that the Islamist parties would not be a radical Talibanizing influence in the Frontier. While their policies and rhetoric continued to trouble many observers, the religious parties were clearly unwilling or unable to press for dramatic Islamist reforms. It is easy to forget that this trend-line toward moderate politics, while apparent in retrospect, was not at all obvious even in 2003. What then accounts for the relatively limited scope of the MMA's program of Islamization? There are four major factors described below — presented in roughly increasing order of importance — which serve to explain how and why the MMA did not govern as many had expected.

Internal alliance politics

From its earliest days, the MMA was an alliance fraught with internal divisions. These fractures played out differently at the local, provincial, and national levels. At the local level the differences between the two dominant parties were not related to strategic objectives so much as jostling for influence: both partie's operatives in a given district sought to take advantage of the political environment for their own ends. It was to the benefit of the MMA as an alliance that such tensions were, in 2002, somewhat obviated by the NWFP's political geography. The power bases of the JUI-F and the JI were largely geographically disjoint, with the former dominant in the southern districts and the latter in the northern Malakand division. The major parties did not altogether avoid electoral tension, but the historic weakness of religious parties in the province made it such that neither party had a strong bench of experienced candidates, particularly for those regions outside their traditional spheres of influence.

At the provincial level, disputes predictably centered around the distribution of patronage, including cabinet positions, in which the JI and especially the smaller parties in the alliance felt excluded.[93] Somewhat less expected was that the pace of the MMA's Islamization agenda would also prove to be a point of provincial-level contention within the alliance. The MMA faced a nearly constant tension between those leaders who were in a governing role, such as members of the provincial cabinet, and those who were not, such as party workers and activists. The former group had a strong incentive to demonstrate the government's credentials as a responsible party committed to the rule of law, while the latter remained primarily focused on appeasing their party's constituent base. When, for example, Jamaat cadres were publicly linked to vigilante action in the summer of 2003 (defacing billboards and burning music shops), the chief minister spoke out against the action, precipitating a feud within the alliance. It was but one of many: the "governing" leadership of the MMA consistently demonstrated greater concern for procedure, for the public reputation of the alliance, and for a gradual reform path than did those without such obligations. This ongoing internal tension made it difficult for the alliance to put forward a common approach to Islamization efforts.[94]

At the national level, the forces acting upon the constituent parties were in some sense reversed from those at the local level. Here the JUI-F and JI shared relatively little in the way of overall objectives, and saw the relationship between the MMA and the state through starkly different lenses. While the JUI-F sought to establish itself as a dominant *status quo* political force in the Pashtun areas of NWFP and Balochistan (even if that meant compromising with the Musharraf government), the Jamaat sought to act on a broader agenda that included structural reforms — changes which necessitated opposition to Musharraf's regime and its philosophy of "enlightened moderation."

Ultimately, the JUI-F's more pragmatic orientation toward the center prevailed. Qazi Hussain threatened frequently to resign from the National Assembly in protest of martial rule, but the JUI-F — seeing a large downside in the potential loss of the Frontier government, and an uncertain upside at the national level — refused to go along. (Qazi Hussain resigned only in August 2007, long after it had ceased to matter.) This internal fragmentation, which was felt at all levels of the MMA's governance, proved to be a constant source of stress on the alliance's ability to pursue its agenda, and a constant inroad by which the military and bureaucracy could exert pressure on the provincial government.

Constituent pressures

One of the most salient factors which limited the MMA's ability to implement its Islamist agenda was the lack of enthusiasm for real reform within sectors of the MMA's own constituency. An overwhelming majority of Pakistanis, when surveyed, express support for "implementing strict *shariah* law" in Pakistan.[95] Actual implementation of strict regulations ostensibly deriving from the *shariah* is decidedly less popular.[96] Even the relatively modest changes implemented by the MMA in NWFP provoked grumbling — and not just among "liberal-minded" Pashtuns.

Prohibitions on traditional music and dance were widely (though quietly) lamented, and the obscuring of women's faces on billboards ridiculed. Proposals to close down dance halls, music stores, and cinemas caused a stir among the urban merchant class. Campaigns to ensure that stores were closed during prayer hours met with discontent by shopkeepers. And purveyors of imported clothing and technology were frequently nervous that the religious parties would, in politically charged situations, call for a boycott of such goods. Given that the petty merchant class in NWFP constituted a key base of support for the Jamaat in particular, the MMA was forced to tread lightly so as not to alienate important domestic constituencies.

The MMA was also forced to backtrack on its promise to shutter cable television in the province, and there is reason to believe that the government's foray into more dramatic prohibitions would have been politically devastating.[97] Although many of the *ulema,* for example, considered smoking to be un-Islamic, once in government they rallied in support of tobacco farmers who constituted a key electoral constituency in Swabi district, where the MMA had made major inroads in 2002. (The MMA later boasted about the aid it had given to help the tobacco industry.)

The alliance discovered that promises of Islamization carry with them certain political benefits, but also risks. As the spreading neo-Taliban insurgency in the southern districts amply demonstrated, the appeal of "Talibanism" often far outweighed the appeal of Taliban presence itself. To a lesser extent, the MMA found — particularly in places such as the Peshawar valley — that promises to get rid of "vice" made for popular electoral politics, but not necessarily popular governance. Although this dynamic is difficult to quantify, it is safe to conclude that at least one reason behind the MMA's stalled Islamization agenda was internal resistance by the very electorate that had brought the Islamists to power. The gulf between expressed preferences and revealed preferences on the part of the electorate created a limited field of action within which the religious parties could actually implement an Islamization agenda.

Interaction with the international community

The MMA ran on an agenda of opposition to foreign interference in the affairs of the Frontier. Western NGOs, foreign governments, and international organizations were all deemed suspect by religious party candidates. The Islamists' rhetoric on these issues changed very little during their tenure in power. But as a practical matter, the MMA's governance was shaped by its interaction with the international community.

Perhaps the most significant interaction in this regard took place on issues of finance and development. The World Bank and the Asian Development Bank (ADB) both had a long history of partnering with the government of NWFP, and the MMA leadership realized very quickly into its tenure that without the financing of the international donor community its religious government would stand little chance of fulfilling its electoral agenda. Just two weeks into his job as senior minister and minister of finance, Siraj ul-Haq of the JI acknowledged that "all planning is dependent on foreign assistance. All our projects are waiting for foreign financial assistance…No work is possible in the present state of affairs."[98] The provincial government's first year of governance, however did little to assuage the concerns of the international donor community. High-profile vigilantism, statements against the West and the "war on terror" (driven largely by the build-up to the Iraq war), a chaotic legislative agenda, a stand-off between the province and the district *nazimeen* over power-sharing, and a host of "ridiculous" efforts by the MMA government all made the World Bank seriously rethink its strategy toward the Frontier. By late 2003, the Bank was considering suspending its giving to the province.[99]

With its government under fire and desperate for World Bank support, the MMA leadership made a surprising pitch: Siraj ul-Haq, in a meeting with the mission director in Islamabad, laid out a "passionate plea" for Bank involvement in the NWFP and, as noted above, proposed that the MMA's top priority would be female education. Coming just weeks after mid-level cadres from Siraj ul-Haq's own party had destroyed billboards portraying women in Peshawar, it was a striking tactic. The MMA's proposal, incongruous as it seemed, "hit at the Bank's soft spot," and Siraj ul-Haq assiduously courted both the Bank staff and the political and bureaucratic leadership in Peshawar.[100] Eventually, the Bank decided in June 2004 to authorize a second structural adjustment credit for $90 million, which not only proved to be a financial boon to the MMA government, but also signaled to other major donors such as the British DFID that the provincial government was prepared to accommodate the interests of the donor community.[101] Looking back on its interaction with the MMA, Bank officials acknowledged that the Islamists engaged in a "very professional dialogue" with the donor community.

The ADB's experience in interacting with the MMA government was not dissimilar from that of the World Bank. ADB staff found the MMA to be "pretty shrewd" and their performance "more or less in line" with that of previous governments. "They know what they want," noted a senior official in Islamabad, and if "anyone thought the

MMA government would be an underdog, they have proved them wrong." Relations between the ADB and the MMA were, nonetheless, strained at times. The Islamists' most significant disagreement with any international donor agency arose over a small ADB Gender Reform Action Programme (GRAP) which constituted a required component of the $300 million nationwide Decentralization Support Program (DSP).[102] When the DSP proposal was submitted to the MMA cabinet, it refused to approve the GRAP, arguing that gender reform was simply not one of its priorities and that it should not be imposed upon them.

Opposition to the GRAP implementation by the MMA endangered the entire second tranche of DSP funds from the ADB throughout Pakistan. It was a delicate political situation for the MMA leadership, which faced strong internal opposition to the gender program, but also intense pressure from the international community and the other provincial governments in Pakistan. The solution to the GRAP stand-off eventually came by way of bureaucratic sleight-of-hand on the part of both the bank and the MMA. The ADB voted to give a waiver allowing the tranche to proceed without the MMA's acceptance of the GRAP.[103] And the MMA chief minister, after almost two years of delays, eventually approved the program, though he did so by submitting a notification directly to the chief secretary without putting the issue before the cabinet for discussion.

The British DFID and German GTZ development agencies held less financial sway over the provincial government than the World Bank or ADB, but sought to leverage their relational and technical influence to help bring MMA leaders into the mainstream. In doing so, these agencies created space for sustained political interaction that often exceeded — both in scope and productivity — the more formal political relationships with the MMA initiated by their respective governments. DFID officials were initially "quite scared" by the MMA's agenda, but decided to press ahead with a strategy that extended technical support to all levels of the provincial government (focusing on government reform, health, and economic development), and sought to initiate dialogue on the alliance's Islamization agenda. Its interaction with the MMA government was therefore quite deep, and DFID officials commented later that the relationship was remarkably "constructive" and "frank."[104]

The Germans took a similar approach, quietly partnering with the MMA at all levels to pursue joint objectives in education and health. It was, by all accounts, a successful strategy. Provincial ministers, bureaucrats, and NGO leaders in Peshawar spoke in glowing terms about the Germans' technical assistance, with one former *madrassah* leader noting that "they have no agenda... and didn't impose their orders on us. They gave us a logical framework."[105] GTZ's non-confrontational approach with the MMA served in a number of ways to moderate aspects of the Islamists' agenda. The agency invested heavily in building relationships with MMA officials including the education minister, whom GTZ brought to Germany for discussions on modern education policy.

GTZ also used these relationships to initiate dialogue with the MMA on the issue of the *madaris*. Although management of the *madaris* fell outside the formal portfolio of the provincial minister of education, the minister's background as a *madrassah* leader meant that the Germans were eventually able to leverage their position as trusted advisors in order to broach sensitive issues of religious education. By 2006, GTZ noted "some breakthroughs" in this dialogue and was able to build relationships among the JUI-F leaders which could prove to be valuable for future joint *madaris* reform efforts. The JUI-F, noted someone in GTZ who worked closely with them, "held a very narrow vision of the world, but their experience in government has helped them to understand some of the issues.... That exposure *does* trickle down [through the party ranks], and it also has an effect at the leadership level."[106]

The MMA's relationship with non-governmental organizations proved to be complex. Foreign NGO leaders were relieved that the Islamists' strong anti-NGO campaign rhetoric did not translate into harsh action against their organizations in the Frontier. The religious parties, by most accounts, came to realize that many organizations in the NGO sector were in fact contributing to the MMA's own health and education priorities, and providing significant avenues for local patronage. Even the NGO work which took place in NWFP following the October 2005 earthquake elicited only a mild reaction from the MMA leadership, and on several occasions the religious government even quietly partnered with American NGOs on health projects in the province.[107]

At the same time, however, the NGO community's relationship with the Islamists was quite strained. Senior MMA leaders often spoke out in public against foreign-funded organizations which spread "obscenity," and argued that they undermined the cultural and religious identity of Muslims in the Frontier.[108] In parts of the southern tribal districts, the term "NGO" (imported into the Urdu lexicon) had gained such a stigma that organizations began labeling themselves as a *ghair sarkari tanzim* (non-governmental organization) in order to be seen more positively as an indigenous institution. The kind of work undertaken by NGOs was also an important factor in the MMA's response. Organizations conducting health, construction, and education programs were given far more latitude by the provincial government than NGOs working to promote gender-oriented reforms.

At the end of the day, the religious parties and the donors both had strong incentives to find a *modus vivendi* that would meet the requirements of the international community, and placate the religious parties' rank-and-file membership. It helped that, with the notable exception of gender issues, the basic agenda of the donors aligned nicely with the MMA's own populist rhetoric and interest in enhancing service delivery — the very slogans on which the religious alliance had run. This alignment of interests, if anything, served to enhance the influence of the international community in mainstreaming the religious parties during their five-year tenure in the Frontier.

Federalism and the martial state

The mild character of the MMA's Islamism is often explained with reference to a single factor: its manipulation and co-option by state elites. Of all of the variables which constrained the MMA's Islamist agenda, this was arguably the most critical. Beginning with the MMA's victory in the NWFP, in which the state itself had a hand, there were profound pressures on the provincial Islamist government to comply with the interests of the martial regime in Islamabad.

Politically, the central government held several key levers of control over the MMA. It appointed the province's chief secretary and inspector general of police, and its approval was required for large development projects. Islamabad was also able to hold out the prospect of governor's rule if the religious alliance did not comply with the central government's wishes. And, most notably in the 2005 Local Body Elections, the central government spent great sums of money to ensure the election of local politicians who would be friendly to the PML-Q, thus putting pressure on the MMA from below.

The Musharraf government also exerted pressure on the religious alliance at the federal level. The *quid pro quos* were considerable: the MMA's support for the Legal Framework Order (LFO) in late 2003, which strengthened the powers of the presidency and gave legal cover to Musharraf's continued rule as both president and chief of army staff, was effectively a precondition for its continued rule in the NWFP.[109] In 2006, the religious government again legitimized Musharraf's rule under pressure by participating in the National Security Council meetings, over the objection of many MMA figures. And in the legal sphere, the military regime's effective control of the federal courts allowed Musharraf to contain the MMA's *shariah* agenda.[110]

Moreover, the central government retained enormous financial leverage over the MMA government. Over 90% of the NWFP provincial budget is derived from fiscal transfers from Islamabad, which are divided between the National Finance Commission (NFC) award, the hydroelectric royalties (known as "net hydel" payments), and other transfers such as the tobacco tax. The province itself has a very weak tax base, as its economy is heavily dependent on transit and other services which operate informally or for historical reasons are not subject to tax.[111] The NFC award to NWFP did increase during the MMA's tenure, and the provincial government was also able to win a longstanding dispute with the central government over the net hydel royalties (but for political reasons Islamabad delayed the back payments).[112]

In the end, the federal structure of Pakistan, the central government's fiscal and bureaucratic leverage, the ability of the security services to fragment the religious alliance, and the MMA's unique role as a "loyal opposition" to the Musharraf government kept the Islamists in Peshawar vulnerable to manipulation by the state.[113] The MMA did not have wide berth to pursue a rigorous Islamization agenda even if it had wanted to, and nor did it have the autonomy to pursue policies which ran counter to significant state interests.

That said, it is too simplistic to dismiss the MMA as nothing more than "puppets" of the central government. Like all political blocs in Pakistan, the MMA found itself constrained by the interests of the ruling elite, and by a system which limited the ability of any one party to significantly change the balance of power between civil and military institutions. But Musharraf's ruling party also had its own political imperatives: virtually devoid of allies in the NWFP, it needed the MMA government's support, and benefited both from the perception of a democratic order, and from fears in the West of a resurgent Islamism in the Frontier.

IN SUMMARY:
THE LIMITS AND LESSONS OF ISLAMIST 'MODERATION'

The virtues of disillusionment

The MMA, contrary to expectations, governed for the most part as a *status quo* political force. Most close observers judged the provincial government to be moderately competent, and its Islamization agenda constrained by both internal and structural factors. There are few commentators outside of the Islamist sector itself who regard the MMA's tenure to have been, on balance, positive for the Frontier: the alliance proposed a number of troubling initiatives, contributed to the further Islamization of political discourse, opposed the participation of women in public life, channeled support to the *madaris,* and was hesitant to take action against new Islamist insurgent groups.

Even so, there is reason to believe that the Islamists' governance experience was not entirely negative. In the first place, five years of MMA rule deflated the "*mullah* mystique" which surrounded the religious parties, and brought about a healthy disillusionment with Islamist governance. For the first time in Pakistan's history, the religious parties were forced to seriously contend with the victor-victim problem. Their religious rhetoric had helped them come to power, but did not prepare them to govern. By 2007, most political analysts in the Frontier agreed that "the myth is gone" and that religious parties would have to be more realistic in the future, both in their campaigning, and in their interaction with the institutions of the state.

Several religious leaders from minority communities also raised an interesting counter-factual: if, in the religiously- and politically-charged context following 9/11, the religious parties in the Frontier had *not* assumed a governance role, but had instead kept away from the formal political space — either by their own choice, or because of state interference — the Islamists might then have caused even *more* problems for the minority communities. That is, some saw the religious parties' participation in provincial governance as a welcome check on their behavior, and a "second-best" solution to dealing with the problematic extra-political activities of the parties and their allies.

Modeling Islamist moderation

There is a great deal of interest in the policy community today in the ways in which Islamist movements are apt to change when they are forced to govern. Although observers in the West are likely to continue to be skeptical about the democratic credentials (and, more to the point, the liberal credentials) of movements like the MMA, the challenge of how to respond to Islamic politics is likely to grow more salient with time. Movements like al Qaeda ultimately have very little to offer local communities, while "democratic Islamist" movements — such as those in Egypt, the Palestinian territories, Turkey, Indonesia, Pakistan, and elsewhere — are able to bring together their Islamic discourse and values with credible programs of local governance.

One could argue that the MMA in the NWFP constitutes a poor case study of Islamist moderation because it was hemmed in by such a great number of political, legal, and fiscal constraints. But in fact, these constraints are precisely what make the case of the MMA realistic and valuable in the Pakistani context. It is exceedingly unlikely that Islamist parties will take power in Islamabad in the foreseeable future; there is simply no mass constituency for such a radical shift. It *is,* however, quite likely that Islamist parties will once again play a significant role at the margins — either in the NWFP or Balochistan, or as a part of a coalition in Islamabad.

In such a scenario, the MMA's case and its limitations become instructive. It is easy to imagine a scenario in which the JUI-F serves as a minor coalition partner at the federal level with the PPP;[114] or the JI and the JUI-F both with the PML-N. (The JUI-F has demonstrated its ability to partner with virtually anyone.) There are, moreover, a number of ways in which the MMA constituent parties could again participate in governance at the provincial level in the Frontier, and in none of these cases do the parties need to form a majority in order to advance their respective agendas: the current state of the party system in Pakistan is such that ethnic and religious parties serve as swing blocs and can garner significant influence by bargaining with the two or three mainstream parties, none of which can form a parliamentary majority outright.

Given the importance of federal constraints on provincial activity, policymakers would be right to be more concerned about the judicial, political, and bureaucratic checks imposed by Islamabad than by the composition of the NWFP government itself. The participation of the Jamaat as a minor coalition partner in NWFP under a PML-N government at the center, for example, might well be more problematic than a scenario in which an MMA-like alliance ruled outright in the Frontier under a PPP government at the center. In either case, internal constituency politics and international donor engagement will exert a moderating influence on Islamic political behavior, but given the state of Pakistan's federalist system, the disposition of the ruling coalition in Islamabad is likely to be the decisive factor.

Specifically, this analysis makes a strong case for engaging the mainstream PML-N. The Nawaz league's right-of-center politics — emphasizing Islamic values, economic growth, and national sovereignty — is likely to be increasingly resonant with the Pakistani public. History suggests that a PML-N government in Islamabad would be less apt to constrain Islamization efforts by religious parties at the provincial level, and may even turn to such efforts itself in a bid to bolster its standing vis-à-vis its left-of-center rivals. The PML-N also has very close ties to the Jamaat, particularly in urban Punjab, which further suggests that if and when the religious parties are to exert substantive political or legal influence, it may well be facilitated by mainstream right-of-center political forces.[115]

Lessons from the Frontier

As the narrative below argues, the MMA as a formal alliance has for now been sidelined in the Frontier — overtaken electorally by Pashtun nationalist politics and rhetorically by new insurgent Islamist movements. Some of the lessons which can be drawn from the MMA's five year tenure may nevertheless have enduring relevance: the mechanisms by which the Islamists adapted to a governance role; the ways in which interaction with the Pakistani state and the international community exerted leverage on religious politics; the divergence between Islamist rhetoric (which moderated little) and actual political behavior (which moderated a great deal); the role that religious parties can play in bringing "backward" areas into the provincial mainstream; and the ways in which religious or sectarian politics can complicate the administration of local governance.

On the level of mass politics, the MMA's use of Islamic populist themes may have continuing implications for the mainstream parties in the Frontier, which are now more vulnerable to being outflanked on the right by Islamic discourse. Parties like the PPP and ANP have learned that they cannot afford to allow the Islamist parties to co-opt religious language and support for the *shariah;* they may, as a result, be pressured to play up their Islamic credentials in order to forestall a return by the Islamist bloc. Although the MMA as a formal alliance is currently moribund, it could easily be resurrected: now that Musharraf's presence in the government no longer drives a wedge between the JUI-F and the JI, the religious parties (and the Deobandis in particular) can revert to form as swing blocs between center-left and center-right politics. A JUI-Jamaat partnership in the NWFP is somewhat less complementary than it was in 2002, but the geographic bases of the parties are still sufficiently disjoint as to make electoral alliances attractive in future contests.

Finally, as will be argued below, it is worth noting a lesson that should *not* be drawn from the decline of the MMA: religious politics is not going away in the Frontier. If anything, it is more relevant than ever. There is a striking resonance between the rhetoric, promises, complaints, and hot-button issues of the MMA in 2002, and the language of neo-Taliban groups in the Frontier today: injustice, corruption, obscenity, government inaction, and foreign intervention, to name a few. The locus of this "discussion," to be sure, has gradually moved outside the bounds of formal electoral politics and into the realm of vigilantism, militancy, and insurgency — but it may yet come back. If and when it does, the religious parties are likely to again play an important role, and the lessons from the MMA's tenure may again be relevant in responding to the religious politics of the Frontier.

NOTES:

1 A comprehensive and methodologically rigorous study of the MMA and its implications for an understanding of "Islamist moderation" has yet to be written. This chapter provides only a high-level overview of the MMA's tenure, and a set of initial policy-oriented conclusions which might be drawn from it. Note that many of the journalistic accounts used below draw from the archives of *Dawn,* which is reputed for its balanced and careful reporting; *The News,* a left-of-center daily; and the *Daily Times,* whose staff in Peshawar consistently provides the most comprehensive coverage of religious politics in the Frontier.

2 Khaled Ahmed, "Three angry Pushtuns," *Friday Times,* August 16, 2002.

3 Religious parties had come together before for other purposes, such as in 1995 when a group of parties formed the Milli Yakjehti Council (MYC) to address sectarian conflicts. The MYC was not, however, able to coalesce as an electoral alliance for the 1997 polls.

4 See, e.g., M. Ilyas Khan, "Inside the MMA," *Herald,* November 2002. Hamid Gul was later described as a "strategic advisor" to the MMA, and in 2006 was involved in an unsuccessful attempt to create a more hardline Islamist alliance which would include organizations of a more militant character than the JI and JUI-F. Arnaud de Borchgrave, "Gulled by Gul," *Washington*

Times, December 2, 2004; and Hasan Mansoor, "New religious alliance in the offing? JUI-S takes fight to the next level," *Daily Times*, March 11, 2006. Some have also suggested that the massive JUI-organized Deoband conference in Peshawar in May 2001 served as a catalyzing force for developing a common platform among the religious parties. See Behroz Khan, "Assembly of Faith," *Newsline*, May 2001. Ahmed Rashid claims that this conference was in fact funded by the ISI. Rashid, *Descent into Chaos*, 53.

5 The party is also referred to as Pakistan Islami Tehrik.

6 The People's Party in the NWFP had seen its political organization atrophy since its period of dominance in the 1990s, and had been weakened by the defection of Aftab Sherpao in 1999, which drained the party of its base in the politically important Charsadda district. The ANP was similarly contesting the elections from a position of internal weakness. The Pashtun nationalist movement, which traces its political heritage to the "Frontier Gandhi" Khan Abdul Ghaffar Khan, had fragmented in the 1990s. By 2002, the nationalists were in disarray and party workers were despondent. Author interviews with ANP party workers, July 2007. Peshawar.

7 M. Ilyas Khan, "Inside the MMA," 45–6. MMA President Maulana Shah Ahmed Noorani (of the Barelvi JUP) later acknowledged that "the government propaganda against the PPP and PML-N" also contributed to the alliance's success in 2002. "Noorani — a binding force," *Dawn*, December 12, 2003.

8 See "Government helped MMA leaders contest elections," *Daily Times*, November 8, 2002. See also Rashid, *Descent into Chaos*, 156.

9 Author interview with a senior NWFP provincial official, July 2007, Peshawar.

10 It was reportedly analysts from the police service's Special Branch who most accurately predicted the MMA's overwhelming electoral gains. Author interviews with federal and provincial officials, 2007, Islamabad and Peshawar.

11 See Mohammad Waseem, *Democratization in Pakistan: A Study of the 2002 Elections* (Oxford: Oxford University Press, 2006), 129. Note also that the MMA's campaign promises were much more extensive than its formal manifesto, which was "critically devoid of specifics" and did not even address Pakistan's relations with the United States. Pakistan Institute of Legislative Development and Transparency, *Election 2002: A Comparative Study of Election Manifestos of Major Political Parties*, October 2002, 34.

12 Quotation by Qazi Hussain Ahmad, from *Mashriq*, October 20, 2002.

13 See, e.g., Rahimullah Yusufzai, "Durrani follows Mufti Mahmud," *The News*, November 30, 2002.

14 Ironically, exit polling conducted during the 2002 elections showed that those who voted for the MMA tended to be richer and more educated than those who voted for the mainstream parties. These data were not broken out by province, so it is impossible to judge whether this pattern also held in the NWFP. But neither the alliance's platform nor its program of governance specifically appealed to educated or upper-class voters. Pakistan Institute of Legislative Development and Transparency, *Election 2002: Who Voted for Whom? Findings from an Exit Poll Survey*, October 2002.

15 "MMA's plan for first 100 days in power," *Dawn*, October 10, 2002.

16 Figures from the Election Commission of Pakistan. The MMA's final party position, including reserved seats, accounted for 68 out of 124. Waseem Ahmad Shah, "MMA tally in NWFP PA rises to 68: Names for reserved seats notified," *Dawn*, November 3, 2002. For detailed studies of the 2002 elections, see Waseem, *Democratization in Pakistan*; and Andrew R. Wilder, "Elections 2002: Legitimizing the Status Quo," in *Pakistan on the Brink: Politics, Economics, and Society*, ed. Craig Baxter (Maryland: Lexington Books, 2004).

17   Some commentators have attributed the MMA's success almost entirely to intervention by the state. See, e.g., Frédéric Grare, *Islam, Militarism, and the 2007–2008 Elections in Pakistan* (Carnegie Endowment for International Peace, July 2006).

18   Author interview with a provincial government official, July 2007, Peshawar. See, e.g., *Express* (Urdu), November 28, 2002. These restrictions generally did not apply to the cantonment areas, which operated under the control of the military. As a practical matter, however, private enterprises in the cantonment, such as hotels, chose to abide by the MMA's restrictions.

19   Author interviews, 2005–7, Peshawar. See also, e.g., "Vigilante action against cable operators continues in Peshawar," *Daily Times*, January 11, 2003; "Editorial: Talibanisation of NWFP," *Daily Times*, May 25, 2003; Iqbal Khattak, "Police warns MMA against talking law in own hands," *Daily Times*, December 29, 2003; and Amy Waldman, "In One Pakistan Province, Reality Tempers Ideology," *New York Times*, January 18, 2004.

20   See *Express* (Urdu), February 1, 2003; Ghafar Ali and Iqbal Khattak, "MMA to set up Taliban-style ministry," *Daily Times*, January 30, 2003; Shafiq Ahmad, "Headscarf for girl students urged," *Dawn*, March 11, 2003; Iqbal Khattak, "NWFP slides closer to Sharia," *Daily Times*, March 19, 2003; and "NWFP Shariat body's proposals on education in 40 days," *Daily Times*, December 19, 2003.

21   The MMA, led by the JUI-F's Maulana Fazlur Rehman, finally acceded in December 2003 to a compromise version of the LFO.

22   In June 2003 a World Bank official was quoted as saying, "We feared the Talibanisation of Pakistan soon after the MMA came to power. Its recent moves have further strengthened our apprehensions. We are now fully convinced that the Alliance is hell-bent on enforcing the Taliban system on Pakistan." Mohammad Shehzad, "MMA causes US$200 million loss," *Friday Times*, June 20, 2003.

23   As noted below, the vigilantism which began circa 2007 in areas such as Malakand, while often associated in journalistic accounts with the early MMA vigilantism in 2003–4, should in fact be considered a separate phenomenon; the MMA generally opposed the later vigilantism, which was organized in part by the TNSM.

24   The MMA justified the introduction of the *mohtasib* on the grounds that the other three provinces in the federation had already established such a position. While this was technically the case, the role of the *mohtasib* as envisioned by the Hisbah legislation far outstripped the largely symbolic *mohtasib* positions that had previously been established in other parts of Pakistan. In other respects, the bill's establishment of the *mohtasib* office was simply redundant (Musharraf's Local Government Ordinance of 2001, for example, allowed for *mohtasibs* at the district level).

25   Ismail Khan, "Force will be raised to prevent 'vice': NWFP cabinet approves draft 'Hisba Act,'" *Dawn*, May 23, 2003.

26   Critics of the bill cited its ambiguity about the means of enforcement of *mohtasib* decisions; its exemption from normal judicial review; and its lack of clarity regarding terminology. (For example, the bill granted powers to the *mohtasib* to "monitor adherence of moral values of Islam at public places," but failed to define any of the key terms.) See "Text of Hasba Bill," *Dawn*, July 16, 2005.

27   "Opinion of the Supreme Court in Reference No. 2 of 2005 (PLD 2005 SC 873) [Hisba Bill case]," Supreme Court of Pakistan. See also Mohammad Kamran, "SC declares key Hasba sections unconstitutional," *Daily Times*, August 5, 2005.

28   Even MMA insiders acknowledged that the bill was not well designed or vetted by the proper legal experts and provincial departments. Author interviews with MMA advisors, 2007, Peshawar.

29　JI senator and party intellectual Khurshid Ahmad framed the opposition to Hisbah as opposition to Islam, warning his readers that "the real target is not the Hisbah bill, but Islam itself...!" Khurshid Ahmad, "Revival of the Hisbah System in Frontier Province: Why All This Hullabaloo?" *Tarjumanul Quran*, August 2005, available at http://jamaat.org/Isharat/2005/ish0805.html (accessed October 1, 2008).

30　Most close observers of religious politics in Pakistan believe that the civil legal structure is in little danger of being overtaken by religious law. Mohammad Waseem notes, "Even after several bouts of Islamisation of laws and institutions during the five and half decades after independence, Pakistan's legal system is based essentially on British common law. In this respect, the state apparatuses in Pakistan display a fundamentally secular character in both structural and operational contexts, even as Islamic ideology gradually dominated the self-image of the people at large." Mohammad Waseem, "Political Sources of Islamic Militancy in Pakistan," in *The Deadly Embrace: Religion, Politics and Violence in India and Pakistan 1947–2002*, ed. Ian Talbot (Oxford: Oxford University Press, 2007), 147.

31　It helped that the resolutions were non-binding. Resolutions in 2003 included: requesting that the federal government release all "freedom fighters" who had been arrested for fighting the Americans in Afghanistan; reverse its decision to revise the *Islamiyat* (Islamic studies) curriculum in public schools; and reject the recommendation of the Womens' Commission to terminate the notorious Hudood Ordinance.

32　In one case, MMA workers apparently visited internet cafes in order to "inform the government if anyone were found violating government orders." This form of civic action no doubt had the intended effect on the proprietors. Ghafar Ali, "MMA workers to police Internet porn," *Daily Times*, May 14, 2004. In another case, district officials in Dir accompanied police to encourage shopkeepers to attend Friday prayers. *Express* (Urdu), February 9, 2003.

33　Both of these bills were introduced in December 2004 by Nadar Shah, a JI MPA.

34　Author interviews with provincial government officials, July 2007, Peshawar.

35　Author interview with a JUI-F advisor, August 2008, Peshawar.

36　See, e.g., Ismail Khan, "Govt's writ weakening in NWFP, tribal areas," *Dawn*, March 29, 2007; Raza Khan, "An intensified Talibanisation," *Weekly Cutting Edge*, May 9, 2007; David Montero, "Pakistan losing territory to radicals," *Christian Science Monitor*, May 29, 2007; "Who is targeting Peshawar?" *Daily Times*, May 31, 2007; Iqbal Khattak, "'Independent cells spreading Talibanisation across NWFP,'" *Daily Times*, June 1, 2007; and Jane Perlez and Ismail Khan, "Taliban Spreading, Pakistani President Is Warned," *New York Times*, June 30, 2007.

37　Author interviews with MMA politicians, July 2007, Peshawar.

38　Author interview with a military officer posted in NWFP, August 2008, Islamabad. See also "NWFP govt calls for army's help," *Daily Times*, September 26, 2007.

39　Author interview with a provincial government official, August 2008, Peshawar. See also "'No Swat operation in MMA rule,'" *Daily Times*, October 29, 2007.

40　Author interview with a JUI-F leader, 2007, Islamabad.

41　Before the MMA came to power, the NWFP government was spending around Rs. 2 million per year on *madaris*. The non-minority expenditures of the Auqaf, Hajj, Religious & Minority Affairs Department was increased under the MMA, but never exceeded Rs. 10 million per year (i.e., less than $200,000). Author interviews with provincial government officials, July 2007, Peshawar. See also "Government sets condition for helping Madaris," *Dawn*, March 15, 2002; and Zulfiqar Ali, "50 Madaris in NWFP to get financial assistance," *Dawn*, June 23, 2002.

42 The propensity of the JUI to consider government support of the madaris to be corrupting can be seen in the reaction of the Ittihad Tanzimat-e-Madaris Dinya (ITMD) — a coalition of the five major Wafaq ul-Madaris boards — to terminate the affiliation of 125 seminaries in NWFP that agreed in February 2007 to receive government funds under the Madrassah Reforms Project. Expressing the consensus opinion of the JUI, ITMD central leader Maulana Hanif Jalandhri argued that "financial aid would provide the government an excuse to interfere in the affairs of the seminaries." Zulfiqar Ali, "125 seminaries agree to receive govt aid," *Dawn*, February 23, 2007. The Darkhawasti faction, now known as JUI-S and led by Maulana Sami ul-Haq, has traditionally been more willing to accept *zakat* funds. Jamal Malik, "Dynamics Among Traditional Religious Scholars and their Institutions in Contemporary South Asia," *The Muslim World* 87, no. 3–4 (July–October, 1997), 199–220.

43 Author interview with a JUI-F advisor, August 2008, Peshawar.

44 There were accusations by political opponents of the MMA that the leaders of the alliance had unjustly directed these funds to their own districts. See, e.g., "PHC seeks NWFP govt reply over MPAs writ," *Dawn*, September 13, 2007.

45 Author review of provincial development documents.

46 The chief minister redesigned the budgeting process to include a large number of "umbrella grants" which he could then direct in a discretionary manner to preferred regions or constituents. Author review of provincial development documents, and interviews with MPAs, July and August 2007, Peshawar. This issue was also debated in the assembly in November 2006. See Pakistan Institute of Legislative Development and Transparency, *State of Democracy in Pakistan: Report for the Year 2006*, January 2007.

47 The Jamaat, to a lesser extent, operated in a similar manner, drawing on its support base among the devout middle class to solicit donations to its own in-house charity, Al-Khidmat Trust.

48 For an in-depth look at these dynamics, see the forthcoming study on Pakistan undertaken by the DFID-funded Religions and Development Research Programme Consortium, http://rad.bham.ac.uk/index.php?section=14 (accessed October 1, 2008).

49 This is a secondary quotation, taken from Iqbal Khattak, "Durrani promises to 'crush' crime in NWFP," *Daily Times*, December 31, 2002.

50 Allocations to the provincial government education sector under the Annual Development Plan (ADP) almost doubled from 2002 to 2006, increasing from Rs. 10.4 to Rs. 20.4 billion.

51 This two year period is FY2004/5 to FY2006/7. Note that Malakand, Nowshera, Swat, Lakki Marwat, Hangu, and Shangla also recorded overall 2-year gains of over 20%. Author analysis of Education Management Information System (EMIS) data, provided by the Directorate of Schools and Literacy, Government of NWFP.

52 Battagram also saw its female secondary enrollments rise dramatically during this period, but they began from a base of only 204 students. Ibid.

53 Computed on age group 5–9. Ibid.

54 This idea was borrowed from the government of Punjab, and greatly expanded by the MMA.

55 Note that education at the primary and secondary levels is gender segregated in Pakistan. See "MMA to resist change in Islamiyat," *Daily Times*, December 23, 2005; "Education Ministry denies deleting prayer chapter," *Daily Times*, December 23, 2005; and "NWFP not to follow centre: minister: Enlightened moderation — MMA style," *Dawn*, January 25, 2007.

56 Islamiyat is Islamic studies. In Pakistan, curriculum is a federal subject, although provincial recommendations are taken under advisement by Islamabad.

57 Members of the provincial bureaucracy and donor communities in general found the MMA's negotiating objective to be a shallow reaction to the central government's modest reforms, but also believed that the MMA acquitted itself well by approaching the negotiations seriously and reasonably.

58 Author interviews with NGO and international experts, and provincial government officials, summer 2007, Islamabad and Peshawar.

59 See, e.g., Declan Walsh, "Polio cases jump in Pakistan as clerics declare vaccination an American plot," *Guardian,* February 15, 2007.

60 Anita Weiss, "A Provincial Islamist Victory in Pakistan: The Social Reform Agenda of the Muttahida Majlis-i-Amal," in *Asian Islam in the 21st Century,* ed. John L. Esposito, John O. Voll, and Osman Bakar (Oxford: Oxford University Press, 2008), 161.

61 See Anita M. Weiss, "Questioning Women's Rights in Pakistan: Finding Common Ground," *Pakistan Vision* 8, no. 1, 110ff.

62 See "NGO accuses MMA govt of coercion, ends collaboration," *Dawn,* June 12, 2003; and "Lack of Islamic teachings blamed for crime against women," *Daily Times,* January 24, 2004. Early in the alliance's tenure, the JI became embroiled in a controversy surrounding one of Aurat's shelters near Peshawar for female survivors of domestic violence, which was funded by the German aid agency GTZ. After a great deal of local politicking, Aurat had to abandon the shelter, and the Germans were very displeased at the MMA's intransigence. For a detailed look at this controversy, see Uzma Khan, *Storm in the Shelter: Lessons Learnt from the Mera Ghar Experience* (Aurat Foundation, n.d. [circa 2003]).

63 Notes provided to the author by Mariam Mufti from her interview with an Aurat Foundation leader, July 2007, Lahore.

64 For a Pakistani woman's perspective on the MMA's gender policy, see Nazish Brohi, *The MMA Offensive: Three Years in Power: 2003–2005* (Islamabad: ActionAid, n.d. [2006]), 56–84.

65 Author interview, July 2007, Peshawar.

66 The MMA was quick to assert that its gender agenda was not synonymous with that of the Taliban. In a 2003 interview, Maulana Fazlur Rehman was asked, "But Maulana Sahib, there are women who cannot sleep well due to the recent policies adopted by the MMA." He replied: "They should not be afraid. They should not view it as Talibanisation, as projected by the west. We also tried to make the Taliban understand the realities of the modern world. There is no ban on working women. But the prime responsibility of women is to look after the household and the responsibility of the men is to earn. But if women want to contribute economically, there is no ban on them in Islam." Owais Tohid, "Interview with Maulana Fazlur Rahman," *Newsline,* July 2003.

67 Author interviews with provincial government and World Bank officials, July 2007, Peshawar and Islamabad. Fazlullah reportedly destroyed 40 girls' schools between July 2007 and May 2008 in the Swat Valley. See Massoud Ansari, "The Ticking Bomb," *Herald,* August 2008, 67–70.

68 Author interview with an Aurat Foundation worker, July 2007, Peshawar.

69 The official 1998 census recorded about 37,000 religious minorities in the NWFP, or about 0.2% of the total population of 17.74 million. It is widely believed that, due to under-counting, the actual percentage is closer to 0.5%.

70 On the electoral front, the MMA included a Shia party in the alliance (although it was only one of many active in the province) in order to bolster its appeal among the small Shia population and project an image of sectarian moderation. The reintroduction of the joint electorate system

71　The MMA maintained steady funding for minority projects in its Annual Development Programmes at about Rs. 12 million per year from FY2003/4 to FY2005/6, and programmed increases to Rs. 19 million and 23 million in FY2006/7 and FY2007/8, respectively. Other minority-related projects were funded out of the Chief Minister's Special Fund. Author review of NWFP Annual Development Programme documents.

72　See "Church in Muslim institution not un-Islamic: Peshawar High Court," *Daily Times*, January 24, 2007.

73　Author interviews with Protestant and Catholic church leaders, 2005–7, Peshawar. *Dhimmitude* refers to perceived attempts by a Muslim majority to subordinate a non-Muslim minority on the principle that they are *dhimmi* (a protected non-Muslim subject within a Muslim state).

74　Even the MPAs holding seats reserved for religious minorities — who were, ironically, appointed by the MMA — often did little to support the communities that they supposedly represented.

75　Author interviews with Charsadda Christian leaders, June 2007, Peshawar.

76　Author interviews with representatives of Christian, Hindu, and Sikh communities in NWFP, 2006–7, Peshawar.

77　Author interviews with PML-N, ANP, and PPP MPAs, July 2007, Peshawar.

78　This created an added burden for the bureaucrats, who not only had to purchase new software that could accommodate Urdu's complex Nastaliq script, but had to learn the Urdu equivalents for technical terms (many of which were neologisms) in place of the commonly-known English terms.

79　Author interview, July 2007, Peshawar.

80　Author interview with a senior NWFP bureaucrat, July 2007, Peshawar.

81　Party workers frequently recounted the story of Amanat Shah, a young MPA who, lacking a car, rode his bicycle around his Mardan constituency; and also that of Senior Minister Siraj ul-Haq, who made a point of traveling to official meetings in Islamabad using a public bus.

82　Author interview, July 2007, Peshawar.

83　The religious parties were explicit about this focus: "The present government has embarked upon a development policy under which less developed areas situated at the extreme north and south of the province have been prioritized for initiation of developmental schemes in order to bring them on a par with the developed ones." Government of NWFP, *Third Year of the NWFP Govt: A Journey Through Heavy Odds*, 5. Note that the MMA government did, by most accounts, respond admirably in the immediate aftermath of the October 2005 earthquake which hit parts of Hazara division; but some observers have argued that the religious parties did not give sufficient follow-up attention to the region in 2006 and 2007, since the non-Pashtun population was unlikely to vote for the MMA in large numbers. Author interviews with NGO workers and U.S. officials, summer 2007, Islamabad and Peshawar.

84　Discretionary grants by the provincial ministers, MPAs, and MNAs were often subject to approval by the bureaucracy, but were generally not made available in the public record. Local journalists had to resort to analyzing the tender proposals for construction projects which appeared in local newspapers in order to ascertain the distribution of development monies.

85　Author interview with a senior JUI-F advisor, July 2007, Peshawar.

86　For a sophisticated analysis of the MMA's use of patronage, see Mariam Mufti, "Ensuring Social

Order: A Case of Islamic Governance under MMA 2002–2007," *Critique Internationale,* January 2009 (forthcoming).

87 They complained, however, about the government's efforts to shield the budget process from input by members of the opposition.

88 Quoted in Ashutosh Misra, "Rise of Religious Parties in Pakistan: Causes and Prospects," *Strategic Analysis* 27, no. 2 (April–June 2003). See also Amjad Mahmood, "MMA promises roti, kapra, makan," *Dawn,* August 25, 2002. "Roti, kapra aur makan" is Urdu for "bread, clothing and shelter."

89 See Younas Kayasi, "Police corruption and advice of the Chief Minister," *Aaj,* September 28, 2006.

90 Government of NWFP, *The Achievements of the Provincial Government of Muttahida Majlis-e-Amal (MMA) (since 30th November, 2002 till date),* n.d. [circa 2003].

91 The day before the election in 2002, MMA leaders Maulana Shah Ahmad Noorani and Maulana Fazlur Rehman outlined their ambitious public-sector job-creation program: "Under the programme, make-shift fibre kiosks would be set up along main roads for 200,000 jobless people while special evening bazaars would be organized in cities for 250,000 more unemployed people. At least 50,000 jobless graduates would be given a six-month military training against a reasonable honorarium." "MMA's plan for first 100 days in power," *Dawn,* October 10, 2002.

92 For more on the ANP, see chapter III, "New Islamists and the Return of Pashtun Nationalism."

93 The JUI-F was the undisputed leader of the alliance in NWFP and received the chief minister slot, while the Jamaat received the senior minister and speaker of the assembly positions. 2006 saw the formation of a "forward block" (dissenting faction) within the MMA opposed to the actions of the chief minister; tellingly, the JUI-F was able to appease the dissidents at minimal cost, bringing them back into the fold with promises of more equitable distribution of funds.

94 At a provincial level, the MMA was also forced to deal with the role of the four smaller parties in the alliance — the JUI-S, JAH, JUP, and ITP — who had between them only two seats in the provincial assembly, and none in the National Assembly from NWFP. The small parties often protested against their exclusion in the alliance's decision-making. Perhaps the most bitter and long-standing internal dispute involving the minor parties revolved around Maulana Sami ul-Haq and his faction of the JUI. Not long after the 2002 elections, Sami threatened to leave the alliance on account of its slow implementation of the *shariah* program. His party was frequently at odds with the JUI-F, accusing it of being too accommodating toward the martial government in Islamabad. For its part, the JUI-F resented Sami ul-Haq's demands for greater participation in the alliance's decision-making on account of the fact that his electoral constituency and vote-bank demonstrably paled in comparison to that of the major parties. They also voiced discontent, apparently without irony, over the supposed ease with which he was manipulated by the security services in Islamabad. In the last several years, the JUI-F and JUI-S have adopted diverging positions toward the neo-Taliban, with the JUI-S taking a more sympathetic line.

95 See the August 2007 and January 2008 surveys by Terror Free Tomorrow, which reported that about three-quarters of respondents said that "strict *shariah*" was "very important" or "somewhat important." (The Urdu word used for "strict" used in this survey is unknown; some common translations in Urdu are far less pejorative than the English word, and have connotations closer to "strong" or "proper.") A survey conducted in September 2007 by World Public Opinion also reported that 75% of respondents thought that *shariah* should play "a larger role" or "about the same role as it plays today" in Pakistani law. C. Christine Fair, Clay Ramsay,

and Steven Kull, *Pakistani Public Opinion on Democracy, Islamist Militancy, and Relations with the U.S.* (WorldPublicOpinion.org and United States Institute of Peace, January 7, 2008).

96   This assertion is based largely on the author's interactions with religiously and politically conservative Pakistanis in NWFP. Surveys conducted in Pakistan tend not to get beyond the surface questions regarding support for *shariah,* and rarely ask about specific practices. Surveys have shown that 90% of respondents affirm the importance of Islamic principles in governing the state, while only 15% support an increase in the "Talibanization of daily life." Fair et al, "Pakistani Public Opinion."

97   The MMA leadership quickly realized that limiting television broadcasts would be exceptionally unpopular. Author interviews, 2005–6, Peshawar.

98   Iqbal Khattak, "Haq raises alarm bells on Frontier govt," *Daily Times,* December 19, 2002. It is worth noting that the MMA's disapproval of *riba* (interest) did not materially dissuade it from seeking out international loans for the province.

99   Author interviews with World Bank officials, July 2007, Islamabad.

100 Ibid.

101 By and large the Bank was pleased with the provincial government's implementation of the SAC-funded reforms. A December 2005 assessment of the SAC-I noted that the parties elected under the MMA's banner "formed a solid coalition which supported the reform program as meeting much of their own agenda, particularly in the delivery of social services." World Bank, *Project Performance Assessment Report, Sindh Structural Adjustment Credit, NWFP Structural Adjustment Credit, NWFP Community Infrastructure and NHA Strengthening Credit,* December 19, 2005.

102 The GRAP program amounted to only $7 million of technical assistance out of the $300 million DSP loan package, but it was enough to put the entire project at risk.

103 The NWFP's portion of the GRAP funds was, of course, withheld.

104 Author interview with a DFID official, July 2007, Islamabad.

105 Author interview, July 2007, Peshawar.

106 Ibid.

107 For example, Save the Children (U.S.) undertook significant post-earthquake projects in Battagram, and was awarded a major grant in early 2007 to revitalize the local health system in the district. The organization had to pull out of the region in November 2007 after attacks by militant groups against local NGO workers. Author interviews with an NGO health expert, July 2007, Islamabad. See also "$2.9 Million World Bank-Administered Japanese Grant for Revitalizing Primary Health Care in Earthquake Areas," World Bank (Islamabad), January 11, 2007. Note that the MMA initially opposed the presence of U.S. forces in the earthquake areas, but their comments were mostly for public consumption. Author interviews with MMA leaders, 2006, Peshawar; and Raja Asghar, "MMA opposes Nato, US forces for quake relief," *Dawn,* October 29, 2005.

108 Shortly after the MMA's 2002 victory, for example, JI leader Qazi Hussain Ahmad explained his position thus: "All those NGOs who have been working for the welfare of the people would be encouraged by the MMA government, but those who want to work according to the agenda of imperialistic powers and indulge in spreading anti-Islamic culture would not be allowed to continue their work." Quoted in "Qazi Hussain Ahmad: Islamic revolution in sight," *The News,* November 10, 2002.

109 The MMA's negotiation with the martial government over the 2002 LFO represented perhaps the prime example of the way in which the Islamist alliance balanced its electoral agenda against

the structural realities of operating in a military-dominated political system. The LFO was subsequently adopted, with minor changes, as the 17th amendment to the constitution.

110 For more on the relationship between the MMA and the martial state, see Ashutosh Misra, "MMA-Democracy Interface in Pakistan: From Natural Confrontation to Co-habitation?" *Strategic Analysis* 30, no. 2 (April–June 2006): 377–388.

111 See World Bank and Government of NWFP, *Economic Report*.

112 For a history of the NFC awards, see Iftikhar Ahmad, Usman Mustafa, and Mahmood Khalid, *National Finance Commission Awards in Pakistan: A Historical Perspective* (Pakistan Institute of Development Economics, 2007). See also Mohammad Ali Khan, "NWFP, Wapda ink agreement on hydel profit; Terms, conditions for arbitration finalized," *The News*, July 29, 2005; and Intikhab Amir, "Interim NFC award to provide relief," *Dawn*, May 22, 2006.

113 Vali Nasr has summed up this dynamic well: "The army's acquiescence to Islamization actually transcends its fear of it, by seeking opportunities in it to establish the military's hegemony and expand its control over society." Quoted in Rashid, *Descent into Chaos*, 158.

114 The JUI-F essentially serves in this role in the present national coalition.

115 While the PML-N and the Jamaat also have close ties in the NWFP, their party demographics in the province are quite distinct; the JI draws strong lower-class support in areas such as Upper and Lower Dir which are not welcoming to the PML. Note that the PML-N also has close ties to the Saudi-backed Jamiat Ahl-e-Hadith (JAH), a party which has been weak electorally but influential in the education sector in NWFP.

III
NEW ISLAMISTS AND THE RETURN OF PASHTUN NATIONALISM

Concomitant with the political decline of the MMA came the rise of new Islamist actors in the Frontier, commonly known as the neo-Taliban, along with the return of Pashtun nationalism. This chapter covers in brief some of the dynamics from 2006 through 2008, during which time the political landscape of the Frontier changed in important ways and the focus of Islamist activity shifted from mainstream religious politics to movements more firmly opposed to the state.

THE RISE OF THE NEO-TALIBAN

Markers of an entrepreneurial insurgency

It is still far too early to present a robust history of the Frontier's new insurgent movements and their relation to the Islamist political establishment. What began circa mid-2006 as a spill-over of militancy from the troubled Waziristan tribal agencies into NWFP's southern settled districts — precipitated in part by the failed peace deals between the government and the Waziri Taliban — became within about a year's time a movement which threatened the political stability of the entire Frontier.[1]

This new movement, known as the neo-Taliban, is distinct from both the Afghan Taliban and from mainstream Pakistani Islamists such as the MMA, though it has critical linkages with both groups.[2] "Neo-Taliban" is itself a term of convenience, and refers not to a coherent operational entity but rather to a loose collection of self-defined Taliban groups which share a number of common features. To the extent that one can generalize about this new form of insurgent Islamism, it can be seen to have several distinguishing characteristics.

First, the movement is politically rejectionist. Unlike the mainstream Islamist parties, neo-Taliban groups tend to dismiss the legitimacy of the Pakistani state, either for ideological reasons, or on account of the state's ostensible failure to live up to its Islamic political commitments. On this point, however, the movement is far from monolithic. Groups with close ties to al Qaeda, such as some Taliban organizations in Waziristan and Bajaur, are more likely to have a transnational Islamist outlook and clear ideological reasons for rejecting the legitimacy of the Pakistani state. Other more locally-oriented movements, such those which emerged in Swat district and Khyber agency, tend toward a language of vigilante Islamism, in which they accept the state's role in theory, but legitimize violence on the basis of its ostensible failings. Needless to say, the latter groups are more amenable to political compromise or co-option, provided that they do not fall under the sway of the former.

Second, the neo-Taliban tend to be somewhat more *takfiri* in their ideology than the mainstream Islamists.[3] That is, they are more willing to sanction *jihad* against other Muslims who reject their sectarian or ideological position.[4] Mainstream Islamist parties do frequently operate along sectarian lines, but are inclined to outsource sectarian violence to affiliate groups in order to retain their democratic credentials. This ideological split is also deeply political: the religious parties in the Frontier recognize that *takfiri* ideology can easily boomerang back upon the more mainstream Islamists. They have, as a result, tried to pre-empt this ideological and political move against them by repeatedly rejecting the legitimacy of suicide bombing within Pakistan (though their position with respect to other locales is less clear cut).[5]

Third, the movement is often linked to criminal networks and the illegal economy. This was, and remains, true for the Afghan Taliban, which is intimately linked to the opium trade. In the Pakistani context, it is becoming increasingly clear — even to the public at large — that the groups which call themselves Taliban are often no more than armed gangs which use religious symbolism to gain a foothold in local communities.[6] Whereas mainstream religious parties such as the JUI-F historically maintained side interests in local transport networks, the neo-Taliban groups have explicitly sought to dominate local services and industries, particularly in FATA and PATA regions. The timber mafia in Swat was reportedly a key backer of the TNSM insurgency, and local leaders in Khyber agency such as Mangal Bagh rose to prominence through their control of transport networks used for smuggling goods across the Durand Line.[7] Some observers have suggested that the neo-Taliban may eventually go the way of the FARC in Colombia, becoming over time less ideological and more criminal in nature.

Fourth, these groups are highly entrepreneurial. The creation of Tehrik-e-Taliban-e-Pakistan (TTP) in late 2007 merely formalized what had become a franchise-oriented model of insurgency. And while the Tehrik eventually took on a coordinating role among the various Taliban groups, it succeeded as a brand more than as an organization. TTP's branding strategy sought to portray the movement as cohesive, and affiliate it with a simple platform of religious and political values. This aggregation function served the TTP leadership in Waziristan by amplifying its voice and reach, but also served the local affiliates by providing them with access to resources, and by discouraging local communities from pushing back against outsiders who claimed to be part of the umbrella organization. Despite this strategy, the TTP remains a loose alliance of convenience; local commanders still play a critical role in the decision-making of these groups, and some localized movements — like that of Mangal Bagh in Khyber — have sought to triangulate their position vis-à-vis the state by staying out of TTP and instead pursuing a parallel Taliban-like agenda.

Fifth, the Taliban groups have proven to be adept at co-opting the state at the local level. Their expansion has often followed a predictable pattern: well-armed groups of young men enter an area with Kalashnikovs and white pickup trucks, calling themselves Taliban; they win the favor of the community by taking on local criminal elements and prohibiting certain un-Islamic behaviors; they establish *qazi* courts for the quick adjudication of disputes; and, having garnered some measure of local support, they set about solidifying their control by marginalizing or killing local notables and government officials, enacting even stricter Islamist measures, and establishing environments conducive to their own criminal networks.[8] By playing off of local discontentment with the judicial system, policing, and other state services, the insurgents are able to gain a foothold which they then use to reinforce their local position.

And finally, this new movement is increasingly in tension with traditional Pashtun norms. At a macro level, the neo-Taliban movement is indisputably a Pashtun-dominated insurgency. Disputes within the movement often fall along predictable tribal lines; and just as often, local tribal blocs leverage Taliban influence in order to compete against traditional rivals. But at the same time, the insurgents are threatening established norms by killing tribal elders, carrying out suicide bombings, and attacking *jirgas*. Other aspects of Pashtun culture (particularly those which have come under conservative Deobandi influence over the last several decades) are amplified perversely by the militants: the destruction of girls' schools, barber shops, and music stores sit uncomfortably with most Pashtuns living in the conservative southern districts of the NWFP.

Vigilante Islamism and the mainstream-militant divide

The nature of the relationship between this new insurgent Islamism and the mainstream religious parties is not well understood. From a distance, commentators in the West have tended to assume that the similar rhetoric of the two groups reflects a commonality of objectives, tactics, and even organizational structures. It is true that the political discourse of neo-Taliban insurgents is often very close to that of parties like the JUI-F and the Jamaat, particularly when it comes to regional and global affairs. It is also the case that just as the religious parties during the MMA era retained linkages to militant Islamist groups, so they continue to interact informally with the neo-Taliban movement, most commonly by way of lower-level cadres who move freely between party and insurgent structures. Nonetheless, these commonalities belie very important differences. In reality, the religious parties are often deeply ambivalent about the neo-Taliban program, and threatened both directly and indirectly by its expansion into areas which were traditionally dominated by religious politics.

These fault-lines began surfacing in 2006, but only came to the forefront in 2007 when neo-Taliban groups began challenging the state in places such as Swat, Bannu, and even Islamabad. It was, in fact, the Lal Masjid (Red Mosque) crisis in the summer of 2007 that exposed the deepening rifts between the religious parties and the vigilante Islamism of the new Taliban groups.[9] The Jamaat, for example, was outspoken in its support for the Lal Masjid leadership, but — somewhat to its shock — found itself disowned by the *madrassah* students who were challenging the government's writ in Islamabad. The JUI-F tried to serve in a mediating role between the state and the militants, but ended up receiving criticism from its own ranks for not supporting the *madrassah* against "interference" by the state. More significantly, a rift formed within the JUI-F and more broadly within the Deobandi Wafaq ul-Madaris al-Arabia (the sect's *madrassah* board) regarding the proper response to vigilante Islamism of the kind carried out by Abdul Rashid Ghazi and his students at the Lal Masjid.

Even before the government's operation against the *madrassah* students in July, dissenters within the JUI-F (many of whom were from the Balochistan wing of the party) had argued that they needed to come out strongly in favor of the Taliban groups.[10] Fazlur Rehman and most senior JUI-F party members from the NWFP demurred, in part because they were more dependent upon the state for patronage in the Frontier, but also because they were more directly threatened by the insurgent expansion in the southern part of the province. After the operation, the conflict burst into the open, and the JUI-F leadership wrestled for several months with internal dissenters who insisted that the party was obligated to support the *madaris* and the Islamization agenda of the neo-Taliban.

Links between the JUI-F and Taliban groups have been well documented, particularly in the southern part of the province where Deobandi politics is strong.[11] But the rise of the insurgency in 2006 and the aftermath of the Lal Masjid crisis in 2007 further complicated the nature of JUI-F interaction with the neo-Taliban and other vigilante Islamist groups. By early 2008, this relationship had become extremely complex. The general elections in February held in district Bannu — a traditional JUI-F stronghold bordering North Waziristan, in which Maulana Fazlur Rehman was contesting the national assembly seat — served as a window into the party's internal turmoil.[12]

On the one hand, Fazlur Rehman was concerned about his party's declining influence in the southern settled districts and adjacent tribal agencies, including North and South Waziristan. The neo-Taliban had established a strong presence in the area, and on more than one occasion had instructed people not to vote, based upon the premise that "democracy is un-Islamic."[13] Fazlur Rehman sought to counter this politically rejectionist message by dismissing Taliban concerns in public, while lobbying in private for them to remain neutral. He reportedly requested a "non-objection certificate" (NOC) from Taliban commanders in the Bannu area, as a result of which he was able to minimize militant opposition to the election process.[14] While Fazlur Rehman clearly required at least tacit support from Taliban groups, he was also wary of siding too closely with the militants: particularly since the relatively liberal PPP seemed poised to do well in the upcoming election, he could not afford to alienate a potential coalition partner.

If anything, the election revealed the complexity of the relationship between formal religious politics and Islamist insurgency. Prior to the polls, the JUI-F had fragmented into at least two factions over what to do about the Taliban; and, in a sense, the Taliban had fragmented into at least two factions over what to do about the JUI-F. Fazlur Rehman avoided campaigning in Bannu out of concerns for his own safety, but eventually won the seat due to the support of neo-Taliban from the nearby Frontier Region Bannu, who commandeered polling stations with rocket launchers and sent election observers packing.[15]

The relationship between religious parties and insurgent groups in Swat proved to be even more complicated. As the TNSM was originally founded by local Jamaat party cadres, the JI was inclined to support the movement in Swat, including the young Maulana "Radio" Fazlullah.[16] The Jamaat's leadership in Punjab saw the Swat case, and the central government's military response, to be a winning issue by which to mobilize its political base. The JUI-F's response was more tepid, as its leadership position in the government made it wary of disruptions which might reflect poorly upon its management of provincial affairs. In reality, all rhetoric aside, *neither* major party of the MMA was pleased to see the return of the TNSM in the Swat valley; its politically rejectionist message ran counter to the religious parties' electoral interests.

The TNSM and its Waziri allies came to develop a similarly bleak view of the religious parties. The TNSM leadership, including Maulana Fazlullah, had close ties with the Jamaat, but also with JUI *ulema* from the Swat valley. Several of these *ulema* went to Fazlullah with the intent of persuading him to moderate his opposition to polio prevention campaigns and girls' schools, but ultimately failed.[17] Fazlullah did not strongly oppose the MMA — particularly so long as the alliance took a hands-off approach to the TNSM — but his supporters from Waziristan reportedly pushed the movement into a more hard-line posture.[18] As the TTP "patrons" from Waziristan became more and more dominant over their TNSM clients in Swat in 2008, the movement eventually took a harder line against the state, and against politically-active religious elements.

The new Islamist 'moderates'

The rise of new Islamist groups over the last several years has served to marginalize the religious parties, but also change their role. Many religious party leaders are now "moderates" within their own Islamist context in the Frontier. Although they share some of the same objectives as the new insurgent groups, their inclination to reject vigilantism and to support the democratic political order marks them as being more similar to mainstream political actors than to militant groups.

Although the religious parties have been weakened, they continue to occupy an important political space between Islamist militancy and relatively liberal democratic norms. Even secular observers interviewed in Peshawar in 2007 and 2008 expressed concern that the religious political establishment — leaders like Fazlur Rehman and Qazi Hussain — might lose their ability to draw young activists into the formal political space rather than see them join militant organizations. (The JUI-F has, in making its case to foreigners, also framed its role in this way: arguing that it is a "wall" holding back the tide of militant influence in the tribal areas.[19]) The religious parties relish the opportunity to play the part of intermediaries between the militants and the state, and will likely continue to do so. Their views on the legitimacy of violence and vigilantism are also apt to prove important means by which they distinguish themselves from more militant Islamist efforts.

Ultimately, the marginalization of the religious parties is likely to induce two contradictory responses. On the one hand, the parties will be pressured to distance themselves from the rising tide of Islamist militancy, both as a means of retaining their democratic legitimacy, and protecting themselves from new (and violent) forms of political competition. On the other hand, the religious parties will face pressure to compensate for their diminished stature by moving further to the right in an attempt to motivate their political base, and insulate themselves from *takfiri* accusations coming from the Islamist fringe.

These contradictory impulses are difficult to finesse. The JUI-F, for example, has allied itself rhetorically with neo-Taliban groups by strongly opposing military action in the FATA, while at the same time speaking out against insurgent tactics and continuing to give tacit support to the civilian government.[20] This kind of balancing act rightly troubles observers in the United States, but also comes with a silver lining: religious parties which can retain their Islamist credibility in areas such as the Frontier stand a better chance over the long-term of being able to co-opt local populations into the formal political process, and away from anti-state insurgent movements.

Assessing state response: the Darra case

By and large, the government of Pakistan has been slow to respond to the gradual expansion of neo-Taliban influence in the Frontier. In Waziristan it undertook deals in 2004 and again in 2006, both of which failed to quell local violence and resulted in an increase in cross-border attacks on coalition forces in Afghanistan.[21] In Swat, the provincial government responded haltingly to the return of the TNSM under Maulana Fazlullah. After considerable delay, it carried out relatively successful army operations in October 2007, which appear to have been spurred by attacks on military targets in the area, capture by insurgents of tactically important sites such as the Saidu Sharif airport, and growing embarrassment that the militant groups were operating openly in defiance of the state. Following the collapse of the May 2008 peace deals, the army again took on the TNSM and their Waziri patrons in Swat, prompted in part by concern over the compromise of critical lines of communication, including the Shangla Pass in northern NWFP.[22] The military also carried out limited (and mostly cosmetic) operations under the aegis of the Frontier Corps in Khyber agency in the summer of 2008, ostensibly to disrupt the activity of Mangal Bagh's Lashkar-e-Islami; and a large-scale campaign in Bajaur and Mohmand agencies, which included both ground and air operations and resulted in the displacement of several hundred thousand refugees into the settled areas of the NWFP.[23]

While recent actions, such as those in Bajaur, suggest the adoption of a more aggressive posture by the military in the Frontier, the overall pattern of the state's response has been quite tentative in the past years. The case of Darra Adam Khel is broadly illustrative of the ways in which the government has attempted to deal with the emergence of the neo-Taliban, and serves as a microcosm for understanding the interaction between insurgents and the state.

Darra Adam Khel, commonly known as Darra, belongs to Frontier Region Kohat. Situated about 20 miles south of Peshawar, it sits along the Indus Highway — the vital road link between the provincial capital and the southern settled districts. To the south is

Kohat, from which Darra is separated by the Japanese-built Friendship Tunnel. The city's bazaar is infamous for its gun markets, which produce an array of hand-crafted small arms. It has also historically been a center for drug smuggling and other illicit trades.

The emergence of the neo-Taliban in Darra can be traced to mid-2005 or early 2006, when a group of "young boys" began attacking fuel convoys destined for coalition forces in Afghanistan. Later, this group began calling itself the "Taliban," initiated programs to curtail "vice" and "obscenity," and threatened girls' schools in the area.[24] The government did nothing when the militants began targeting local *khassadars* in early 2007, and by the summer of that year the neo-Taliban group was patrolling roads and enforcing its own brand of "justice" against local criminals.[25] Following a wave of vigilante action against "anti-social elements," there were a number of failed attempts to negotiate with the militants by the local MNA and senator, as well as both the JUI-F and the banned sectarian group Sipah-e-Sahaba.[26]

Finally, the government in Peshawar decided to convene a *jirga*, which convinced the neo-Taliban to withdraw on the condition that the members of the *jirga* would continue the fight against un-Islamic activity, and with the understanding that both sides retained the right to use force if needed.[27] Not surprisingly, the agreement broke down, and by September 2007 the neo-Taliban had again taken control of most of Darra. A second *jirga* was convened in December to exchange prisoners, but the government made no major effort to challenge the *status quo*.

The situation changed dramatically in late January 2008, when militants seized four ammunition trucks in a surprise attack, captured Frontier Corps personnel, and took control of the Kohat FC Fort.[28] After *jirgas* failed to secure the return of the trucks and the soldiers, the FC launched a robust attack with helicopter gunships and ground forces.[29] The militants attempted to cut off FC supply lines at the Kohat Tunnel, but were eventually rebuffed.[30] The FC also had to deal with attacks in Darra emanating from Khyber agency in the north.[31] Local tribesmen in nearby Kohat were known to be supportive of the government, but would not speak out openly in favor of the operation for fear of being targeted by neo-Taliban groups.[32]

A number of the militants retreated after several days, reportedly leaving for more hospitable areas in Bajaur.[33] The neo-Taliban, however, retained a presence in and around Darra. In February, an "underground" anti-Taliban organization formed in an attempt to spur local action against the militants.[34] And in March, local leaders convened a peace *jirga* of over 1,000 tribesmen to discuss the growing threat. Tragically, the *jirga* was attacked by a suicide bomber, killing 42 people.[35] Throughout the spring of 2008, the neo-Taliban groups continued to press their position in Darra. When the military pulled back in late April, the militants returned to the area, retook control of the Indus Highway, and began exacting "taxes" on local vehicles.[36]

Officials attempted yet another round of negotiations in late May. Revealingly, the outlines of the government's demands were exceptionally narrow: the military would cease its operations in exchange for a cessation of Taliban activities "on the stretch of Indus Highway passing through Darra."[37] By early June, the militants put forward a more comprehensive set of demands to the government — not only the withdrawal of security forces, but also the provision of "health and education facilities, special quota[s] ... in engineering and medical colleges, payment of royalty for the Kohat Tunnel ... establishment of a medical college, construction of small dams," and the exemption from several fees and taxes.[38] The negotiators for the Taliban side, in fact, included local *maliks* and former politicians, suggesting that the movement had gained real support among local influentials, or at the very least that political leaders were pressured into opposing the government.

These negotiations also broke down, and in mid-August militant leaders in Darra brazenly established their headquarters in the residences of senior politicians (a former MNA and sitting senator), and threatened local *khassadar* forces.[39] When the government arrested a prominent Taliban leader in late August, the Darra-based militants once again retook the Kohat Tunnel, spurring yet another military action. This time, the army claimed that 50 militants had been killed and hundreds of other "foreign militants" had fled.[40] After being closed for nearly a month, the tunnel finally reopened in late September.

The rise of militant influence in Darra illustrates a number of the neo-Taliban characteristics described above. The local militant movement, by most accounts, emerged in an *ad hoc* way and only later established linkages with other networks in the Frontier. It built goodwill by targeting local criminals, but soon engendered resentment for its own criminality and brutality. It took advantage of the poor governmental oversight of the FR areas, and co-opted elected officials into its camp, thus allowing it to frame its agenda in terms of local development and not simply Islamization or power politics.[41] It used religious parties and local tribesmen as intermediaries, while recognizing that the government lacked the capacity and the will to follow through with sustained paramilitary or military operations. And it fostered relationships with outside groups, including Lashkar-e-Jhangvi, a Punjabi sectarian organizations whose members reportedly established militant training camps near Darra.[42]

The response of the state to the violence in Darra was also illustrative of the broader challenges it faces in the Frontier. The government repeatedly negotiated with neo-Taliban militants, usually through *jirgas*, and these negotiations repeatedly failed. One basic problem was the lack of credible state capacity to enforce its agreements. The system of managing the FR areas relies heavily on indirect rule by the political agent through the tribal leaders, and is ill-equipped to deal with a robust militant movement like that of the neo-Taliban. The state was able to displace the militants for a short while, but had no robust system of local governance through which to maintain order.

Compounding the problem, the government often waited to take action until the point at which it became nearly too late; or did so only reactively in response to provocative action on the part of the militants. Perhaps most significantly, the government consistently took a very narrow view of its objectives: its goal was to keep the strategic Indus Highway open between Peshawar and Kohat, not to dismantle a militant infrastructure in Darra. As a result, the military operations in FR Kohat were undertaken with a short-term focus on preserving key lines of communication rather than bringing any semblance of long-term stability to a strategic region of the Frontier. To its credit, the military began to move beyond this minimalist approach in the second half of 2008 with its operations in Swat and Bajaur, which appear to have been less narrowly tactical than those undertaken in Darra. It remains to be seen whether the army will continue this trend, or revert to minimalist objectives in and around the FATA.

THE RETURN OF PASHTUN NATIONALISM

The 2008 Frontier elections

Despite an array of problems, the February 2008 general elections were widely acknowledged as being the fairest since 1970.[43] Postponed following the assassination of Benazir Bhutto in December 2007, the polls were held amidst growing anger at the Musharraf government and growing fears about the spread of extremist influence into the Pakistani heartland. The voters delivered a resounding defeat to the PML-Q, and at the national level a clear narrative emerged tying the election results to a rejection of Musharraf's rule and an embrace of the mainstream democratic politics of the PPP and the PML-N.

In the Frontier the results appeared to tell a different, but related, story. The MMA was defeated soundly by its rivals, garnering only 10% of provincial assembly seats (down from about 50% in 2002). The Pashtun nationalist ANP delivered the strongest showing, with 32% of seats, followed by independent candidates with 23%, and the PPP with 18%.[44] The PPP-S, PML-N, and PML-Q each polled about 5%. Despite widespread fears of terrorism, overall turnout appeared to be comparable to that of the 2002 election. (Participation was somewhat depressed in Malakand division due to fears about Taliban presence, and somewhat inflated in the areas around Bannu due to Taliban ballot-stuffing.[45])

Overall, the contests were more competitive than in the previous general election: the average margin of victory was just under 10%, compared with 15% in 2002. The performance of the leading parties was even more striking. The MMA's average margin in 2002 was over 20%, while the ANP's margin in 2008 was about 9%. The overall trend toward more competitive races in 2008 can largely be accounted for by the presence of more competitive contests in the central areas of the province — the Peshawar valley, Mardan division, and Malakand division — where the MMA had made surprising inroads in 2002, rather than in the southern or eastern districts, where the average margins were virtually unchanged.[46]

On the strength of their combined showing, the ANP and PPP formed a governing coalition which was supported by the PPP-S and the independents. The ANP selected Amir Haider Khan Hoti, nephew of party chief Asfandyar Wali Khan, as the new NWFP chief minister, and the cabinet positions were divided between ANP and PPP politicians.[47] The JUI-F chose not to participate in the coalition government in Peshawar, but its party's participation in the PPP-led coalition at the national level meant that its role in the Frontier assembly was essentially that of a "loyal opposition."

Explaining the MMA's defeat

The electoral success of the ANP and PPP brought about a flood of news reports hailing the rise of secularism and the rejection of religious politics and "Talibanization" in the Frontier. While this narrative captured one important dynamic of the poll results, it did not tell the entire story. The religious parties' defeat was due to a number of factors. Public anger over American action in Afghanistan was no longer a driving force as it had been in the 2002 elections, and anti-Western sentiment was no longer the province only of the religious parties. Moreover, the MMA's standing had been weakened by rifts within the alliance over the extent of its cooperation with Musharraf's military government, and following the imposition of the Emergency in late 2007, the JI had decided to boycott the elections. (While it is doubtful that the Jamaat would have returned a strong showing in the polls, its participation might have cut somewhat into the ANP's success in urban areas, and districts such as Upper and Lower Dir.) The mainstream and nationalist parties were also given much wider latitude to contest the elections than in 2002, and there was by all accounts significantly less government interference in the election process.

At a more granular level, the February 2008 results can be seen as the product of four separate trends in voter behavior, each of which played a role in shaping the outcome of the NWFP elections:

The first trend was one of *specific opposition* to the MMA. Part of the anti-MMA vote was clearly tied to concerns about the alliance's ineffectual response to the creeping militancy in the NWFP. Many voters felt that the religious government was too sympathetic to the new Taliban movements to be able to respond decisively to security threats in the province. At the same time, MMA also lost credibility with its conservative religious constituency, which was upset that the alliance had not done enough to implement a program of *shariah* in the province.

The second trend was one of *general opposition* to the MMA. Anti-incumbency has traditionally been a very powerful determinant of voter behavior in the Frontier. It is a fact that the ruling party nearly always loses in the NWFP. In part this is attributable to voter frustrations about corruption and ineffective governance, but in part it reflects a systemic problem. The provincial government's role in the Pakistani federation is such that it does not have sufficient autonomy or resources to allow incumbents to deliver on most of their promises. In this case, the MMA's undoing was in large part its perceived failure to deliver on education, health, and clean government — the same things that brought down many of its predecessors. That the Islamists raised expectations by promising to be righteous and incorruptible simply reinforced voter disenchantment with their rule.

The third trend was one of *specific support* to the ANP and PPP. Both of these parties ran on platforms promising to deal with the rising militancy in the Frontier, and the ANP in particular was able to draw on its heritage of non-violence and its reputation for relatively competent governance. The ANP had rebuilt its party operations after years of internal strife, and was able to mobilize strong patronage networks, especially in the Peshawar valley.

The fourth and final trend was one of *general support* to the ANP and PPP. As Andrew Wilder has argued, voting behavior in Pakistan is often driven less by policy considerations than by public perceptions about which candidate or party is most likely to win.[48] Since voters rely on their representatives for political favors and patronage, it is in their interest to vote for winners rather than simply for those who share their political outlook. In the run-up to the 2008 elections there were widespread expectations, voiced in the media, that the ANP and PPP would return strong showings in the NWFP polls, and the PPP would be the leading party at the national level. This incentivized local voters to cast their lots in with these parties, in the hope that they would have the best access to state resources.

While none of these factors can easily be quantified, one can make a case that the *general* trends described above carry with them a more robust explanatory power than any *specific* anti-MMA or pro-ANP/PPP sentiments. The historical salience of anti-incumbency voting patterns, combined with the strong trend toward voter bandwagoning with expected winners, should give pause to those who would see the 2008 elections as a resounding defeat for religious politics, or an embrace of secular Pashtun nationalism.

Taking the long view, the MMA's defeat in 2008 is best seen as a return toward the mean, in which political fragmentation in the NWFP is the norm rather than the exception. What does this mean for the religious parties in the Frontier? Both the JUI-F and the JI used their five-year tenure to gain valuable experience into the workings of government and are likely to remain significant, but not dominant, players in the NWFP political scene. An MMA-like alliance may prove useful to these parties in the future as a means of amplifying their collective influence in the national political debate. But that being the case, the trend toward a party system in Pakistan with two dominant mainstream parties and a number of smaller religious and ethno-nationalist parties makes it likely that the JI and the JUI-F will each prefer to adopt a more flexible and independent electoral strategy so that they can remain free to bargain their way into a mainstream alliance after voting has taken place.

The place of Pashtun nationalism

Largely absent from the above historical narrative has been the Pashtun nationalist movement. This movement, which operated mostly on the margins of Frontier politics between 2001 and 2007, has nonetheless historically played a much more significant role in the NWFP than any religious party or alliance. As the nationalists are today a leading electoral force in the province, it is worth understanding their role and their political objectives in the Frontier.

The movement traces its roots to the Khudai Khidmatgars (Servants of God) who, led by Khan Abdul Ghaffar Khan, launched a non-violent campaign against the British in 1929. Known as the Red Shirts, these Pashtuns later later allied themselves with the Indian National Congress, with Khan dubbed the "Frontier Gandhi." On account of their affiliation with the Congress, the Red Shirts were sidelined after the creation of Pakistan in 1947 and intermittently banned until the early 1970s. The movement nominally continued during this period under the leadership of Khan's son Wali Khan, who joined the leftist National Awami Party (NAP). The NAP, as noted above, formed a coalition government in NWFP in 1972 with Mufti Mahmud of the JUI, but this alliance was short-lived.[49] Wali Khan's NAP was banned during the latter years of Bhutto's rule, and he eventually took up the leadership of the National Democratic Party (NDP) in 1984, which in turn merged into the Awami National Party (ANP) in 1986.[50]

The ANP participated in several coalition governments between 1988 and 1999. It briefly joined a PPP coalition in 1988, then decided to side with Nawaz Sharif and joined a Frontier coalition with his party after the 1990 elections. In 1993 it again formed an alliance with the PML, but was forced out when the PPP regained power in NWFP in 1994. It formed yet another a coalition with Nawaz Sharif after the 1997 polls, but the partnership broke up in 1998 over a dispute regarding the renaming of the province as Pakhtunkhwa.[51] In each of these coalitions the ANP took ministerial positions rather than the chief ministership. The recent 2008 elections were, therefore, the first time that the ANP had chosen to formally lead a coalition in the Frontier.

In leading the current Frontier government, the party brings with it a number of strengths. It can draw on the legacy of the Khudai Khidmatgar movement by using *jirgas* and other traditional mechanisms to bring together Pashtun traditions with an ideology of peace and non-violence. It can call upon a strong base of well educated and politically astute supporters who are active in key professional sectors such as education, health, and development. It is willing to be pragmatic in its dealings with the central government and the military. And it can serve as a bridge to the Karzai government in Kabul, with which it has close relations.

The party also brings with it notable weaknesses. It does not have significant influence in many of the areas which have come under insurgent threat, such as the southern settled districts, or FATA agencies outside of Khyber and parts of Mohmand and Bajaur. It has a history of vicious infighting, manifested in ongoing disputes between Asfandyar Wali Khan (son of Wali Khan, and uncle of the current chief minister) and the Bilours, a long-established Hindko-speaking political family from Peshawar. Its leadership is often uncomfortable and ineffective in using Islamic language that appeals to the religiously conservative population, particularly outside of the Peshawar valley. (Although, in its efforts to promote the Nizam-e-Adl Act in Malakand division, it has been more proactive in enacting religious legislation than the MMA government.) And its pro-Karzai policy is deeply unpopular throughout the Frontier, where Karzai is widely ridiculed to as a "fake Pashtun."[52]

The Pashtun nationalism of the ANP is frequently thought to be more ambitious and consequential than it actually is. It remains the case that the ANP, like the government of Afghanistan, does not recognize the Durand Line, considering it an artificial boundary which unjustly divides the ethnic Pashtun population.[53] And on the domestic front, the party has continued to insist on renaming the NWFP in accordance with its ethnic Pashtun majority, demanding greater provincial autonomy, and arguing for the inclusion of FATA into the Frontier province.[54] But despite these far-reaching demands there is very little motivation, even among most ANP party members, to pursue a broader "Pakhtunkhwa" state which incorporates Pashtun areas of Pakistan and Afghanistan. And contrary to hyperbolic predictions that Pakistan is in danger of coming apart under the strain of ethno-nationalism, regional parties such as the ANP are arguably more interested in gaining concessions at the margins than pursuing a radical political restructuring of the region.[55]

The ANP's nationalist agenda, while generally consonant with U.S. interests in the near-term, is therefore more complex than it is often portrayed. The party has spoken out strongly against American strikes in the FATA, and has pushed, against U.S. pressure, for peace deals in Swat. Taking the long view, the ANP's enthusiasm for Western military intervention in Afghanistan is also likely to be contingent. This support, as one party leader has argued, is based on the premise that "the U.S. and NATO in Afghanistan are not as dangerous as Persians and Punjabis."[56] To the ANP, the American support for Karzai is, on the one hand, a check on Tajik (i.e., Dari-speaking Afghan) influence and, on the other, a check on Pakistani state hegemony over the Pak-Afghan frontier areas. This perspective suggests that the ANP will continue to be viewed with suspicion by the military-bureaucratic elites in Islamabad. It also suggests that any substantive attempt by the international community (together with the government of Pakistan) to negotiate with the Taliban in Afghanistan may put the party in the awkward position of having to weigh its its support for Pashtun dominance of Afghan politics against its secular political orientation and its abiding fear of a "Punjabi" proxy in eastern Afghanistan.

NOTES:

1 See, e.g., Behroz Khan, "Settled NWFP areas also under threat of Talibanisation," *The News*, September 30, 2006; and Nicholas Schmidle, "Next-Gen Taliban," *New York Times Magazine*, January 6, 2008.

2 Some observers refer to the present-day Taliban movement in Afghanistan as the neo-Taliban, but for the purposes of this work the term is limited to the self-described Taliban groups which arose in the Frontier after 2001. For an insightful analysis of the new Taliban movement in Afghanistan, see Antonio Giustozzi, *Koran, Kalashnikov, and Laptop: The Neo-Taliban Insurgency in Afghanistan* (New York: Columbia University Press, 2008).

3 *Takfir* is the practice of accusing other Muslims of apostasy.

4 They claim, of course, that these other groups are in fact not truly Muslim.

5 Typical of this view are comments made by JUI-F Maulana Rahat Hussain: "No religious scholar, organization, or mufti has ever declared suicide attacks in Pakistan as legitimate. There is a different background of such attacks in Palestine, Afghanistan, and Iraq." Mohammad Riaz Akhtar, "Why No Notice Has Been Taken of Mischievous Statements About Usama's Presence in K2 Region (Interview with Maulana Rahat Hussain)," *Nawa-e-Waqt*, June 9, 2008, translation by World News Connection.

6 Author interviews, Peshawar, August 2008.

7 Mushtaq Yusufzai, "Route of law," *The News*, May 18, 2008.

8 Author interviews, Peshawar, August 2008.

9 For a more detailed analysis of the religious parties' response to the Lal Masjid crisis, see Joshua T. White, "Vigilante Islamism in Pakistan: Religious Party Responses to the Lal Masjid Crisis," *Current Trends in Islamist Ideology* 7 (Autumn 2008).

10 Syed Saleem Shahzad, "Taliban's call for jihad answered in Pakistan," *Asia Times Online*, June 16, 2006, http://www.atimes.com/atimes/South_Asia/HF16Df01.html (accessed October 1, 2008).

11. See, e.g., Imtiaz Gul, "The fog of war in Waziristan," *Friday Times*, March 17, 2006.
12. At the time of the elections, the party was still facing internal dissention. See "Postponement of polls won't be accepted, says Fazl," *Dawn*, January 17, 2008.
13. Iqbal Khattak, "Taliban leader warns against using religion for electoral gains," *Daily Times*, December 28, 2007.
14. "JUI (F) seeks Taliban NOC for elections," *Frontier Post*, December 1, 2007.
15. Author interview with an election observer based in Bannu, February 2008, Islamabad.
16. Fazlullah is often seen as the face of the "new" TNSM, even though there are some who deny that he represents the organization. See Farooq Azam Khan, "The Next Trap?" *Herald*, August 2007, 44. For a perspective on the JI-TNSM relationship, see "March on Islamabad?" *Dawn*, October 30, 2007.
17. Author interviews with JUI-F clerics, August 2007, Islamabad.
18. Author interview with a provincial ANP leader, August 2008, Peshawar.
19. Author interviews with JUI-F clerics, July 2007, Islamabad.
20. See, e.g., Irfan Bukhari, "Fata operation pressing JUI-F to leave coalition," *Nation*, July 12, 2008; and Javed Afridi and Asim Yasin, "Fazl, Sherpao back Zardari," *The News*, August 31, 2008.
21. See, e.g., Frontline, "Cutting deals with the Taliban," http://www.pbs.org/wgbh/pages/frontline/taliban/pakistan/deals.html (accessed October 1, 2008); and Ismail Khan and Carlotta Gall, "Pakistan Lets Tribal Chiefs Keep Control Along Border," *New York Times*, September 6, 2006.
22. Author interview with a U.S. military official, July 2008.
23. See Ismail Khan, "Battle to be won or lost in Bajaur," *Dawn*, September 21, 2008; and Jane Perlez and Pir Zubair Shah, "Confronting Taliban, Pakistan Finds Itself at War," *New York Times*, October 3, 2008.
24. Abdul Sami Paracha of *Dawn* has provided the most reliable reporting on the situation in Darra. See Abdul Sami Paracha, "Taliban take the law into their own hands in Darra," *Dawn*, December 14, 2006; and "Girls' education under threat in NWFP, says UN," *Dawn*, December 22, 2006.
25. Abdul Sami Paracha, "'Decree' issued against girls education," *Dawn*, April 11, 2007; "Security man killed in ambush," *Dawn*, April 17, 2007; and "Militants impose night curfew in Darra," *Dawn*, June 5, 2007.
26. Akhtar Amin, "Darra Taliban launch drive against 'criminals,'" *Daily Times*, August 11, 2007; Zulfiqar Ali, "Talks with militants remain inconclusive," *Dawn*, August 11, 2007; and Akhtar Amin, "Efforts to secure Darra Adamkhel: Govt wants talks with Taliban through jirga," *Daily Times*, August 13, 2007.
27. Akhtar Amin, "Taliban hand over control of Darra Adam Khel to govt," *Daily Times*, August 14, 2007.
28. These trucks were reportedly headed to South Waziristan agency.
29. According to the governor, the government had sent "six jirgas in fifteen days" in unsuccessful attempts to resolve the dispute through peaceful means. See "Administrative system changes in NWFP, Fata likely," *Dawn*, February 1, 2008.
30. For more on this conflict see Rahimullah Yusufzai, "New frontlines," *The News*, February 3, 2008.
31. Abdul Sami Paracha, "Tense calm prevails in Darra Adamkhel," *Dawn*, January 29, 2008.
32. Munawar Afridi and Abdul Sami Paracha, "Troops on the offensive in Darra, occupy militants' stronghold," *Dawn*, January 26, 2008.
33. "Darra calms down after 3 days of clashes," *Daily Times*, January 29, 2008.
34. "The Taliban nemesis in Darra," *Statesman*, February 11, 2008.
35. Munawar Afridi and Zulfiqar Ali, "Tribal peace jirga attacked: 42 killed, 58 injured in Darra Adamkhel," *Dawn*, March 3, 2008.

36 Abdul Sami Paracha, "Militants retake Darra Adamkhel," *Dawn,* May 1, 2008.
37 This report is taken from the comments of a local Taliban commander, as reported in Abdul Sami Paracha, "Taliban declare truce in Darra Adamkhel," *Dawn,* May 29, 2008.
38 Abdul Sami Paracha, "Taliban's 12 demands for peace in Darra," *Dawn,* June 6, 2008.
39 Abdul Sami Paracha, "Militants retake control of Darra," *Dawn,* August 14, 2008.
40 Abdul Sami Paracha, "50 militants in Darra killed, claims ISPR," *Dawn,* September 24, 2008.
41 The lack of local government institutions meant that there were only two such officials to co-opt, the MNA and the senator.
42 Sectarian organizations found it useful to establish bases in Darra, from which they had easy access to Kohat, Kurram, and other areas with contested Sunni-Shia relations. See Iqbal Khattak, "Six key militant outfits operating in Darra," *Daily Times,* January 29, 2008. Linkages between Darra-based Taliban organizations and violence in Mardan also points to the role of the Darra militants in the larger neo-Taliban movement. See Akhtar Amin, "Mardan residents say paying price for delay in Taliban-govt peace pact," *Daily Times,* May 20, 2008.
43 For a balanced summary of the election process, see Democracy International, *U.S. Election Observation Mission to Pakistan General Elections 2008: Final Report,* May 2008; and reports by the Free And Fair Election Network (FAFEN), available at http://www.fafen.org/.
44 These figures and those which follow are calculated from Election Commission of Pakistan data on the basis of elected provincial assembly seats, and do not include the reserved seats for women and minorities which are selected proportionately after the polling on the basis of party lists. In those cases in which a provincial assembly seat was not contested in the general election due to the death of a candidate, the results of the bye-election has been included for purposes of tabulation.
45 Overall provincial turnout was 33% in 2008, compared with 34% in 2002. Malakand division registered an 8% drop in turnout compared to 2002; and Bannu division nearly a 5% increase.
46 Average margin of victory in Peshawar, Mardan, and Malakand divisions (taken as a whole) fell from 18% to 9%, while the change in the other four divisions was less than 1%.
47 "NWFP cabinet takes oath," *The News,* April 3, 2008.
48 See Andrew R. Wilder, *The Pakistani Voter, Electoral Politics and Voting Behaviour in the Punjab* (Oxford: Oxford University Press, 1999).
49 Bhutto supported the NAP-JUI alliance in NWFP and Balochistan because his own PPP had a weak base of support in both provinces.
50 For an excellent history of the Khudai Khidmatgars, see Mukulika Banerjee, *The Pathan Unarmed: Opposition & Memory in the North West Frontier* (Karachi: Oxford University Press, 2000).
51 The PML's stronghold in the NWFP is in Hazara division, a primarily non-Pashtun area that was not willing to accept a new name for the province that referred to a single ethnic group.
52 This phrase was heard repeatedly by the author during travels in NWFP in 2006–8.
53 "Durand Line unacceptable to Pukhtuns, says ANP," *Dawn,* September 27, 2004.
54 See Manifesto of the Awami National Party, August 9, 2004. Available at http://awaminational-party.org/news/index.php?option=com_content&task=view&id=2&Itemid=27.
55 For a more pessimistic take, see Selig S. Harrison, "Putting Pakistan together again," *International Herald Tribune,* January 31, 2008.
56 Author interview with a senior ANP leader, July 2007, Peshawar.

IV
U.S. POLICY TOWARD THE FRONTIER

Apart from the substantial American contribution in support of the Afghan *jihad* in the 1980s, the United States has appeared only on the margins of the preceding narrative. That reflects not an intentional omission, but a political and historical reality: until recently, the Frontier was simply not a major focus of attention by Washington policymakers. This inattention, however, is clearly beginning to change. A 2007 U.S. National Intelligence Estimate, which corroborated speculation that al Qaeda had "regenerated" itself in the Pakistani tribal areas, has focused U.S. attention as never before on the problems and challenges of the Pak-Afghan border areas, and on their integral relation to overall U.S. interests.[1] The following sections examine the history of U.S. policy toward the Frontier, with particular emphasis on American political engagement and various forms of assistance provided to the government after September 11, 2001.

PRE-2002 HISTORICAL CONTEXT

U.S. presence in the Frontier has historically been oriented toward the situation in Afghanistan rather than toward the settled areas of the Pakistani Frontier itself. To the extent that the U.S. had a pre-9/11 policy pertaining to the NWFP proper, it was focused largely on counter-narcotics and on dealing with the Afghan refugee crisis.

The 1980s: Narcotics, refugees, and Afghanistan

U.S. strategic interest in the Frontier dates back principally to the early 1980s, when it channeled assistance through the Pakistani intelligence services to the *mujahidin* in support of their anti-Soviet operations in Afghanistan. The activity of the consulate in Peshawar during this period was focused almost exclusively on support to the Afghan operations, along with counter-narcotics programming. At the height of the Afghan *jihad* in the late 1980s, Peshawar fielded U.S. reconnaissance aircraft and served as a listening post for U.S. intelligence activity into Afghanistan and Central Asia. The consulate in Peshawar scaled up dramatically, as did the presence of the international community, which arrived *en masse* to deal with the flow of several million Afghan refugees into the settled areas of the Pakistani Frontier.

Even after the withdrawal of Soviet troops from Afghan territory in 1989, U.S. efforts in the Frontier continued to be focused on both the humanitarian and security aspects of the refugee crisis. Dozens of NGOs set up operations in Peshawar to serve the refugee community, and USAID provided funds for education and health initiatives in support of these efforts.[2] The other major thrust of U.S. activity in the Frontier was its counter-narcotics efforts. These, in retrospect, are widely seen as being among the most successful programs ever implemented by the United States in the Frontier. Throughout the 1980s, the U.S. funded efforts in both the settled and tribal areas to promote alternative livelihoods. These included direct counter-narcotics activity such as the spraying of poppy crops in the northern settled districts and the tribal areas; and indirect activity such as the building of roads to allow farmers to bring licit produce to market.

The 1990s: Scaling back

U.S. engagement with the Frontier took a dramatic turn following the October 1990 decertification of Pakistan under the Pressler Amendment, which imposed sanctions on Pakistan on account of its nuclear program. With the end of the Afghan war and the collapse of the Soviet Union, the U.S. felt that it had less incentive to turn a blind eye toward Pakistan's nuclear ambitions. The implications of the decertification were dramatic, and the bulk of U.S. aid assistance to Pakistan was suspended for over a decade.

Throughout the decade of turbulent civilian rule that followed the death of Zia ul-Haq in 1988, the U.S. continued to fund some education and health programs indirectly in NWFP and Sindh provinces through a new Pakistan NGO Initiative, but did so at a much-reduced level of expenditure.[3] The consulate in Peshawar continued to operate as a hub of anti-narcotics programming and humanitarian efforts to serve the swelling refugee population, which was exacerbated by Afghanistan's descent into a decade of warlordism and civil war following the retreat of the Soviets.

The victory of the Taliban in Afghanistan in 1996 shifted the focus of U.S. Frontier policy even further away from the NWFP proper: from 1999 to 2002, the U.S. principal officer in Peshawar devoted less than 10% of his time to issues relating to the NWFP.[4] Once again, the consulate became engrossed in dealing with eastern Afghanistan. Mullah Mohammad Omar's regime in Kabul posed not only human rights concerns but, by refusing to give up Osama bin Laden, growing strategic concerns as well. For understandable reasons, the U.S. policy focus in Peshawar was oriented almost entirely outside the Pakistani Frontier itself, and toward the Taliban government in Kabul.

Post-9/11 reengagement

After September 11, 2001, the focus on Afghanistan only intensified. The war in support of the Northern Alliance drove Taliban and al Qaeda militants from eastern Afghanistan into the tribal areas of Pakistan, where they settled beyond the immediate reach of U.S. or Pakistani forces. With the establishment of the Hamid Karzai government in Kabul, the U.S. began to pour resources into Afghan reconstruction projects; refugees slowly began to return from the Pakistani Frontier to Afghanistan; and scores of international aid workers based in Peshawar began relocating to Kabul.

Ironically, this exodus of aid workers from Peshawar came at the very time that the U.S. was beginning to orient, for the first time in decades, a significant portion of its Frontier policy toward the Pakistani Frontier itself. The reopening of the USAID mission in Pakistan in 2002 resulted in the rolling out of several small projects in the Frontier, each of which was centrally managed from Islamabad. And the October 2002 general elections which brought the MMA to power drew fresh attention to the possibility that — absent countervailing efforts — the settled areas of the NWFP might become the sort of repressive Taliban enclave that the U.S. had just worked to dismantle in Afghanistan.

POLITICAL ENGAGEMENT

In keeping with its post-9/11 privileging of the military-bureaucratic elite, the U.S. interacted regularly but very selectively with both mainstream and Islamist political elites in the Frontier. This policy of narrow engagement, which continued until approximately mid-2007, was counterproductive in that it hampered public diplomacy efforts, resulted in missed opportunities for substantive interaction with influential religious elites, and handicapped later attempts to encourage a broader basis of political legitimacy in Pakistan.

Early responses to the 2002 elections

The U.S. was surprised and concerned by the strong showing returned by the Islamist parties in the October 2002 general elections, particularly in the Frontier. Initially, the response of the State Department was muted; a spokesman in Washington noted that "the Pakistani people and the government have already demonstrated their strong opposition to terrorism and extremism, their desire to move their society in a more moderate and stable direction" and expressed the hope that "all the parties will be committed to moving in that direction."[5]

On the whole, the early American response to the MMA was predictably mixed: the U.S. refrained from criticizing the alliance directly, fearing that criticism would simply buttress its popularity. But the U.S. also kept a distance from the MMA leadership, at least in public. Assistant Secretary of State Christina Rocca in a December 2002 visit to Pakistan pointedly declined to meet with the MMA leadership, including Chief Minister Durrani, in Peshawar.[6] The cautious

U.S. stance in many ways mirrored the MMA's own ambivalence about how to adopt a conciliatory approach toward the international community without alienating its electorate.

The U.S. posture toward the MMA hardened somewhat during the tumultuous first year of the Islamists' tenure, which saw a surge of vigilante violence and occasionally fierce anti-American statements by party members outside the senior tier of leadership (for example, a November 2002 *fateha* in the NWFP provincial assembly which included a prayer that God "destroy the United States").[7] Assistant Secretary Rocca, when asked in July 2003 whether she considered the MMA to be "the Taliban of Pakistan," responded diplomatically, but with evident concern:

> I'm not sure that the exact thing can carry from one country to the other. Every country has its own peculiarities. But certainly, a situation where women are kept from working, kept from school, and kept in the home is something that we would like to not see happen to Pakistan.[8]

It is telling that even after the first, tumultuous year of the MMA's governance, the U.S. showed signs of trying to engage with the Islamist leadership. Ambassador Nancy Powell visited Peshawar in October 2003 and met with the MMA leadership, prompting speculation that the U.S. was trying to co-opt the religious leadership into more pragmatic governance.[9] In reality, that transformation was already underway — the alliance, as argued above, had turned a corner after the crisis over federalism and internal opposition to vigilantism — and the U.S. engagement with the MMA was never substantial enough to have influenced its political direction.

Engagement with mainstream and nationalist parties

Despite frequent diplomatic protestations to the contrary, there is ample evidence to suggest that U.S. engagement with Pakistani political actors during the first eight years of Musharraf's rule was focused overwhelmingly on the ruling party, to the exclusion of other mainstream, nationalist, and religious political blocs. The stated American policy was to support democratization in Pakistan, but the *de facto* policy of the Bush administration was to bolster Musharraf's rule at the expense of Pakistan's democratic parties and institutions.[10] Senator Joseph Biden's oft-quoted quip that the U.S. was pursuing "a Musharraf policy and not a Pakistan policy," while simplistic, ably captured the basic dynamic of U.S. political engagement in post-9/11 Pakistan.

The fruits of this policy of narrow political engagement are now well known, at least in general terms: the precipitous decline in Pakistani state legitimacy under the Musharraf government; the perception that American talk about democracy was a rhetoric of convenience and not conviction; and the further entrenchment of the military into Pakistan's political and economic life, as well as the U.S.-Pakistani bilateral relationship itself.[11]

This policy not only had far-reaching consequences for the overall American relationship with Pakistan, but it brought about unique implications for the Frontier, which was the only province in which Musharraf's ruling PML-Q party (or its close ally the MQM) did not have significant parliamentary or public support. The PML-Q, as noted above, was quite unpopular in the Frontier, and garnered close to no support in the Pashtun-dominated areas of the province. U.S. political engagement was therefore focused on the other mainstream and nationalist parties which operated in the NWFP. But this interaction too was limited. American diplomats were wary of developing close contacts with the PPP and PML-N, both of whose leaders were effectively exiled by the martial government. The U.S. had traditionally enjoyed warm relations with Aftab Sherpao, who broke from Benazir Bhutto's PPP in 1999, contested the 2002 elections under the banner of his own PPP Sherpao Group (PPP-S), and later allied his party with the PML-Q coalition in Islamabad. But Sherpao's political base in the NWFP was confined mostly to his native Charsadda and nearby districts, and did not extend substantially to the areas abutting the tribal belt.

Along with the PPP and PPP-S, the Awami National Party was in many ways the most natural ally of the United States in the Frontier. Despite its irredentist dismissal of the Durand Line, it was pro-West, pro-Karzai, and wary of religious politics. Ever since the end of the Cold War had made irrelevant its former affiliations with communists, the ANP had found favor in Washington as a potential bulwark against the spread of religious-inspired militancy in the Frontier. Even so, U.S. interaction with the nationalists remained cautious. For one, the ANP's devastating loss in 2002, and its history political infighting, did little to inspire confidence in its ability to project a moderate Pashtun politics in the NWFP. Moreover, U.S. officials were skeptical about its potential for gaining political traction in the conservative areas of the southern Pashtun belt. And finally, the ANP's strong federalist stance on provincial autonomy often set it in fierce opposition to the ruling elites in Islamabad, which further put a damper on U.S. engagement with the party.

Following Asfandyar Wali Khan's consolidation of the nationalist movement in 2005 under the ANP banner, he visited Washington in 2006 along with Afrasiab Khattak. They were received for meetings at the State Department and the Office of the Vice President, but later became disappointed that the communication channels with Washington did not develop as they had hoped.[12] U.S. officials remained quietly supportive of the ANP's efforts, but cognizant of the party's limits. Asfandyar traveled again to the United States shortly after the 2008 elections for discussions in Washington and with CENTCOM in Florida.[13]

Engagement with Islamist parties

If the U.S. was cautious in its engagement with the mainstream and nationalist parties, it was even more reticent toward the Islamists. U.S. diplomatic interaction with the MMA, while more or less consistent from 2002 through the end of their term in 2007, was selective and shallow. The U.S. principal officer in Peshawar called on the NWFP chief minister on a regular basis, and Ambassadors Powell and Crocker paid visits during the course of their tenures. In Islamabad and Lahore the U.S. maintained contacts with MMA figures, particularly senior JI leaders.[14] There was much more limited official interaction, however, with other important

MMA figures including provincial ministers in Peshawar; MPAs and MNAs from the *ulema* class; and senior figures in the JUI-F, most notably its leader Maulana Fazlur Rehman.

The choice of U.S. interlocutors reflected in part the post-9/11 orientation toward focused political engagement with the military-bureaucratic elite and its PML-Q ruling party. All the same, the narrow pattern of U.S. interactions with the Islamist parties was striking. USAID projects were structured in such a way as to require minimal interaction with the NWFP provincial government (a point not lost on MMA officials).[15] And interaction with MMA members of the provincial and national assemblies was similarly limited. Many such members interviewed in the summer of 2007 — including several who led key provincial ministries — had not met an American representative in the previous three years. U.S. officials acknowledged that the American consulate in Peshawar had "very little contact" with MMA members, as the majority of its efforts were focused on the problems of the FATA, and not on the NWFP as such.[16]

Although the provincial and national assemblies were arguably institutions of little consequence in the military-dominated Pakistani political system, the same was not true of their constituent members. Many of the assembly members, while new to politics, were important religious figures in the Frontier. Most of the JUI-F assembly members, for example, were senior *madrassah* teachers or administrators, often from the most influential and religiously conservative institutions in the province. Seen from the structural perspective of their role in the formal institutions of governance, these politicians were not particularly important. But their informal political influence was undeniable. The U.S. made little apparent attempt to take advantage of the presence of so many influential religious leaders in the assemblies in Peshawar and Islamabad, most of whom lived in parliament lodges just minutes from the U.S. consulate and embassy.

The U.S. choice of interlocutors among the MMA leadership was occasionally puzzling. Embassy officials had, for example, regular interaction with Liaqat Baloch, an outspoken senior JI leader known to be something of a showman, and a figure who lacked a strong constituency within the movement. But it chose not to deal with Maulana Fazlur Rehman, who while equally outspoken in his opposition to U.S. military action in Afghanistan, was a much more pragmatic politician with a considerable constituency in the southern Pashtun districts and tribal areas.

U.S. interaction with both leaders presented similar political difficulties: Liaqat came from the Jamaat's sometimes-violent student wing Islami Jamiat-e-Talaba (IJT), and the Jamaat itself historically had close ties with the Kashmiri militant groups and, indirectly, with al Qaeda.[17] Fazlur Rehman, who chaired the Senate Foreign Relations Committee under Benazir Bhutto, had multivalent links to the original Taliban movement, and retained questionable ties to Libya and financiers in the Gulf Emirates.[18]

Rightly or wrongly, the U.S. refusal to meet with Fazlur Rehman exemplified to many leaders in the MMA the extent to which the U.S. sought to avoid interaction with the Islamist political elite.[19] In spite of Fazlur Rehman's status as the leader of the opposition in the Pakistani National Assembly (and a rather docent opposition figure at that, playing the part of the loyal opposition), the U.S. went to great lengths to avoid the encounter. When pressed repeatedly by Pakistani reporters as to why he would not be meeting with leader of the opposition Fazlur Rehman on his visit to Islamabad in 2006, Assistant Secretary Boucher unconvincingly demurred: "[There are] several hundred million Pakistanis that I am not going to see, and I don't want to have to explain why I am not seeing each one."[20]

Limitations on Islamist interaction

There are several explanations for the American reluctance to interact with elected Islamist leaders, particularly in the Frontier. To begin with, engagement with the Islamists posed a problem of political optics. Both the JUI and the JI have a long history of anti-American statements, and of support — at times direct, and at times indirect — for Islamist insurgent groups in Kashmir, Afghanistan, and the tribal areas. Their social agenda was no less controversial. Particularly following 9/11, when the Taliban became a declared enemy of the United States, it became politically awkward for U.S. officials to meet with members of the Deobandi parties. Other events, such as the lead-up to the Iraq War, and U.S. Predator drone strikes in the tribal areas, ratcheted up Islamist rhetoric in ways that complicated attempts at political engagement.

Second, there was an evident though not unexpected gulf in relational norms between American diplomats and members of the Islamist parties. Several former U.S. officials recalled specific inflammatory statements made by Fazlur Rehman against the United States, or instances in which he misrepresented private conversations in public fora in order to show up his American interlocutors.[21] American diplomats came to believe that engagement with the Islamists was too risky and often counterproductive. Senior members of the JUI-F, on the other hand, repeatedly expressed confusion as to why the Americans would be so upset about statements which were merely "political" in nature and intended only for public consumption.

Finally, and perhaps most fundamentally, the hesitancy on the part of American officials to interact with the MMA in the Frontier is attributable to a simple policy calculus: for the first eight years of the Musharraf government, the Bush administration saw few compelling reasons to engage Islamist parties. This was especially true beginning in roughly 2004, when it became clear that the MMA government in the Frontier would not pose a strategic threat to U.S. interests in the region. Ambassador Ryan Crocker, whose tenure began in November of that year, brought with him a policy which reinforced this outlook. More so than his predecessor Nancy Powell, Crocker developed a reputation in diplomatic circles for focusing U.S. attention on Musharraf and his political allies, and restricting diplomatic contact with other political parties. This policy orientation continued until roughly 2007, when both political realities and personnel changes began to bring about a more open strategy of political engagement.

By early 2007, U.S. policymakers were aware that the general elections scheduled for later that year might result in a political realignment. Musharraf's popularity was slipping, and there was pressure to allow the return of Benazir Bhutto and Nawaz

Sharif in advance of the polls.[22] American officials served as brokers between Bhutto and Musharraf, seeking to arrange a deal by which Bhutto might stand for elections and come to a post-election *modus vivendi* with Musharraf.[23] At the same time, there was a growing realization among U.S. officials during the summer of 2007 that the Islamist parties, and particularly the JUI-F, might constitute a key electoral swing bloc in the forthcoming polls, and could no longer be ignored.[24]

Crocker's successor, Ambassador Anne Patterson, was sworn in during July 2007, and shortly thereafter began a set of high-profile meetings with a wide array of opposition politicians, including Maulana Fazlur Rehman.[25] The shift in approach toward engaging the full spectrum of opposition parties was in part precipitated by political expediency and the Pakistani election timetable, and in part by a more open diplomatic approach brought by the new ambassador.

Evaluating U.S. political engagement

Those who defend the Musharraf-oriented policy have argued that the U.S. had little to gain from dealing with the mainstream and nationalist parties in NWFP, which were weak; or with the Islamists, whose interests were sharply at odds with U.S. policies on a spectrum of key issues. Indeed, the short-term returns on broader engagement may well have been limited. The mainstream and nationalist parties were in disarray during the Musharraf era, and the MMA government — even as it was gradually moving toward a mainstream politics — proposed a number of troubling Islamization initiatives about which Washington was rightly concerned.

Taking the longer view, however, broad-based interaction could have proved fruitful on several levels. Two of Ambassador Powell's six high-level priorities during her tenure included anti-terrorism programs, and preventing Islamist political dominance in Pakistan.[26] On both counts, engaging with political elites outside the ruling party could have been of value. Deeper engagement with opposition parties would, at a minimum, have insulated the U.S. from the widespread charges that American policy was focused solely on supporting the Pakistani military, and that Musharraf was fighting America's war. The U.S. policy of avoiding contact with opposition political figures of whom the Musharraf regime might disapprove opened the U.S. to charges of hypocrisy and severely undermined support for *Pakistani* state action in the NWFP.

Second, American engagement with the nationalist bloc in the Frontier was inconsistent and overly cautious. The nationalist movement emerged from the 2002 elections fragmented and politically weak, and took three years to get its house in order. Despite its impressive showing in 2008, the party still has a number of internal fault lines, and lacks capacity to serve as an effective counterweight to the Islamization trends in the Frontier. More robust indirect support to the ANP for capacity building within the party, funding of ANP-managed initiatives on education and development, and leveraging ANP-affiliated professional networks to devise practical test beds of reform within the FATA could have set up the nationalist movement to be in a stronger position following its electoral victory.

Third, broader U.S. engagement with the Islamist parties could have served American strategic objectives in the mid-to-long–term. Critics of U.S. interaction with Islamists like the MMA argue that such encounters serve only to buttress Islamist political legitimacy; that such engagement ignores the lessons of the 1980s, in which the United States supported Islamist movements only to have them boomerang back with tragic consequences; and that Islamist parties essentially represent fronts for militant organizations. These are all legitimate concerns, but fundamentally misread both the political history of the MMA in the Frontier, and the ways in which current political realities have created a space for constructive interaction.

What could the U.S. have gained from such engagement? In the first place, deeper engagement would almost surely have accelerated the moderating effects associated with the Islamists' interaction with the international community. The experience of the British and German aid agencies in the NWFP was that Islamist figures in the government benefited from, and welcomed, foreign interaction; and that the benefits of that interaction occasionally spilled over into areas outside their official portfolios. Representatives from DFID and GTZ engaged the MMA leadership on a host of sensitive issues such as vaccinations for women and children, birth control, and *madrassah* curriculum.[27]

Regular U.S. interaction with MMA members of parliament at the provincial and national levels could have provided an opening for constructive dialogue on issues surrounding the *madaris*, particularly given that the JUI leaders were deeply concerned over the government of Pakistan's proposed *madaris* reform plans, and deeply suspicious of U.S. intentions toward religious education in Pakistan. This would not necessarily have been a fool's errand: in contrast to the conventional wisdom, Deobandi *madrassah* leaders have in recent years become increasingly willing to discuss in private fora the negative perceptions of *madaris* education in both Pakistan and the West, and the problems associated with educating a clerical class for which there are few legitimate job opportunities.[28] By their own admission, however, U.S. officials had little contact with these MMA members, and thus little impact on this front.

Perhaps the most compelling argument for engaging substantively and regularly with Islamist elites is that it is difficult to predict when interests will converge. The shortsightedness of the U.S. approach toward the religious parties became apparent only when ground realities began to shift in the Frontier. High-level interaction with parties like the JUI-F would likely have made little difference in the first two or three years of the MMA's tenure. But by 2005 the strategic landscape had shifted, and there was increasingly a convergence of interests — if only, at first, at the margins — between Islamist political leaders and broader U.S. and Pakistani objectives. By 2005 the JUI-F, increasingly threatened by the spread of decentralized violence in the settled areas, was eager to expand its interaction with the West, and felt rebuffed.[29] The U.S., having failed to regularize its relationships with the full spectrum of opposition politicians in Pakistan, did not have the relationships in place, or the credibility, to be able to respond politically.

No one would suggest that the U.S. would have found broad areas of common ground with the JUI leadership. The point, rather, is that by initiating political contacts with opposition parties only in advance of elections, American diplomacy becomes reactive and appears exploitative. Few observers could have predicted that by 2007, many analysts would become deeply worried about the JUI's *declining* influence in the Frontier — not because they were amenable to Islamist politics, but because the party, however unpalatable, had come to occupy an important "centrist" ground in the Islamist political space and an important role in restraining more militant Deobandi activity. By regularizing its contact with parties such as the JUI-F, the U.S. might have been better prepared to take advantage of these kind of strategic realignments in Frontier politics.

U.S. ASSISTANCE TO THE FRONTIER

Development assistance

It is by now widely known that American assistance to Pakistan since September 11, 2001 has been heavily skewed toward security assistance and budget support rather than development programming. The most comprehensive review to date generously estimated that about 11% of overt U.S. aid between FY2002 and FY2007 went to development assistance.[30] The U.S. government is only now beginning to make up for seven years of under-investment in key areas such as education, health, and livelihoods, all of which have a bearing not only on development indicators but also on local security and government legitimacy.

USAID restarted its programs in Pakistan in July 2002, after nearly a decade of absence. It chose initially to undertake work in four sectors: education, the economy, health, and democratic governance.[31] It chose also to focus many of its efforts on the provinces of Sindh and Balochistan so as to complement the work of its British counterpart DFID, which was active in the NWFP and Punjab.[32] USAID efforts in the NWFP have therefore been relatively limited, particularly in the education sector.[33] Neither USAID's previous flagship education initiative, the Education Sector Reform Action program, nor its current one, Links to Learning (ED-LINKS), focus on the NWFP.[34] USAID devoted somewhat more attention to health programs in the province, particularly reproductive and child health initiatives. It also carried out small governance programs, including a legislative strengthening project, and a local governance capacity building initiative which recently expanded its scope from one district (Mansehra) to seven.[35]

U.S. aid officials focused somewhat more attention on the FATA. USAID launched a School Rehabilitation and Construction Program in the tribal areas in 2004 which, in partnership with the Japanese, set out to build a total of 130 schools in the FATA and FR areas. The U.S. also funded several health, teacher training, and microenterprise initiatives in the tribal areas. Unfortunately, these programs struggled to meet their objectives. The school construction project was hampered by poor security, lack of oversight, and questionable buy-in by local leaders.[36] (U.S. officials found it so difficult to gain access to the FATA that they discussed at one point the possibility of using unmanned aerial drones to monitor the project sites.[37]) Health projects ran into similar roadblocks, and the microenterprise initiative ended up disbursing only 4% of the targeted number of loans.[38]

In retrospect, it is apparent that the United States was slow to align its development programming with a comprehensive strategy for countering extremism in the region. Not only were development expenditures small relative to military outlays, but it was not until 2006 that the Frontier began to figure prominently in U.S. development planning.[39] Efforts were also plagued with implementation challenges. A full three and a half years after the USAID mission reopened, well-placed U.S. officials and NGO leaders in Pakistan were lamenting that American development programs in the NWFP and FATA remained chaotic and woefully under-staffed. They also had trouble catching the attention of the bureaucracy. Complained one official, "Everyone in Islamabad is spending their time tracking the helicopters" and other security-related initiatives.[40] In addition, USAID's efforts in the Frontier suffered from a shortage of office space at the embassy and consulates; a lack of capacity, both within USAID and within the NGO community; high turnover in personnel; and security threats, which severely limited staff travel and oversight.[41] While a number of these problems were eventually taken up by senior U.S. officials in 2006, they could do little to make up for nearly five years of lost time.[42]

Security assistance

The United States took a number of steps after 9/11 to solidify its defense relationship with Pakistan.[43] It made Pakistan eligible for Coalition Support Funds, which ostensibly constituted direct reimbursements for anti-terrorist military operations, but which also served as an important political mechanism for incentivizing cooperation with U.S. security objectives.[44] A recent GAO report on U.S. government policy toward the Frontier revealed that about 96% of funds expended for "efforts in the FATA and border region" from 2002 through 2007 went toward these reimbursements.[45] The United States also recognized Pakistan in 2004 as a Major Non-NATO Ally, and made available for purchase sophisticated and politically-sensitive military equipment.[46] It restarted the International Military Education and Training (IMET) program, which was popular among Pakistani army officers, and expanded military liaisons.

Apart from military support, U.S. security assistance to Pakistan since 2001 has focused on border control, buttressing the government's investigative capacity, and pursuing counter-narcotics objectives.[47] Most of these programs are run by the Department of State or the Department of Justice. They have included, *inter alia*, efforts to improve international visitor processing, train Pakistani police in forensic sciences and "civil disorder management," construct outposts along the Pak-Afghan border, promote eradication and alternative livelihood programs in poppy-growing areas of the FATA, and teach courses in counterterrorism and SWAT techniques.[48]

Over the last year, CENTCOM has taken the lead in formulating a FATA Security Development Plan aimed at building counterinsurgency capacity for the Frontier Corps and improving internal and bilateral coordination on border issues.[49] This plan received an initial appropriation of $75 million for FY2008, along with the formal authorization from the Congress to "provide assistance to enhance the ability of the Pakistan Frontier Corps to conduct counterterrorism operations" along the Pak-Afghan border.[50] As part of this initiative, the Pentagon also plans to establish FC training centers near Peshawar and Quetta, border coordination centers to improve information sharing and rapid decision-making, and programs to train and equip the 21st Quick Reaction Squadron of the Pakistan army's elite Special Services Group.[51]

NOTES:

1. The NIE assessed that al Qaeda had "protected or regenerated key elements of its Homeland attack capability, including: a safehaven in the Pakistan Federally Administered Tribal Areas (FATA), operational lieutenants, and its top leadership." U.S. National Intelligence Council, "National Intelligence Estimate: The Terrorist Threat to the US Homeland," July 2007, available at www.dni.gov/press_releases/20070717_release.pdf (accessed October 1, 2008).
2. These funds were programmed through State Department's Bureau of Population, Refugees, and Migration, and included funding for NGOs and IOs doing work with refugee communities in Balochistan and the NWFP. See Rhoda Margesson, *Afghan Refugees: Current Status and Future Prospects* (CRS Report for Congress, January 26, 2007).
3. The majority of these funds were provided to the Asia Foundation and the Aga Khan Foundation; they totaled about $10 million over the period 1994–2003. Thomas Lum, *U.S. Foreign Aid to East and South Asia: Selected Recipients* (CRS Report for Congress, May 1, 2008), 32.
4. Author interview with a U.S. State Department official, March 2007, Washington D.C.
5. Richard Boucher, State Department Daily Press Briefing, October 11, 2002, available at http://www.state.gov/r/pa/prs/dpb/2002/14340.htm (accessed October 1, 2008).
6. See "Senior US official arriving for talks with Pakistan," *Agence France-Presse*, December 15, 2002; and "No plans to meet MMA leaders: Rocca," *Press Trust of India*, December 17, 2002.
7. Iqbal Khattak, "Rumpus rules NWFP Assembly," *Daily Times*, November 28, 2002. Later, in June 2006, the house offered *fateha* over the death of Abu Musab al-Zarqawi. Pakistan Institute of Legislative Development and Transparency, *State of Democracy*.
8. "Christina Rocca discusses Pakistan with Mishal Husain," PBS, July 17, 2003, http://www.pbs.org/wnet/wideangle/shows/junoon/transcript.html.
9. Iqbal Khattak, "US planning to co-opt MMA?" *Friday Times*, October 24, 2003.
10. See for example the joint statement between President Bush and President Musharraf in March 2006, declaring that the U.S. "supports Pakistan as it develops strong and transparent democratic institutions and conducts free and fair elections to ensure sustainable democracy." Quoted in Ryan C. Crocker, "US assistance dedicated to Pakistani priorities," *The Statesman*, March 29, 2007.
11. The military's involvement in business has come under withering critique, most notably in Ayesha Siddiqa, *Military Inc.: Inside Pakistan's Military Economy* (Pluto Press, 2007). Chief of Army Staff General Ashfaq Kiyani has taken a number of steps to pull the military back from high-profile political activities and offices, but has not yet made efforts to restructure the political economy of the military and its foundations.
12. Author interviews with ANP members, August 2007, Peshawar.
13. "US silent on visit of Asfandyar," *Dawn*, May 10, 2008.
14. Author interviews with U.S. officials, August 2007, Pakistan.

15 To be fair to USAID, the agency was faced with a lack of capacity, particularly in Peshawar.
16 Author interviews with U.S. officials, August 2007, Pakistan.
17 For more on the IJT, see David Montero, "Islamist voices rise on Pakistani campuses," *Christian Science Monitor,* March 22, 2006; and Haider Mullick, "Towards a Civic Culture: Student Activism and Political Dissent in Pakistan," *Georgetown Journal of International Affairs* 9, no. 2 (Summer/Autumn 2008): 5–12.
18 Recent documents uncovered in Iraq suggest that Fazlur Rehman may also have served at one time as a liaison between the Taliban and the government of Iraq. See Kevin M. Woods and James Lacey, *Iraqi Perspectives Project: Saddam and Terrorism: Emerging Insights from Captured Iraqi Documents, Volume 1 (Redacted)* (Institute for Defense Analyses, November 2007), 15; Ray Robison, "Terror Links to Saddam's Inner Circle," *Fox News,* June 12, 2006, available at http://www.foxnews.com/story/0,2933,199052,00.html (accessed October 1, 2008); and Ray Robison, "Documents Support Saddam-Taliban Connection," *Fox News,* June 16, 2006, available at http://www.foxnews.com/story/0,2933,199757,00.html (accessed October 1, 2008).
19 Author interviews with senior JUI-F parliamentarians and party advisors, 2006–7, Peshawar.
20 Richard Boucher, media roundtable with senior Pakistani editors, November 7, 2006, Islamabad.
21 Author interviews with U.S. officials formerly posted in Pakistan, 2007, Washington D.C.
22 Between September 2006 and September 2007, Musharraf's approval rating plummeted from 63% to 21%. International Republican Institute (IRI), *Pakistan Public Opinion Survey,* January 19–29, 2008.
23 See, e.g., Zaffar Abbas, "The emerging contours of PPP-govt deal," *Dawn,* April 21, 2007.
24 Author interviews with U.S. officials, July and August 2007, Islamabad and Peshawar.
25 "US envoy calls on Fazl," *The Statesman,* September 29, 2007.
26 In addition to counterterrorism, the ambassador's other priorities reportedly included "securing supply lines for American and allied forces in Afghanistan, shutting down the network of nuclear proliferator A.Q. Khan, preventing a nuclear war between Pakistan and India, and forestalling a radical Islamic takeover of the government of Pakistan, a key American ally." This list is taken from a somewhat sensational article in the *New York Sun* criticizing Amb. Powell for failing to vigorously pursue a counterterrorism agenda. The State Department disputed the article's conclusions, but not the ambassador's priorities, which are likely accurate. Richard Miniter, "How a Lone Diplomat Compromised the Hunt for Bin Laden," *New York Sun,* March 25, 2005.
27 Author interviews with DFID representatives, July 2007, Islamabad; and a GTZ representative, July 2007, Peshawar.
28 Author interviews with JUI-F party leaders, 2005, Islamabad and Peshawar.
29 Author interviews with JUI-F party leaders, 2005–6, Peshawar.
30 This is a relatively generous calculation, as it includes budget support which was designated for development programs, but which is "not transparent to public oversight." See Craig Cohen, *A Perilous Course: U.S. Strategy and Assistance to Pakistan* (Washington, DC: Center for Strategic and International Studies, August 2007), 30–3. A somewhat different compilation of the figures has been put together by the Congressional Research Service. See K. Alan Kronstadt, *Direct Overt U.S. Aid and Military Reimbursements to Pakistan, FY2002–FY2009* (CRS Report for Congress, August 7, 2008), available at http://fas.org/sgp/crs/row/pakaid.pdf (accessed October 1, 2008).

31 See USAID, *USAID/Pakistan Interim Strategic Plan, May 2003–September 2006,* May 2003.
32 Ibid.
33 Author interviews with USAID officials, summer 2007, Islamabad and Peshawar. See also http://www.usaid.gov/pk/education/index.htm, http://www.usaid.gov/pk/health/index.htm, http://www.usaid.gov/pk/governance/index.htm, and http://www.usaid.gov/pk/ec-growth/index.htm (accessed October 1, 2008).
34 See USAID, *Education Sector Reform Assistance (ESRA) Program End-of-Project Report,* January 31, 2008; and USAID, *Request for Applications USAID-Pakistan 391-07-012,* March 19, 2007.
35 See Pakistan Districts That Work Project, *Quarterly Performance Report (Project Quarter 7),* April 30, 2008, available at http://cybervision.com.pk/USAID/7-QPR_Project_report_08.pdf (accessed October 1, 2008).
36 Author interviews, summer 2007 and 2008, Peshawar.
37 Author interview with former a State Department official, March 2007, Washington.
38 Author interviews with NGO workers, July 2007, Peshawar. See also Jane Perlez, "Aid to Pakistan in Tribal Areas Raises Concerns," *New York Times,* July 16, 2007; and USAID, "Pakistan Economic Growth Program Evaluation Summary Report," June 2008.
39 This took place concurrently with other interagency planning efforts which began in 2006. See Government Accountability Office (GAO), *Combating Terrorism: The United States Lacks Comprehensive Plan to Destroy the Terrorist Threat and Close the Safe Haven in Pakistan's Federally Administered Tribal Areas,* April 2008, 5.
40 Author interviews, 2005–2006, Islamabad and Peshawar.
41 USAID's support of ESRA, for example, came under criticism by the agency's inspector general, which attributed a number of the mission's oversight problems to high "turnover in mission personnel and precarious security conditions … ." USAID, *Audit of USAID/Pakistan's Education Sector Reform Assistance program,* March 28, 2008.
42 Testimony by USAID officials in the summer of 2008, for example, acknowledged many of the challenges that the agency faces in implementing programs in the Frontier. Mark Ward, testimony before the Senate Committee on Foreign Relations, June 25, 2008.
43 For a discussion of the status of the bilateral defense relationship, see David O. Smith, "Facing Up to the Trust Deficit: The Key to an Enhanced U.S.-Pakistan Defense Relationship," *Strategic Insights* 6, no. 4 (June 2007).
44 For discussion and critique of the Coalition Support Funds program, see GAO, *Preliminary Observations on the Use and Oversight of U.S. Coalition Support Funds Provided to Pakistan,* May 6, 2008.
45 GAO, *Combating Terrorism,* 11.
46 See T. Christian Miller, "U.S. to Reward Pakistan With New Arms Status," *Los Angeles Times,* March 19, 2004; and Smith, "Facing Up to the Trust Deficit."
47 For a thorough review of U.S. security assistance to Pakistan, see C. Christine Fair and Peter Chalk, *Fortifying Pakistan: The Role of U.S. Internal Security Assistance* (Washington, DC: United States Institute of Peace, 2006).
48 Several of these examples are drawn from U.S. Department of State, *Pakistan 2007 Performance Report,* 2007, available at http://dec.org/index.cfm?p=search.getCitation&rec_no=149522 (accessed October 1, 2008).
49 Markey, *Securing Pakistan's Tribal Belt,* 19. See also See Eric Schmitt, Mark Mazzetti and Carlotta Gall, "U.S. Considers Enlisting Tribes in Pakistan to Fight Al Qaeda," *New York Times,*

November 19, 2007; Eric Schmitt and Thom Shanker, "U.S. Plan Widens Role in Training Pakistani Forces in Qaeda Battle," *New York Times,* March 2, 2008; and Jane Perlez, "Pakistani Fury Over Airstrikes Imperils Training," *New York Times,* June 18, 2008.

50 See section 1206 of P.L. 110-181, available at http://frwebgate.access.gpo.gov/cgi-bin/getdoc.cgi?dbname=110_cong_public_laws&docid=f:publ181.110.pdf (accessed October 1, 2008).

51 John Negroponte, testimony before the Senate Committee on Foreign Relations, May 20, 2008.

V
POLICY RECOMMENDATIONS

The sections which follow provide recommendations as to how the United States, working with the government of Pakistan, might respond intelligently to the changing political, social, and security dynamics in the Frontier. Following a brief summary of the strategic context, the first two sections discuss political engagement and suggest a path forward for American diplomacy. The third section examines security policy, and provides recommendations as to the options available for supporting counterinsurgency strategies which target the drivers of political instability and militancy. The fourth and fifth sections look at governance and structural reform in the Frontier, including the FATA, and review the ways in which structural reforms might contribute to a more stable politics in the Frontier. And the sixth section highlights the challenges and opportunities available through aid and development.

There is already a widespread perception that America wields outsized influence in the Pakistani political process. This perception is based in part on a long history of U.S. influence in Pakistan, and in part on a persistent myth of America's "hidden hand." Regardless of the reasons, this perception is detrimental to the development of a strong democratic political culture in Pakistan, and to constructive U.S.-Pakistani bilateral ties. None of the recommendations which follow are meant to suggest that the U.S. take unilateral action in Pakistan, or seek to micromanage Pakistani decision-making. Rather, these recommendations cover areas in which the U.S. is already heavily invested — such as aid, security cooperation, and political engagement — and are meant to focus attention on policies which contribute to joint U.S. and Pakistani objectives. While they are framed in terms of U.S. actions in a bilateral or multilateral context, many of these recommendations are also equally relevant to Pakistani policymakers looking to address the structural weaknesses of the state.

STRATEGIC CONTEXT

Although this report focuses specifically on one region of Pakistan, it is clear that the Frontier cannot be understood apart from its wider domestic and regional strategic contexts. Many of the policy recommendations which follow, should they be implemented, would succeed or fail based not on their policy minutiae, but on the macro political environment — on Pakistani political will and state structures of civil-military cooperation; on American military, political and economic leverage; on regional cooperation; and on the situation in Afghanistan. These extant political and structural realities no doubt limit the effective scope of both Pakistani and U.S. policy toward the Frontier. But they also serve to highlight the importance of macro political factors in the future stability of the region.

Domestic factors

A successful Frontier policy requires, at a minimum, state legitimacy, political will, and civil-military coordination. In the first place, state legitimacy is a prerequisite for any successful and humane counterinsurgency program. The government must be able to convince the public at large that its actions are carried out for the good of the country, and constitute a just and proportionate response to insurgent activity. There is substantial evidence, particularly in the Frontier, that the transition to civilian governance following the February 2008 elections created just such a political opening. The fragmentation or even collapse of coalition politics at the national level in Pakistan could, however, quickly erode the legitimacy of civilian rule, and make it difficult for both Pakistan and the United States to carry out coherent policies toward the Frontier.

A second challenge is the problem of political will on the part of state elites. Pakistan's willingness to deal seriously with security challenges in the Frontier has been a subject of much debate in Washington: many have suggested that the Pakistani military has tolerated and at times supported militant groups in the Pak-Afghan borderlands in an attempt to destabilize Afghanistan, counter Indian influence on their western border, and make the case for expanded U.S. aid. The Pakistan army's ambivalent contacts with Taliban leaders such as Jalaluddin Haqqani and Baitullah Mehsud have raised questions about its commitment to acting against those insurgent leaders who have close ties to the Pakistani state.[1] American officials have also suggested that the military's objectives are often more attuned to displacing militant activity from Pakistan's settled areas (into the FATA, or Afghanistan) than to eliminating militant networks outright.

The nature of coalitional politics at the federal level has also created few incentives for leading political figures to formulate coherent policies toward the Frontier. Most political elites from Punjab and Sindh are thoroughly unfamiliar with, and often dismissive of, the cultural and political dynamics of the Frontier, and are faced with few electoral incentives to focus attention on the problems of the region. The PPP-led civilian government in Islamabad, for example, has demonstrated inconsistent political will in addressing the most pressing security and governance challenges in the NWFP and the FATA, and has instead become mired in political maneuverings, infighting, and dealings unrelated to the pressing security issues facing the state.

Third, the success or failure of Pakistan's Frontier policy — and, by extension, that of the U.S. — will turn on the ability of state elites to coordinate civil and military action. Scholars have written at length about the dysfunctions of the Pakistani state, and the troubled history of civil-military relations.[2] Successful counterinsurgency operations of the kind that are now clearly needed in the Frontier require a level of civil-military cooperation that is infrequently seen in the Pakistani political context. This cooperation is important for both policy formulation and execution. Unless the state can coordinate district-level government and police responses with military planning, it will be ineffective at dismantling insurgent influence at the local level.

In light of these three factors, which are largely structural in nature, the United States has only limited leverage by which to influence the underlying drivers of Pakistan's Frontier policy. The U.S. should, as argued below, maintain strong support for civilian governance, and use its financial and political clout to encourage holistic and structural reforms in the Frontier. In addition, American officials should strongly encourage the formation of a regular, visible, and functioning forum for civil-military interaction in Pakistan. The National Security Council, which was formalized by President Musharraf in 2004 as tool to bolster his democratic legitimacy and co-opt opposition politicians (including those in the Frontier), was never institutionalized as a decision-making forum.[3] But it might nonetheless serve as a template for an institution which brings together key leaders — the prime minister, chief of army staff, chief ministers of the provinces, and senior bureaucrats. In the short-run, the optics of such a forum could be just as important as the substance: by presenting to the public a visible focal-point for high-level discussion and coordination, the NSC could do a great deal to bolster the legitimacy of state action against militants, and improve accountability by highlighting the role of elected political leaders.

Regional factors

This study, with its focus on political Islam in the Pakistani Frontier, addresses in only a peripheral way the security nexus between the Pakistani and Afghan frontier areas. But clearly, a stable and constructive Pak-Afghan relationship is fundamental to the success of any U.S. Frontier policy.[4] The state of this bilateral relationship, which reached its nadir in the summer of 2008 with accusations by the government of Afghanistan of ISI complicity in the attempted assassination of Hamid Karzai, is of tremendous import to the United States.[5]

In the first place, American concerns about the Pakistani government's contacts with Taliban groups in Afghanistan, and about its overall policy orientation toward the Afghan regime, have been well documented.[6] That a great many Pakistanis, including some in the security services, remain deeply skeptical about the longevity and credibility of the Karzai government in Kabul should come as no surprise. There remains a widespread perception throughout the Frontier that Karzai is politically impotent; that his government is overwhelmingly dominated by Tajik figures loyal to the Northern Alliance; and that the Afghan Taliban are representing the exploited Pashtun majority.[7]

Pakistani security planners scoff at the suggestion that the military still sees Afghanistan through the lens of a policy of "strategic depth." But that policy undeniably figures into Pakistani defensive calculations, and for obvious reasons. The nuclear standoff with India in 2002 (which began with an Indian troop build-up in response to the militant attack on its Parliament in December 2001) and, more recently, India's proposed Cold Start doctrine, have not diminished the concerns of Pakistani defense planners over the implications of a confrontation with India.[8] In this context, close Indian ties to the Karzai government pose a real challenge for the United States due to their second-order effects on Pakistan's strategic orientation toward its western border.[9]

American policymakers have, to date, been frustrated by Pakistan's dismissive attitude toward the Karzai government and its apparent unwillingness to sever institutional ties with Islamic militant groups operating in connection with the Afghan Taliban. At the same time, the United States has done a remarkably poor job of addressing the geopolitical realities which drive Pakistani strategic behavior. Until American policymakers do more to engage Pakistani concerns about the growing Indian influence in Afghanistan, they are unlikely to see the Pakistani state elite change its strategic posture vis-à-vis the Karzai government.[10]

There is also a need for much more active and direct engagement by the U.S. in dealing with the dysfunctional Pak-Afghan-NATO tripartite relationship. High-level military contacts among the three parties have been intermittent, and focused largely on tactical cross-border problems.[11] A senior U.S. envoy devoted to addressing issues on both sides of the Durand Line would help to improve coordination on a broader set of issues than simply cross-border militancy.

Ultimately, the situation in the Pakistani Frontier is linked with the success or failure of the U.S. and NATO project in Afghanistan. The Pakistani insurgency is funded in part by the burgeoning narcotics trade in Afghanistan, and the Afghan Taliban movement is in turn being supported by Pakistani militant groups and the presence of a safe haven in the FATA. However distinct the political contexts may be on either side of the Durand Line, these linkages are such that U.S. policy cannot afford to focus on the Pakistani Frontier alone.

POLITICAL ENGAGEMENT

U.S. policy has evolved considerably since 2006, with a Musharraf-centric political engagement giving way to a more balanced and broad-based policy of interaction with Pakistani political leaders. As part of this continuing shift, the U.S. should adopt the following policies which pertain to Pakistan at large, but particularly to Frontier politics.

Signal long-term support for civilian governance

The single most important thing that the United States can do to deal constructively with the challenges posed by Islamist groups in the Frontier is to support civilian governance in Pakistan. The pre-eminence of the army in Pakistan's political order virtually guarantees that military-to-military interaction will and ought to remain a critical part of the bilateral relationship. But American support for democratic institutions ultimately furthers U.S. interests by contributing to the legitimacy of the central government in Islamabad and enhancing the credibility with which the state takes action against extremist groups within its territory.[12] The continuation of civilian governance is especially important in the Frontier, where opposition to military action runs high, and the mainstream parties lack strong political bases.

The U.S. should signal its long-term support for civilian governance by conditioning expanded U.S. aid assistance on the continuation of civilian rule. While conditions-based aid programming usually runs the risk of undermining Pakistani confidence in the longevity of American commitment, this case is different, as it represents an alignment of long-term American and Pakistani strategic interests and coincides with public support for democratization. The Biden-Lugar legislation is a positive first step in this direction, in that it institutionalizes the U.S. commitment, and preempts policymakers from allowing short-term considerations to override the long-term U.S. interest in legitimate, democratic rule in Pakistan.[13]

The U.S. must make both short-term and long-term investments in civilian governance in Pakistan. Most immediately, this means finding ways to signal on a routine basis American support for civilian rule. High level military-to-military contact which excludes elected civilian leaders or senior bureaucrats, such as the secret meeting conducted aboard the USS Abraham Lincoln in August 2008, gives the strong impression that civilian governance remains a secondary concern of U.S. policymakers.[14] Similarly, American diplomats should make efforts to interact with civilian institutions — such as the elected cabinet — rather than bypassing them in favor of one or two senior leaders. Over the long-term, the U.S. can increase its support for programs which will foster an informed, civilian-led, issue-oriented political culture. Both the polling programs run by the International Republican Institute (IRI) and the work by the National Democratic Institute (NDI) to strengthen policy development capacity among parties are very important, and should be scaled up in Islamabad and the provincial capitals.

Institutionalize indirect support to the ANP

The Pashtun nationalist Awami National Party is the political bloc in the Frontier whose interests are most closely aligned with those of the United States. Despite concerns over the party's irredentist policies with respect to Afghanistan and its ethnic nationalist rhetoric, the ANP in fact supports a rather mild form of nationalism — seeking only marginally greater autonomy for the Frontier province, and closer ties with the Karzai regime in Afghanistan. The party has received intermittent and indirect capacity building support from the United States, especially in the lead-up to elections.

The U.S. should institutionalize its political support for the ANP in a way that is not dependent upon the Pakistani election cycle. Specifically, the U.S. should support long-term capacity building programs which would benefit the party; encourage the extension of the Political Parties Act to the FATA, which would benefit the ANP in the northern tribal areas; and consider providing funds to the party's affiliated development organizations, such as the Baacha Khan Trust, for their efforts in promoting moderate education in the NWFP. Given that ANP cadres have a relatively rich expertise in law and governance, the U.S. should explore ways to support reform efforts which would benefit both the party and the province at large.

Engage with the right-of-center PML-N

One of the surprises of the February 2008 general elections was the unusually strong showing by Nawaz Sharif's right-of-center PML-N in urban Punjab. If history is any guide, the current coalition in Islamabad led by the PPP is unlikely to serve out its full term. By joining the governing coalition but staying out of the federal cabinet, Nawaz Sharif has positioned his party to take advantage of political turmoil, the deteriorating economic situation, and missteps by the current government. The PML-N, favored by the Pakistani military and by the Saudi royal family, is well positioned to make a return to power within several years, if not sooner.

The U.S. should take steps to engage the PML-N while it is still in the minority. In particular, further engagement with the Nawaz league may help to forestall the party from adopting strident anti-Western positions in its attempt to outflank the PPP on nationalist and Islamic grounds. Nawaz Sharif is aware that he is viewed with suspicion by the majority of American policymakers, but also recognizes that financial and political support from both the U.S. and Saudi Arabia are essential to Pakistan's economic stability, and to his own future political success. A PML-N government in Islamabad would undoubtedly be troubling to the United States, but it could bring with it a silver lining: the party has tremendous street credibility, and if it were so disposed (and so incentivized), could take firm action against extremist groups while eliciting relatively minimal public backlash.

In addition, U.S. engagement with the PML-N is a means by which to indirectly mitigate the potential influence of the Jamaat-e-Islami. The PML-N would be likely to bring Jamaat ideologues into its governing coalition, and introduce Islamist measures as a means of shoring up its own political standing. The prospect of the Jamaat as a minor coalition partner at the central level is one which has historically caused far more concern among U.S. diplomats than the more far-fetched possibility of an "Islamist takeover" of the government.[15] The JI, by virtue of its bureaucratic organization, is often quite accessible to American diplomats and adept at interacting with the international community; it is also, however, quite ideologically rigid, and U.S. engagement with the party is not likely to be particularly constructive over the long-term. Substantive engagement with its mainstream patron the PML-N might therefore constitute a more productive approach.

Regularize interaction with the JUI-F

The limited nature of U.S. engagement with Islamist parties during the MMA era resulted in a number of missed opportunities for substantive dialogue regarding the parties' Islamist agenda and its role in religious education; and for acting as a moderating influence on the behavior of the Deobandi political leadership. The U.S. was also left unprepared for the political shifts brought about by the rise of the neo-Taliban, which forced the JUI-F toward the political center.

The U.S. should gradually regularize its interaction with the JUI-F and adopt a policy of more consistent diplomatic engagement. Such a policy, while likely to be unpopular in some quarters, is a vital part of a wider policy of consistent interaction with Pakistan's opposition parties and an important avenue for dialogue with influential religious figures in the Frontier.

In particular, U.S. interaction with the JUI-F could focus on areas of common agreement such as programs to discourage suicide bombings and vigilantism; on issues of interfaith and sectarian harmony in Punjab and the Frontier; on providing pedagogical training to *madrassah* instructors and skills training to *madrassah* students; on promoting greater JUI-F participation in parliamentary and civil society training programs; and, broadly, on encouraging the party to play a responsible role in democratic politics and foreign policy.[16] An American policy of regular, consistent engagement would also serve, ironically, to normalize and depoliticize interaction with parties such as the JUI-F, and would allow the U.S. to be better prepared for strategic political realignments in the Frontier which may bring about unexpected convergence of interests.

Retool the U.S. bureaucracy for long-term engagement

In spite of the growing importance of Pakistan to U.S. foreign policy, the American bureaucracy remains under-equipped to engage Pakistan over the longterm. This has little to do with individual government servants, many of whom are capable and impressive. But the tight security restrictions imposed after the 2002 bombing against an expatriate church in Islamabad (and, more recently, against the Marriott Hotel) have severely handicapped the ability of the United States to carry out its mission in Pakistan. Most Foreign Service officers, and many military and aid officials, spend only one year posted in-country. As a former State Department official has noted with respect to the Foreign Service, the "standard practice of personnel rotation is inappropriate to the mission in Pakistan and Afghanistan."[17] It should not be surprising that there is today a notable lack of regional expertise and institutional memory.

This is beginning to change, but only at the margins. Despite the poor security environment, the U.S. now more than ever needs to focus bureaucratic resources on the Pak-Afghan region. In the Pakistani theater, this means taking the difficult step of extending diplomatic tours in Pakistan in order to foster a cadre that has the expertise and relationships necessary to carry out American policy objectives.[18] Training for Foreign Service officers, area experts, and aid workers should also be expanded to include a more substantive focus on religious issues. Pakistani political figures have noted that American diplomats are often uncomfortable discussing religion and its role in international relations — subjects which are likely to be of increasing relevance in the Pakistani-American bilateral relationship.

In Washington, the U.S. needs to establish new coordinating mechanisms focused on the Pak-Afghan region. The State Department has taken initial steps in this direction by creating posts devoted to cross-border issues. But the most pressing challenge remains interagency cooperation. Although coordinating mechanisms may exist on paper, the interagency process has lacked a consistent high-level forum for integrating political, military, and development strategy with respect to the Frontier.

PUBLIC DIPLOMACY

Implementing an effective public diplomacy strategy in Pakistan is a major challenge for the United States. The global media environment is such that segmented messaging — that is, targeting a message narrowly to a Pakistani audience — is increasingly unrealistic. Security constraints on public diplomacy officers also limit the reach and depth of American diplomatic initiatives. The U.S. has taken some positive steps in the last two years to hone its messaging strategy, but much more can be done.

America's public diplomacy strategy in Pakistan should not be geared primarily toward reducing anti-Americanism as such; that is a worthwhile secondary goal. The focal objective of the U.S. strategy should, rather, be that the Pakistani public sees it to be in Pakistan's own interest to partner with the United States and other allies against militancy and extremism. The "hearts and minds" language of U.S. public diplomacy efforts is often overly focused on increasing America's standing among Pakistanis, rather than on increasing the standing of the Pakistani government vis-à-vis its own population. This latter metric is ultimately a more critical component of counterinsurgency planning than Pakistani views of America at large.

Adopt a language of common interests and common threats

It would seem to be obvious that U.S. diplomats should seek to frame American engagement with Pakistan through the lens of common interests and common threats. And while many American diplomats do present messages which resonate with the Pakistani public, high-level statements in the years following 9/11 were strikingly tone deaf to Pakistani sensibilities. The "war on terror" remained the rhetorical focal point of American discourse toward Pakistan long after most Pakistanis — even those sympathetic to the United States — had rejected it as inimical to their country's own strategic interests.

In light of this experience, the U.S. should continue the trend, begun under Ambassador Patterson, of framing bilateral relations in terms of a wide set of common interests, to include not only cooperation against extremism and terrorism — which pose a common threat to both countries — but also a stable and prosperous Afghanistan; the prevention of nuclear war with India; expanded regional trade; improved health and education indicators; and democratization. In a country in which nearly every American statement is parsed and debated in the local papers, the diplomatic tone set by the ambassador and other senior officials has an extraordinarily broad impact on public opinion. President Bush's rhetoric, while slow to adapt to the post-election environment in the spring of 2008, eventually underwent a transformation and effectively struck a balanced tone during the July 2008 visit of Prime Minister Gillani to Washington.[19]

Even so, American officials must make greater efforts to avoid language which reinforces the perception of Pakistani dependence on, or subservience to, the United States. Comments from the White House, for example, suggesting that "President Zardari is going to have to do what he thinks is right for his country, regardless of public opinion" serve only to drive a wedge between the Pakistani civilian leadership and the public at large, rather than contribute to Pakistani "ownership" of the problem of militancy.[20] Similarly, while U.S. officials may be frustrated by the activities of the Pakistani intelligence services, it is plainly counterproductive to press for reform of the ISI by way of public statements, as this only reinforces the perception that the United States manages the internal workings of the Pakistani state.[21]

Use rhetoric that isolates Islamist insurgent groups

The Pakistani press is exceptionally attentive to statements made by Americans — not only diplomats, but also U.S. policymakers and members of Congress in Washington. It is not uncommon for a statement by a junior congressman to make the front page of Pakistani newspapers.[22] American rhetoric on Pakistan from all quarters therefore plays an important role in framing common interests and common threats.

The U.S. should take care to follow the recommendations recently given by the National Counterterrorism Center to avoid labeling Islamic insurgent groups as "jihadists," "mujahidin," or "Islamofascists."[23] Outside of a relatively narrow liberal elite class, many moderate Pashtuns in the Frontier retain positive associations with the term "jihadi," and many continue to associate the idea of the "Taliban" with that of a morally upright, anti-imperialist movement in Afghanistan in the 1990s. These terms should be avoided in reference to militants. Instead, the U.S. should follow the lead of the government of Pakistan, which has wisely chosen to label insurgents in the Frontier as "extremists," "terrorists," and "criminals" in an attempt to isolate these groups from the Islamic mainstream.[24]

American officials also need to be careful in speaking about the role of religion in public life. Many Pakistanis believe that the U.S. intends to undermine Pakistan's religious character and advance a Westernized and secular vision of the nation state. Pakistan's religious parties effectively play on this rhetoric to create a perceived gulf between Pakistani and American interests. The U.S. can work to debunk the perceived "secularization agenda" by taking care to affirm that the U.S. has no intention of changing Pakistan's religious character, and by avoiding the use of the word "secular," particularly in reference to the Pakistani educational system. (The concept of "secularism" is often translated pejoratively as *ladiniyat*, which roughly translates as "without religion.")

As religious education is integrated into the public school system of Pakistan, reference to "secular" education is read as an assault on the religious character of the state itself.[25] Early versions of the bill H.R. 1, introduced in January 2007 in the U.S. House of Representatives, called for "building effective government institutions, especially secular public schools" in Pakistan.[26] Although the language of the legislation was later changed to refer simply to "public education," the earlier version referencing secular education was widely commented upon in the Pakistani press. American officials should, for similar reasons, also refrain from publicly referring to parties such as the PPP and ANP as "secular" — a label which sometimes tarnishes their credentials in the public square.

Highlight the bleak realities of Taliban governance

The paradox of Taliban governance in both the settled and the tribal areas of the Frontier is that "Talibanism" is often popular as an idea, but deeply unpopular as a reality. Taliban insurgents are frequently brutal, killing tribal elders, disrupting commerce, closing schools, and bringing with them a reign of fear. Both Pakistan and the U.S. need to make greater efforts to highlight the disjuncture between Islamic values and the harsh methods employed by the Taliban.

U.S. officials are obviously not well suited to deliver this message. But the United States can partner with the government of Pakistan to fund local programs which publicize un-Islamic behavior by insurgent groups, and encourage respected clerics to speak out — even obliquely — against militancy and vigilante Islamization. The U.S. has done a particularly poor job in highlighting the brutality of the Afghan Taliban; press reports in the Frontier focus overwhelmingly on U.S.- and coalition-inflicted collateral damage to Afghan civilians, and only marginally on the ways in which Taliban fighters violate both Islamic and Pashtun norms.[27]

Assist in shutting down insurgent propaganda

Illegal FM radio stations continue to act as vehicles by which Islamist insurgent groups rally support, both in the tribal areas and in provincial districts such as Swabi, Swat, and Charsadda.[28] The low-power stations, which likely number over a hundred, have proven popular with women and have helped clerics to mobilize local communities in favor of strict *shariah* laws.[29] The U.S. should provide technical assistance in radio jamming to the government of Pakistan, which has struggled to suppress the proliferation of banned stations.

Moreover, the U.S. should encourage and incentivize Pakistan to set up counter-messaging programs on FM frequencies. This approach was proposed by U.S. officials in Pakistan as early as 2005, but received little traction within the U.S. bureaucracy due to concerns over American involvement in "religious" programming.[30] While the U.S. must of course take care not to have a direct hand in religious programming, there is no reason why the U.S. cannot promote joint programs with the government which both disrupt and counter a primary channel of insurgent mobilization in the Frontier.

Encourage exchanges between people of faith

It is not only the Islamists in the Frontier who believe that the conflict between the Muslim world and the West is fundamentally religious in nature; this belief is widespread throughout the NWFP and the tribal areas.[31] Ironically, many Muslims in the Frontier have an inverted view of American religion: they tend to believe that the American government operates in large part from religious motivations, while the American public is for the most part secular.[32] This perception is problematic on two levels. It reinforces the tendency, in the words of Anna Simons, for Muslims to look at America and "see a religion pretending to be an ideology."[33] And it ignores the value of Muslims coming to understand Americans as a religious people, and America as a country uniquely accepting of religious practice. In such a context, people of faith can play an important "track two" role in shifting public perceptions — both Pakistani perceptions about America, and American perceptions about Pakistan.

The U.S. should promote track two dialogues along several fronts. First, American policymakers should scale up lecture and exchange programs which bring American Muslims into dialogue with Pakistanis. There is intense interest in the Frontier about the Muslim experience in America.[34] Such dialogues create a public space in which to debunk "clash of civilizations" rhetoric, and also provide a compelling framework in which to discuss a state's obligation toward religious minorities.[35] Second, the U.S. should encourage dialogues between American and Pakistani faith leaders. Even very conservative Muslims in the Frontier, including those who supported the Taliban in Afghanistan and advocate for expansion of *shariah,* are often eager, for both religious and political reasons, to interact with Christians from the West.[36] These dialogues can provide indirect channels through which to discuss cultural and even political issues, and — particularly when amplified by the media — can serve to disarm the rhetoric which frames the ongoing conflict in religious and civilizational terms.[37]

More broadly, American public diplomacy needs to move beyond its narrow preference for interacting with "moderate Muslims." The existing programs, while not without value, too often fail to engage those leaders who actually exert social and political influence.[38] As Anna Simons cogently argues, "While moderates may vote, they cannot seize attention, let alone galvanize youth or sway public opinion, unless they are willing to speak or act with as much passion as partisans — and by definition they don't."[39] Rather than selecting Islamic leaders who are likely to perform well on interfaith panels in Washington (that is, those who are moderate by the standards of American liberalism), the U.S. should engage with those leaders who are moderate within their own spheres of influence. Although these interlocutors often bring with them a great deal of baggage — anti-Americanism, support for troubling Islamist agendas, dubious linkages with more radical groups, etc. — Americans should reject the trope that such interaction "legitimizes" Islamist actors, and instead find creative ways to bring them into contact with a wider array of religious and political leaders.

Meet tangible needs

The U.S. response to the October 2005 earthquake, which devastated parts of both the NWFP and Pakistani-held Kashmir, was arguably its most successful public diplomacy effort in the region following 9/11. The relief efforts resulted in an uptick in favorable opinion toward America, and may have had a lasting positive impact on local perceptions of both domestic and foreign NGOs.[40] More recently, the U.S. provided over $115 million in food assistance to relieve the pressures of dramatic food inflation caused primarily by supply-side shocks.[41] And it gave a token amount of emergency assistance funding (with more promised from the international community) to support those who had been displaced by the military operations in Bajaur and Mohmand agencies.[42]

The U.S. should broaden its assistance programs in Pakistan to meet perceived needs, particularly in the energy sector. Highly visible infrastructure projects such hydroelectric generation and roads should be an important part of the U.S. aid portfolio.[43] The American experience in Iraq demonstrated the value of providing discretionary funds to political officials on the ground, so that they are able to respond rapidly and effectively to changing needs.

SECURITY AND COUNTERINSURGENCY

Much of the talk about U.S. support for counterinsurgency efforts in the Frontier has focused on American provision of equipment and training in irregular military tactics for the Frontier Corps in the FATA. This support is worthwhile and should continue, since the FC constitutes a key part of Pakistan's border defense policy and a necessary vehicle through which to conduct joint counterterrorism activities.

Most actions undertaken by the FC, however, should not be confused with actual counterinsurgency activities. Any review of the literature on insurgency will suggest that successful counterinsurgency efforts are fundamentally about a *political contestation* over the legitimacy of a given government. Absent a strategic program of coordinated political reforms in the FATA, there is essentially no government in the tribal areas to contest. FC activities, while useful, are maneuver-oriented and tactical rather than politically-oriented and strategic. Counterinsurgency activity in the FATA — whether by the FC or the army — will not achieve overall political objectives until and unless the government begins to conduct such activities in the context of a coordinated program of governance reform, such as the one outlined below.

In the meantime, the U.S. should direct some attention to the settled areas of the Frontier — a region in which there *is* a government whose legitimacy can be contested, and in which insurgent groups have sought to expand their writ at the expense of the state. A focus on the settled areas is complementary to a FATA policy in that it focuses on helping Pakistan to contain the insurgent threat, and prevent its spillover into areas which might threaten the stability of the state itself.

Facilitate counterinsurgency planning in the settled areas

Any counterinsurgency plan in the settled areas must grapple with a basic question: What should the state do in the first 24, 48, and 72 hours following a movement by "Taliban" into a village, or a threat against a government or civilian target? Response by the state needs to be unpredictable enough that the militants cannot easily thwart it, but also predictable enough that locals will choose to bandwagon with the state and not the outsiders. Such a response also requires close coordination between local government, police, paramilitary, and military leaders.

Faced with a rising tide of insurgent activity in Swat, the southern settled districts, and parts of the Peshawar valley, the Pakistani government has, in large part, responded slowly and ineffectively. In the Swat valley in 2007, the state responded to an increasingly-confident Islamist movement with long periods of indecision, followed by a dramatic military escalation involving helicopter gunships and ground troops. Although the military operations proved to be impressive and moderately successful, the striking gap between tepid government inaction on the one hand, and highly kinetic military response on the other, highlights the need for a more graduated and coordinated state response that brings both political and military pressures to bear in a manner that leverages the legitimacy of the state.

Toward this end, the U.S. should work with the government of Pakistan to conduct a needs-assessment on the ways in which American support could aid the development of a robust counterinsurgency response in the settled areas. Such a program could include, per the below, police and judicial measures; targeted political efforts; and structural reforms. These changes must be locally-owned, and developed with input from political, military, bureaucratic, and religious stakeholders. But insofar as the U.S. takes an interest in containing the spread of neo-Taliban groups in the settled areas of the Frontier, it can and should assist in building the capacity of the Pakistani state to carry out these kinds of reforms.

Fund rapid-response police units

Police forces constitute the first line of defense against militancy in the NWFP. Unfortunately, police in the Frontier have been under-equipped, under-trained, and under-staffed to respond to the growing Talibanization. Most often, police forces simply capitulate when militants enter into a village. "The police are scared," lamented former interior minister Aftab Sherpao. "They don't want to get involved."[44] So long as local populations believe that police forces will not take timely and decisive action against insurgents, public support will continue to work against government efforts at controlling state territory.

The ANP-led government in the NWFP has put forward proposals to create an elite police force of 7,500 which could be deployed on short notice to secure areas which had come under the influence of "miscreants" or militants.[45] Building this capacity is long overdue. Earlier in 2008, the outgoing provincial police chief noted that the lessons from the Swat insurgency were that "[we] have to respond to emerging situations at an earlier stage and should not delay action."[46]

Such delays have facilitated a stunning expansion of militant influence; in only two months in 2008, the under-equipped police forces in NWFP seized nearly two thousand small arms, eight rocket launchers, three thousand detonators, over a hundred kilograms of explosives, and more than 200,000 rounds of ammunition.[47]

U.S. efforts to date in support of policing in the Frontier have been piecemeal, and focused predominantly on the Pak-Afghan border rather than on the threats within the NWFP itself.[48] In light of the current environment, the U.S. should take steps to fund, equip, and support (perhaps in cooperation with other international donors) a new rapid-response police force which would be tasked with responding to militant threats within the first 24 or 48 hours of an incident. The force should also be given authority to operate in the provincially administered tribal areas, at the direction of the appropriate political officer.

Further, the U.S. should consider supporting an innovative program which has been put forward by the government of NWFP to raise volunteer youth forces (labeled a "Special Police Force") which would be deputized at the local level to report on militant activity and take basic preventative action.[49] These kinds of programs are particularly important in areas such a Swat, in which the government must eventually backfill policing capabilities when the military forces withdraw to their barracks.[50]

More generally, the government of Pakistan should focus on supporting local communities if and when they choose to mobilize against the insurgents. This community mobilization is beginning to happen sporadically in places such as Dir, Buner, and Peshawar.[51] Citizen mobilization programs which raise *lashkars* against local militants might represent a very effective counterinsurgency model in the Frontier, since most communities have both the legitimating mechanisms (*jirgas*) and means (small arms) to mobilize quickly. Almost by definition, the state cannot direct these *lashkars*, but it can encourage and support them. In some areas and in some cases, consistent and timely state support of *lashkars* has the potential to induce a cascading effect in encouraging other communities to take up arms against militant organizations.[52]

Establish a Joint Justice Working Group

Neo-Taliban groups which have established a foothold in the Frontier have often proven to be unpopular on account of their brutality and their seizure of local assets. One key area, however, in which these insurgents have effectively played on local discontent is on matters of justice. The judicial system in the Frontier, inherited from the British, comes under nearly constant criticism for its partiality, corruption, and slow processing of cases.[53] Taliban groups have proven adept at exploiting frustration over the judicial process by establishing *qazi* courts which adjudicate disputes and award punitive judgments on the spot. These courts have blossomed in almost every Pashtun-majority part of the Frontier — including the tribal agencies, PATA regions, the Swat valley, and even in Peshawar district itself. According to reliable reports, "the Taliban have been campaigning in the Tribal Areas and asking locals to submit their complaints in the Qazi courts rather than the country's courts if they want 'quick and easy' justice."[54] The use of *qazi* courts by Islamist movements as a means by which to bypass or challenge the writ of the state is long-established in the Frontier, particularly in areas such as Swat.[55]

There are two compelling reasons why the U.S. should focus on justice issues in the Frontier. First, these issues constitute a powerful means by which Taliban groups win "hearts and minds" and encourage local populations to bandwagon against the state. Counterinsurgency is a competition for constituent loyalty, and without targeted reforms to the judicial process, insurgents are bound to find the populations amenable to *ad hoc* Islamist justice and not to that of the state. Second, an orientation toward justice issues could contribute to a public diplomacy strategy that resonates with the Islamic mainstream. While American rhetoric tends to emphasize "freedom," the concept of "justice" is in fact a much more stirring idea among Muslims in the Frontier (and, arguably, in the Muslim world as a whole).[56]

The U.S. should work with the government of Pakistan to establish a Joint Justice Working Group which would explore tangible and immediate ways in which to deal with the competition in judicial services which is threatening to undermine the legitimacy of the state. Specifically, the group could identify high-risk areas (at the district or *tehsil* level) in which discontent over the local judiciary has reached critical levels; provide expanded resources to the judicial system to expedite caseloads; and support voluntary alternative-dispute mechanisms — perhaps framed in Islamic terms, but adjudicated by state-regulated clerics — which could supplant the *ad hoc qazi* courts of the Taliban.[57] While there are inevitable trade-offs between considerations of due process and judicial expediency, the Pakistani government should be aggressive in experimenting with new judicial frameworks which might address the dangerous and widening gap between public expectations and state services.

Selectively support peace negotiations

Pakistan's peace deals with Taliban groups in the Frontier have been widely ridiculed by foreign observers for proving to be more advantageous to the insurgents than to the state. In some instances, this has clearly been the case. The deals in Waziristan in 2006 resulted in an increase in cross-border activity into Afghanistan, and simply served to provide the militants with breathing space in which to reestablish tactical advantage. The government has often negotiated from a position of weakness or cut deals when it needed breathing space for political objectives of its own — such as prior to the February 2008 elections.[58] Taken by themselves, these deals have amounted to little, and justly invite skepticism by American officials.[59]

That said, while peace negotiations are plainly insufficient to deal with the growing Islamist insurgency in the Frontier, they can nonetheless be necessary. On a political level, these deals reflect a deep-seated cultural norm among the Pashtun population, which expects that the government will — and *must* — engage in one or more rounds of negotiated agreements before resorting to more direct police or military action. The *jirga* culture of the Frontier is such that the government is often under intense pressure to engage in talks, even if the resulting agreements are bound to fail.

More strategically, however, negotiations can serve to bolster the credibility of the state, and pave the way for more effective and kinetic action. Counterinsurgency operations work best when they cultivate the perception of state legitimacy, and simultaneously diminish the profile of the insurgent as unreasonable, unreliable, and ignoble. Whatever tactical concessions a negotiation process might provide to insurgents — and often those concessions are not insubstantial — the government can gain the upper hand by demonstrating its forbearance, and then leveraging that gained legitimacy to take targeted measures against the insurgents.

At its best, this strategy requires certain conditions, none of which are politically infeasible, but which together demand a level of political-military coordination which to date the government of Pakistan has not demonstrated. These conditions include, first, that the agreements be made public and are publicly intelligible, such that it is clear when and how the insurgents violate the terms. Second, that the state respond in some way to the political demands made by the insurgents (even if those demands are not the underlying drivers of the insurgency), in this case, demands for a more just, Islamic system of governance. And third, that the state be prepared to break off the cycle of negotiations once it has demonstrated its good faith, and bring police and military pressure to bear against anti-state forces.[60]

The U.S. should also recognize that not all peace deals are created equal. As the narrative above argues, there are important historical and political differences between various Islamist movements in the Frontier: although, for example, insurgents in Swat established an alliance of convenience with militants in Waziristan, the two cases require responses which, while coordinated, sit at two ends of a spectrum. Even though Swat has a history of small Islamist uprisings led by charismatic leaders, it is an area which is basically not amenable to strict Islamist rule, and one in which negotiated peace deals — coordinated with targeted military and police action — stand a good chance of being successful over the long-run. In fact, while the peace deals negotiated by the ANP-led government in Swat in the spring of 2008 lasted no more than a few months, the government's negotiating strategy served to buttress its own legitimacy with the population in the Frontier, and pave the way for stronger state action against the militants that summer.[61]

Further along the spectrum, provincially administered tribal areas such as Darra Adam Khel and some FATA regions such as Khyber agency present a more challenging case in which the government has to rely on tribal leaders to enforce agreements, and must contend with Taliban tactics which have disrupted traditional social norms. In these areas, the government can still gain from negotiations and from co-opting insurgent demands, but is more likely to find peace deals to be of tactical rather than strategic value. In areas such as Waziristan, the state is presented with a different situation altogether: faced with a longstanding governance void and a systematic program by insurgents to debilitate traditional structures of social and political accountability, the tactical downsides of peace deals are often likely to outweigh strategic gains in terms of government legitimacy.

The U.S., while remaining skeptical of Pakistan's negotiations with neo-Taliban insurgents, should nonetheless balance short-term tactical concerns over these peace deals against the importance of long-term political solutions. If the state is to succeed in politically isolating insurgent Islamist movements — particularly in the settled areas and northern tribal areas — it will have to use negotiations to its advantage, and account for regional variation in devising strategies which target local movements and local demands.

Curtail American operations in the FATA

Air strikes by American Predator drones in the FATA are often viewed as a classic tradeoff between counterterrorism and counterinsurgency objectives. This is largely true, as the gains which accrue from the killing of senior al Qaeda operatives come at the expense of further inflaming local opinion.[62] These targeted killings are viewed by residents of the Frontier as particularly unjust, not only because they technically violate Pakistani sovereignty, but because they are seen by Pashtuns as a cowardly and dishonorable form of retaliation.[63] The attack at Damadola in January 2006, in Bajaur agency, killed over a dozen civilians and elicited a wave of protests against Pakistani cooperation with the United States.[64] A subsequent strike in Bajaur in October of that year, which killed an estimated 80 people, also garnered a strong reaction, in large part because the religious parties in the NWFP chose to exploit it as a political issue.[65]

Beginning in late 2006 the strikes, while still not formally acknowledged by the U.S. government, slowly became an accepted part of the political landscape. Protests against the attacks generally waned, and during periods when the religious parties were distracted by other political activity — such as the run-up to the February 2008 elections — the strikes received only modest attention. At the same time, the Predator program became increasingly important for U.S. policy objectives, and seen as a vital element of American counterterrorism capability against both al Qaeda and Waziri Taliban networks. In early 2008 the rules of engagement were reportedly relaxed, permitting U.S. agencies a wider rein in conducting the drone operations inside Pakistani territory.[66]

In the late summer of 2008, the U.S. began escalating the frequency of drone attacks in the FATA. This increased pressure on the civilian government in Islamabad, which was forced to account for growing domestic discontent with the covert strikes. In spite of this discontent, it is expected that the United States, in accordance with its legitimate counterterrorism objectives, will continue to conduct these operations in the tribal areas. And although it no longer appears likely that an individual drone attack will spark widespread political disruption in the Frontier, these strikes do set back America's broader efforts to slow militant recruitment and mobilization, and should therefore be limited.[67]

Ground incursions introduce a much more dangerous dynamic. The American special forces operations in Waziristan in early September 2008 generated a wave of protests from senior political and military leaders, followed by a spate of reports which alleged that Frontier Corps soldiers fired on U.S. aircraft in the tribal areas.[68] It is unclear whether the Pakistani military's vocal opposition to the ground incursions was in fact genuine, or staged for domestic consumption. It is equally unclear whether the American actions were conducted primarily for their counterterrorism value, or to send a signal to the Pakistani government about the seriousness with which the United States views the cross-border incursions.[69] In any case, such actions serve to weaken the civilian government; strengthen the hand of right-of-center and religious parties, which often leverage external events for domestic political gain; and complicate efforts to bolster pro-government tribal elders throughout the FATA.

GOVERNANCE REFORM IN THE NWFP

Observers who trace the rise of extremism in the Frontier tend to focus on exogenous factors, such as the Afghan *jihad* and the American war in Afghanistan following 9/11. These are of course critical events. But comparatively less attention has been paid to the internal, structural weaknesses of the state which have facilitated the rise of radical Islamist movements. This section and the one which follows examine these weaknesses and the crises of governance in the settled and tribal areas, respectively.[70]

Encourage Pakistan to revisit devolution reforms

One contributing factor to the lackluster response by the government of NWFP to the rising tide of Talibanization has been former President Musharraf's overhaul of the local government system in 2001. The Local Government Ordinance (LGO), commonly known as the Devolution plan, devolved powers from a class of elite deputy commissioners — each of whom oversaw several administrative districts, and wielded broad discretionary authority — to a class of local elected officials. The reforms were intended to encourage local ownership and decision-making; boost delivery of health, education, and other government services; buttress the military's democratic credentials; and bypass the provincial government so that elites in Islamabad could exert direct political influence on local government.[71]

Devolution did, to some extent, further each of these substantive and political goals. But by dramatically remapping the relationships among civil authority, the police, and elected politicians, it also created real challenges to social and political stability. As state authority under Devolution became simultaneously more rigid and more diffuse, the government was increasingly unable to deal effectively with emerging threats to law and order. Elected local leaders, particularly those with ties to religious parties, succumbed to political pressures and refused to take action against Islamists to whom they were sympathetic; local government officers, stripped of their discretionary powers, had to wait days or even weeks for authorization from Peshawar to act against new threats. Furthermore, police forces emerged unconstrained by clear civilian chains of command, and became increasingly independent and often politicized.[72] Musharraf's hand in formulating the Devolution plan made it politically infeasible to revisit the reforms while he held power. Now that the civilian leadership is exercising greater authority, both the federal and provincial governments have begun a critical reexamination of the LGO and have taken preliminary steps to reestablish the authority of the civil officers.[73]

Amendment of the Devolution plan is ultimately a matter for the Pakistani government to resolve. But it has broader implications which concern the international community — both in terms of maximizing the effectiveness of development monies, and in building the capacity of the state to respond to movements which threaten Pakistan and its neighbors. The provincial government's initial steps in reforming the local government system in the Frontier have been positive, but the true test of the revised system lies in the details. The U.S., along with the World Bank, ADB, and other international stakeholders with experience in structural reform, should work closely with the Pakistani government to encourage amendments to the governance system which reestablish a decisive chain of command and provide reasonable discretionary authority to local officials who need to be able to respond quickly in the face of insurgent activity.[74]

Support coordination across settled-tribal boundaries

The Frontier today is a complex patchwork of governance systems — of settled districts, provincially administered tribal areas, frontier regions, and federally administered tribal areas. Each of these has its own unique history and logic. But the amalgam of frameworks has also made it difficult to manage anything resembling a coordinated counterinsurgency response to the growing radicalization of the Frontier. Prior to the Devolution system, the provincial home secretary in Peshawar served as the link between the settled areas, the PATA, and the FATA. This critical link was broken in 2002 when, following the promulgation of the LGO, the government began transferring administrative oversight of the FATA from a special cell in the provincial government to a new FATA Secretariat in Peshawar. Although the establishment of the FATA Secretariat was justified, not unreasonably, on the grounds that it would improve the state's management of the tribal areas in both the security and development sectors, this seemingly-obscure bureaucratic reorganization in fact handicapped the government's ability to deal with insurgent groups which crossed freely between settled and tribal regions.[75]

In the area around Bannu in southern NWFP, for example, neo-Taliban groups moved frequently between Bannu city (governed under the LGO, with elected representatives from both mainstream and religious parties), the buffer areas of the Frontier Region Bannu (a territory nominally managed by the district coordination officer, on behalf of the governor), and North Waziristan agency (part of the FATA, administered by the FATA Secretariat). By many accounts, this fragmentation of authority contributed to an environment which was conducive to the entrenchment of local insurgent groups, particularly in the border areas stretching from Peshawar in the north to Dera Ismail Khan in the south.[76]

The state has begun taking steps to address this coordination failure, but much more aggressive actions are required. In January 2008, NWFP Governor Owais Ahmad Ghani announced the establishment of Regional Coordination Officers (RCOs) who would be tasked with overseeing the government's law and order initiatives in both the settled and tribal areas.[77] And in October 2008, the provincial government announced its intention to restore the post of Deputy Commissioner (DC) and revive aspects of the former system of governance.[78] These new civilian offices are a welcome development, but their authority needs to be strengthened, and their functions need to be integrated even more broadly with joint border management programs, such as the U.S.-funded border coordination centers and the command-and-control authority for the Frontier Constabulary which patrols the international border.

Encouraging this kind of "deep coordination" — extending from the heart of the settled districts to the Durand Line (and beyond) — needs to be at the forefront of U.S. planning, as both governments partner to integrate political and military counterinsurgency activities throughout the Frontier. Given that the neo-Taliban groups regularly disregard both internal and international boundaries, it is in the U.S. interest to see that the government of Pakistan has a robust capability to deal with insurgent movement across internal administrative lines as well as international ones.

Discourage substantive shariah expansion

Faced with demands by Islamist groups for implementation of *shariah*, the government of NWFP has historically sought to accommodate the spirit of these demands without unduly carving out substantive exceptions to the state's established judicial process. This approach is wise insofar as most Pashtuns express strong support for *shariah*, yet reject the extreme interpretations of Islamic law associated with the Afghan Taliban. To most Pashtuns, *shariah* simply means good governance carried out by leaders who share their religious values — not, as those in the West might expect, a draconian theocratic state.

There are both advantages and dangers to accommodating demands by Islamist groups for the expansion of *shariah* in the Frontier. Given the reality that even most conservative Pashtuns support *shariah* but not theocracy, the state can sometimes co-opt Islamist movements by recommitting itself to Islamic values, and making modest concessions on nomenclature. Although, for example, the 1999 Shariah Nizam-e-Adl act in Malakand division (instituted after the TNSM uprising of 1994) was not without its flaws, it did not fundamentally reorder the system of justice: civil magistrates were dubbed "qazis" and litigants under the *qazi* system still had recourse to the High Court in Peshawar. Even mostly-symbolic government concessions in this domain can sometimes be enough to drive a wedge between the population at large and the hard-core Islamists, paving the way for a reestablishment of the writ of the state.

At the same time, the U.S. ought to be wary of any changes which create islands of *shariah* regulation that are detached from established judicial processes; which offer preemptive concessions in areas which have not seen significant Islamist agitation or have no history of alternative Islamic judicial systems; or which might adversely affect the judicial recourse available to women and minority groups. While modest *shariah* concessions may at times simply reflect a pragmatic policy by the state in its negotiations with Islamist insurgents, they also set a troubling precedent by reinforcing the belief that the civil system of justice is neither sufficiently Islamic, nor sufficiently legitimate.

Weighing these considerations, both U.S. and Pakistani observers were right to criticize the Shariah Nizam-e-Adl amendment which was proposed in early 2008 by the caretaker government of NWFP for application in the Malakand division. As originally drafted, it would have delinked the *qazi* courts from High Court oversight; extended *shariah* regulations to districts such as Chitral in which there was little demand for such changes; and may have empowered local clerics — serving as Muavin-e-Qazi (helper to a *qazi*) — to press for judgments inconsistent with Pakistan's commitments on gender and minority rights.[79] The amendment was ultimately revised by the new provincial government following the February elections and finalized in late September 2008, but retains several troubling features.[80]

GOVERNANCE REFORM IN THE FATA

Following the February 2008 elections, there have increasingly been calls for regularizing the system of governance in the tribal areas, which continues to be ruled under the Frontier Crimes Regulation (FCR).[81] There are four reasons behind the advocacy for FATA reform. First, the region is rightly seen by security planners as an "ungoverned" space conducive to the development and perpetuation of insurgent and terrorist safe havens.[82] Following the reestablishment of al Qaeda operations from FATA, this has become a preeminent national security issue for the United States. Second, the Pakistan army's failed intervention in Waziristan in 2004, combined with actions taken by the neo-Taliban insurgents targeting political agents and tribal *maliks*, has resulted in the collapse of the political agent system in several of the southern tribal agencies.[83] There is a recognition among some military and civilian leaders that it may be more profitable to move forward with FCR reforms than to attempt a reinvigoration of the now-discredited political agent system.

Third, civil society advocates have proposed FCR reforms in order to bring FATA governance into conformity with international civil and human rights norms.[84] The FCR system lacks basic civil protections; allows for collective punishment of individual crimes; and places extraordinary discretionary powers in the hands of the political agent, who often faces perverse incentives to collude with tribal elders for their mutual financial gain.[85] And finally, there are political pressures behind the current agitation for reform: the ANP would like to see the FATA integrated into the NWFP, as it believes that integration will serve both its ideological aspirations (for pan-Pashtunism), and electoral prospects.

FATA reform is a highly complex subject, and a variety of proposals have been put forward to bring the region into the governance mainstream.[86] U.S. officials were slow to recognize the importance of FATA governance reform to overall U.S. security and development objectives in the tribal areas, but to the credit of both the U.S. and Pakistani bureaucracies, the subject began to be seriously raised in late 2007 and early 2008 in bilateral fora.[87] Governance reform ought to be at the center of U.S. political, security, and development strategy with respect to the FATA, and American officials would be wise to take a keen interest in several of the current proposals and their implications.

Support extension of the Political Parties Act

Universal suffrage was extended to the FATA in 1997, and residents of the tribal areas now elect members to the National Assembly in Islamabad. Political parties, however, are officially banned in the tribal areas. Candidates for the National Assembly therefore campaign on a non-party basis, even though their implicit party affiliations are widely known.

The U.S. should support extension of the Political Parties Act to the FATA. This legal change would be largely symbolic, but nonetheless politically meaningful. The current political environment, in which party activity is formally suppressed, favors parties such as the JUI-F which can mobilize via *madrassah* networks. Allowing formal party activity would send an important signal to residents of the FATA about their political rights and their place in the larger Pakistani polity, and would provide incremental benefits to mainstream and nationalist parties seeking to compete for votes in the tribal areas.

Promote institution-building paradigms

Much of the discussion over FATA reforms has focused on repeal of the most egregious sections of the FCR which violate universal norms of civil and human rights. Repeal of these outmoded regulations should be high on Pakistan's reform agenda. But the most critical reforms are those which focus on institutions of governance. Aside from the office of the political agent, and the relatively moribund "agency councils," the FATA lacks institutions through which political power and state resources can be channeled. Absent institutional development, FATA reforms will have little effect in integrating the tribal areas into the Pakistani mainstream, or addressing the governance vacuum which has proven to be so advantageous to neo-Taliban groups.

The U.S. should strongly promote the development of institution-oriented reform plans. These might include the establishment of local government structures (directly or indirectly elected) which feed into a FATA Council on the model of a provincial assembly; courts which establish a right of appeal to Peshawar or Islamabad; and modest civil institutions through which to coordinate development programs.[88] Of these, a local elected government is perhaps the most important. Such a system need not mirror the local government system in the settled areas, but at the very least the state should begin a process by which to establish a baseline set of government functions, and build up institutions which, over time, can constitute legitimate alternative centers of local power.

Both Pakistani and American officials have repeatedly raised objections to pursuing a robust, institution-oriented reform path in the FATA. In the first place, they have argued that such reforms are at odds with the *riwaj* (custom) of the tribal areas, and inconsistent with Pashtunwali social norms. It is true that the long history of indirect governance of the tribal areas — first by the British, and today by Islamabad — has cultivated an aversion among the FATA population to interference in tribal matters. But rather than reflecting an unchanging Pashtunwali, the preference in the FATA for local tradition and non-interference is historically conditioned and constantly in flux. Millions of Pashtuns live today under modern systems of governance, not only in the NWFP, but in Karachi and the Gulf states. The cultural reductionists contribute an important word of caution to the debate over FATA reforms, but ultimately fail to account for the dynamism and adaptability which Pashtun society has demonstrated over the last three decades.[89]

Second, some officials fear that institutions of local government would end up being dominated by the religious parties, or even representatives of the Taliban. These fears are not without merit, but they ignore the significant potential for local institutions to serve as mechanisms by which the state can exert political and financial leverage. The history of the MMA government in the NWFP demonstrates the ways in which the state can co-opt and in some instances moderate religious party participation in governance. Even a local government system which, for a time, was dominated in areas by the religious parties would be preferable to the present governance void in the FATA, in that it would help to channel religious energies into the formal process rather than into militancy; would incrementally expand the footprint of the state in the tribal areas; and would create avenues through which new politically-minded groups could obtain state patronage.

Institution-oriented reform, in short, has its risks. But it is considerably less risky than trying to counteract an Islamist insurgency in the context of practically no institutions whatsoever. The creation of well-bounded, culturally-adapted, representative political institutions would send a signal to the local population that the governance *status quo* in the FATA can and must change, and would lay the groundwork for meaningfully integrating the tribal areas into the political and economic life of the state.

Encourage a gradual reform path

The only governance policy worse than continuing the *status quo* would be one of abrupt change. Even in light of the current instability in the tribal areas, officials in the FATA Secretariat are right to worry about the potentially destabilizing effects of reform. Surveys and anecdotal evidence suggest that there is a desire for political change in the FATA, but as yet no clear sentiment on precisely what kind of change should be implemented.[90] Any reform plan should therefore pursue a gradualist approach, taking local leaders into confidence and phasing-in changes based on conditions on the ground.

The U.S. should encourage two kinds of gradualism. First, it should use its leverage with the Pakistani government to promote a geographically phased program of reform. Some areas of the FATA such as Waziristan are simply not amenable at the present time to major political reforms, particularly institution-building. Other tribal agencies, such as Orakzai, Mohmand, Kurram, and even Khyber — while not without their own security problems — are better candidates for reform. Beginning governance reforms in several small regions, and coordinating that reform with development and security incentives, would create a positive demonstration effect which could then be extended to the FATA at large.[91]

Additionally, the U.S. should discourage the government from implementing "comprehensive" reforms which might further destabilize the FATA in the near-term. In particular, some observers have proposed reforms which would essentially repeat the mistakes of the Devolution plan in the settled areas — that is, devolving powers to local elected representatives while simultaneously weakening the discretionary authorities of government officers. A program, for example, which transferred powers to local elected councils, while at the same time curtailing the powers of the political agent, would likely result in a dysfunctional system even less equipped to deal with the rising tide of militancy.

Instead, the state should pursue a gradualist approach focused on long-term investment in political institutions, while in the short-term retaining some important discretionary powers of the civil authority.[92] One possible approach would be to establish an intermediate state structure between the FCR and the settled system, modeled in part on areas of the provincially administered tribal areas. Malakand district in the NWFP, for example, was once under the FCR, but later was adapted in the 1970s into a PATA region. As such, it retained a political agent and a system of "levied" police, but was also given a system of courts, and eventually an elected district council. A hybrid system such as this one would not be without its own challenges, but it represents one possible intermediate path which both defers to local sensibilities, and incrementally advances the reach of the state and the set of shared interests between the tribal region and the country at large.

Account for local sensibilities

When Prime Minister Gillani announced in his inaugural address in March 2008 that his government would abolish the FCR, the response from the FATA was decidedly mixed. While some tribal leaders celebrated the announcement, others, concerned perhaps about their own continued access to state patronage, expressed reservations. Some of those reservations were expressed in Islamic terms, as tribal leaders suggested that the FCR should be replaced by some form of Islamic law.[93] Clearly, there will be pressure on the state to ensure that whatever succeeds the FCR conforms with local custom and with Islamic sensibilities.[94]

It is quite possible that the government will choose to frame the revised system of governance in the FATA in Islamic terms. This should not necessarily trouble U.S. observers, as again there is often a wide gap between the rhetoric and the substance of *shariah* regulations. The U.S. should recognize that it is the substance of FATA reforms which are critical, and that if nascent state institutions are to compete politically with insurgent institutions such as *qazi* courts which have the sheen of religiosity, they may need to appeal to religious legitimacy as well. That said, American observers would rightly be troubled by *shariah* systems which preclude or replace existing systems of civil law; which give clerics from religious parties substantial influence over social policy or matters relating to law and order; or which disadvantage women or minority communities.

AID AND DEVELOPMENT

President Bush announced in March 2006 an ambitious U.S. commitment to support a multi-year development program for the FATA. This program was designed to address the poor developmental status of the tribal areas, and support strategic U.S. objectives by making the FATA less amenable to terrorist and insurgent activity. The FATA plan, budgeted at $750 million over five years, complements other USAID programs which have been ongoing in Pakistan since the mission reopened in the summer of 2002.

It is too early to say whether the U.S. FATA Development Program will be successful in its objectives, which include "enhancing [the government of Pakistan's] legitimacy and writ in FATA, improving economic and social conditions for local communities, and supporting sustainable development."[95] The program faces a number of challenges, including a highly restrictive security environment, insufficient indigenous development capacity, and the challenge of scaling up a huge program on short notice. (Remarkably, there were no USAID staff based in Peshawar until mid-2006.[96]).

Structure aid for the long-term

At the bilateral level, it is imperative that the U.S. structure its aid commitment for the long-term. Given the vagaries of the congressional appropriations process, this is easier said than done. But U.S. aid efforts, particularly in the Frontier, are hampered by the perception that America is an unreliable partner. The withdrawal of U.S. aid to Pakistan under the Pressler Amendment is seen in the Frontier, to the present day, as a betrayal of the friendship between the two nations, and is taken as evidence of a supposed double standard in the U.S. treatment of India and Pakistan. Many senior bureaucrats in the NWFP have expressed skepticism over the seriousness of U.S. aid efforts, and tell stories of U.S.-funded projects left uncompleted in the early 1990s.[97]

The five-year FATA commitment is a positive step in demonstrating U.S. commitment to the Frontier. Moreover, the bipartisan Biden-Lugar plan to authorize $7.5 billion in development assistance over five years as a "democracy dividend" (and to advocate for another five years of assistance at the same level) demonstrates to the Pakistani public and bureaucracy that America intends to provide more than simply short-term assistance.

Long-term, sustainable development will, however, require investment in local capacity. On account of the weakness of local development capacity for the tribal areas, the still-small U.S. staffing presence in the Frontier, and the pressure which USAID is under to produce results in the near-term, contracts for the FATA Development Program have gone to established American and international firms rather than the Pakistani bureaucracy or local organizations.[98] USAID is working to build capacity so that future projects can be disaggregated into smaller pieces for local contracting, or provided to the FATA Secretariat for direct implementation.[99] This process of localization is critical to overall U.S. development and security objectives in the Frontier, and ought to be a focus of continued oversight by the Congress.[100]

Lastly, the U.S. should consider ways to bring Pakistan's allies into the FATA development efforts. Specifically, the multilateral Friends of Pakistan initiative, inaugurated in September 2008 to assist Pakistan in staving off a balance of payments crisis, should be extended into a full-fledged consortium which would become the public face of U.S. and allied development efforts in the FATA.[101] Visible, public participation in the consortium by Saudis, Turks, and Emiratis would help to cast the FATA initiatives as a global program and not simply an American initiative. While the United States would undoubtedly provide a bulk of the funding and the operational programming, such a consortium could, over time, help to overcome the impression that aid efforts in the FATA are designed to subvert Muslim values and interests.

Align aid policies with structural changes

Until very recently, U.S. officials have been wary of pressing the government of Pakistan to address the governance void in the FATA. Addressing this void, as argued above, is a key component of any robust counterinsurgency program. But it is also critical to the success and sustainability of U.S. development efforts in the Frontier. There is little evidence to suggest that either Pakistan or the United States has seriously and systematically considered the interaction effects between governance reform and development policy in the FATA.[102] The government of Pakistan's FATA Sustainable Development Plan, for example, acknowledged the importance of governance in framing the FATA development goals, but demurred on any substantive discussion of that nexus.[103] And U.S. policymakers chose until recently to keep governance reform off the table in deference to the pre-February 2008 Pakistani *status quo* on the FCR.

The governance-development nexus is important for the simple reason that a massive influx of funds will inevitably bring about profound *de facto* changes to the governance and power structures of the Frontier. Aid can easily be destabilizing, as local players compete for foreign funds, and it is therefore imperative that the development programs are designed to reinforce governance objectives.[104] If the governance objective, for example, involves "doubling down" on the traditional system of tribal *maliks* and political agents in the FATA, it is worth asking whether U.S. aid delivery is reinforcing or undermining that objective. If, on the other hand, the objective is to build up local institutions of governance, such as agency councils modeled on *jirgas*, the question should be whether U.S. is aid institutionalizing and incentivizing such structures. As a practical matter, the effects of U.S. aid *cannot* be neutral on these matters.

Already, the U.S. aid programs in the FATA are having an *ad hoc* political impact. In some PATA regions, the government is now consulting local councils in developing priorities for development projects. And in those areas in which U.S. funds are being distributed, the office of the political agent and its subordinate institutions are, by some accounts, being strengthened, while the *maliks* — even those participating in local councils — are finding their influence diminished.[105]

The U.S. should press the government of Pakistan to develop, in consultation with stakeholders in the NWFP and FATA, a revised Sustainable Development Plan which addresses this lacuna by thoroughly integrating governance issues with aid planning. In the meantime, Congress ought to exercise its oversight role to examine the political impact of the ongoing U.S. development efforts; the degree to which aid programs are properly incentivizing governance objectives; and the extent of both interagency and bilateral coordination in addressing this critical governance-development nexus.

Leverage settled-tribal boundary areas

Following President Bush's public commitment in 2006 to a $750 million program of aid for the FATA, U.S. efforts have focused on scaling up USAID programming in the tribal areas. Now that this effort is underway, the U.S. should also begin examining the benefits of programming aid in the nearby settled areas in such a way as to benefit American objectives in the FATA.

The U.S. administration and Congress, moving forward, should consider authorizing a portion of FATA-designated aid to be used in areas of the NWFP which sit adjacent to the tribal areas. Several of these settled areas, stretching from Kohat district in the north to Dera Ismail Khan in the south, have emerged as frontline regions in the government's contest with Islamist insurgent groups. The U.S. government could, for example, authorize a trial program under which a portion of FATA development funds could be used in settled areas which are within 15 or 20 kilometers of the settled-tribal boundary line, provided that these projects serve and employ the tribal population.

Such an approach would have several advantages. Projects in the settled areas are generally easier to monitor than those in the FATA; Pakistani businesses are more likely to establish job-creating industries in regions which fall under the civil code rather than the FCR; and on a social level, there is already a great deal of transit back and forth by extended families on either side of the boundary. Some kinds of projects, such as health and primary education initiatives, clearly need to be located within the FATA itself. But others, such as employment-generation programs designed to deal with the problem of mass unemployment among the FATA youth population, might be more successful were they situated nearby the FATA rather than within the tribal areas themselves.[106]

Unlike the funds committed to the FATA, the proposed Reconstruction Opportunity Zones (ROZs) do provide the U.S. with wide discretion to promote employment-generation programs in the FATA, NWFP, or parts of earthquake-affected Kashmir.[107] The ROZs, while they may prove to be worthwhile, are not in their current form targeted narrowly enough to significantly benefit the FATA population. The tariff-free zones are likely to be placed in the Peshawar valley or even the non-Pashtun areas in the eastern part of NWFP, where they will struggle to attract residents of the FATA.[108]

Focus more aid on the NWFP proper

After the USAID mission to Pakistan reopened in 2002, American aid officials made a decision to focus on Sindh and Balochistan provinces as a way of complementing the ongoing development work by other international partners in Punjab and the NWFP. The focus by USAID on the NWFP was and remains relatively small.

In light of the strategic significance of the Frontier province, U.S. officials should step up development programming in the districts of the NWFP, not only those which border the FATA, but also areas of the Peshawar and Swat valleys which have seen a rise in extremism.[109] Fairly or not, the U.S. has a reputation for undertaking development work in Pakistan without thoroughly coordinating its efforts with international or local government institutions and objectives.[110] Development in NWFP is an area in which the U.S. can and should work closely with the provincial government and other international donors to align aid spending with the government's own objectives in education, health, and other sectors.

There are also opportunities to fund high-impact work outside of the core development sectors. As noted above, the Pakistan Legislative Strengthening Program funded by USAID from 2005–2008 was well received in the NWFP by both mainstream and religious party MPAs, and should be considered for renewal.[111] The U.S., in consultation with international lending organizations, should also explore supporting and financing small- and medium-scale hydroelectric projects.[112] These projects would provide high-visibility opportunities to demonstrate the U.S. aid commitment, would help Pakistan meet its growing energy needs, and would provide revenue to the Frontier province which would in turn likely be invested in the health and education sectors.[113]

As the U.S. prepares for a possibly dramatic increase of non-military aid to Pakistan, it should also consider creative and non-traditional projects which might complement efforts in NWFP and the FATA. The U.S. could expand funding for innovative interagency approaches such as the State Department's Economic Empowerment in Strategic Regions, which seeks to encourage entrepreneurship in the Pak-Afghan border areas, and serve as a clearinghouse for linking opportunities with public and private partners (both donors and investors) in the U.S.[114] American aid officials could also explore the possibility of funding, on a trial basis, skills training centers in cooperation with select *madaris*. A number of clerics in NWFP have expressed interest in providing marketable skills to their *madrassah* graduates, and it would not be infeasible to design a vetting process which satisfies U.S. grantee certification requirements and also incentivizes *madrassah* leaders to work more closely with Pakistani and international donors.

And finally, the U.S. should seek out ways to leverage the universities in southern NWFP to further long-term economic development objectives. Taking advantage of a pool of students from the settled and tribal areas now studying at the University of Peshawar (est. 1950), Gomal University in Dera Ismail Khan (est. 1974), Kohat University of Science and Technology (est. 2001), and University of Science and Technology Bannu (est. 2005), the U.S. could fund skills courses on accounting, project management, and economic development which would help to build local capacity for aid programs in the Frontier; and could sponsor entrepreneurship competitions for business students focused on local small and medium enterprise.

CONCLUSION: TOWARD POLITICAL MAINSTREAMING

U.S. policymakers dealing with the Frontier are routinely torn between short-term objectives, which are primarily oriented around preventing attacks on U.S. forces in Afghanistan, and America's long-term interest in seeing a stable Frontier which denies Islamist insurgent groups the physical and socio-political space to carry out operations against Pakistan and its allies. This mismatch unavoidably entails certain trade-offs between counterterrorism and counterinsurgency objectives. Ground incursions by U.S. troops into the FATA, for example, may disrupt key terrorist networks, but also undermine long-term efforts to stabilize the Frontier.

In general, though, these tradeoffs are far from absolute. Despite widespread militancy and growing concerns about Pakistan's strategic ambivalence regarding the neo-Taliban insurgency, there is no reason why the U.S. cannot pursue a two-track approach that addresses the short-term terrorist threat and at the same time lays the groundwork — even incrementally — for more comprehensive counterinsurgency efforts. This approach is critical because solutions to the problems posed by illiberal or insurgent Islamism ultimately require political mainstreaming. This, in turn, calls for legitimate and capable state institutions — both civilian and military — which can set the political boundaries for Islamist participation and respond effectively to new and unexpected forms of "religious" insurgency.[115]

To begin with, a successful counterinsurgency track will be one that is able to leverage political and social fragmentation in the Frontier. The Pakistani government has a long history of taking advantage of cleavages within and among tribal structures.[116] In the wake of the "Anbar Awakening" in Iraq, American policymakers have discussed whether similar strategies might be successful in Pakistan. Carrying out a tribe-oriented Anbar model in and around the FATA would pose real challenges on account of the internally fragmented, egalitarian, and increasingly entrepreneurial nature of the Pashtun tribal system. Although tribal *lashkars* may prove to be useful in pushing back neo-Taliban advances in some areas, and should be supported by the state when they do so, these *ad hoc* alliances are likely to disintegrate quickly or even turn against the government.[117] Any effort to take advantage of fragmentation in the Frontier must integrate political strategy with tactical approaches *from the outset* and should be oriented around a concerted program to incentivize tribal communities and relatively moderate Islamist groups to integrate into the political mainstream.

Ultimately, the kinds of cleavages that matter most are those that divide politically accommodationist groups which accept the authority of the state from politically rejectionist groups which contest it. This is true within tribal communities as well as within ideologically-driven Islamist movements. And here again, the United States can play a significant but indirect role by supporting policies which help to delegitimize and isolate rejectionist groups, and encourage local populations and relatively moderate Islamist leaders (such as those who supported the "old" Taliban but are threatened by the neo-Taliban movement) to throw in their lot with the state rather than the insurgents.

This requires the use of "soft power" initiatives, particularly in the area of FATA development. But it also requires that such initiatives be more thoroughly integrated with security efforts and robust governance reforms. Integrated approaches — even if they are, at first, implemented only in small demonstration areas (such as the MRZ concept outlined below) — are likely to be the only effective means of translating development assistance into support for state authority.

These policies will obviously take time. But their potential impact is not confined to the long-run. They can also have immediate relevance as a means of assisting the government of Pakistan in solidifying its near-term military gains in the Frontier. Recent campaigns in Swat, Bajaur, and Mohmand, for example, will prove fruitless unless the state is able to use the operations to drive a wedge between the insurgents and the local populations, and implement governance structures which can provide security and development after the army returns to its barracks.

There are signs that both the security establishment and the political leadership within Pakistan increasingly see the spreading militancy as an internal challenge, and not simply a regional problem which can be externalized. Their resolve in dealing with this challenge may yet grow, so long as the insurgents continue to target government interests and civilian populations. While American officials are, for good reason, likely to remain skeptical about the capacity and the will of the Pakistani government to deal with these problems, the United States as a practical matter has no choice but to work with Pakistan in addressing the rise of the neo-Taliban, and laying the groundwork for a more comprehensive and holistic strategy in the Frontier.

NOTES:

1. See Carlotta Gall and David Rohde, "Pakistan Struggles Against Militants Trained by Agency," *New York Times,* January 15, 2008; Dexter Filkins, "Right at the Edge," *New York Times Magazine,* September 7, 2008; and "Backgrounder: The ISI and Terrorism: Behind the Accusations," Council on Foreign Relations, September 29, 2008, available at http://www.cfr.org/publication/11644/pakistans_isi.html (accessed October 1, 2008).

2. See Hasan-Askari Rizvi, *Military, State and Society in Pakistan* (New York: St. Martin's Press, 2000); and Saeed Shafqat, *Civil-Military Relations in Pakistan: From Zulfikar Ali Bhutto to Benazir Bhutto* (Boulder, CO: Westview Press, 1997).

3. The legal basis of the council was the National Security Council Act of 2004. Following its adoption, the constituent parties of the MMA were split over whether their participation would constitute an endorsement of the military's role in politics. Throughout 2005 the JI was firmly opposed to the alliance's participation, while the JUI-F was, characteristically, eager for a compromise with the martial government. After the earthquake struck in October 2005 the JUI-F saw its opening, and allowed Chief Minister Durrani to attend an NSC meeting in the "best interest of the province and the five districts destroyed in the earthquake." See Ihtasham ul Haq, "Authority set up for rehabilitation: Durrani attends NSC meeting," *Dawn,* October 13, 2005; Zakir Hassnain, "Akram Durrani speaks in NWFP Assembly: '29,360 dead, 7,000 missing, Rs 32b loss,'" *Daily Times,* November 16, 2005; Ismail Khan, "A grim year for the Frontier," *Dawn,* January 1, 2006.

4. For an ambitious but clear-eyed view of where the U.S. might take its Pak-Afghan policy, see Barnett R. Rubin and Ahmed Rashid, "From Great Game to Grand Bargain: Ending Chaos in Afghanistan and Pakistan," *Foreign Affairs,* November/December 2008.

5. See, e.g., Abdul Waheed Wafa and Graham Bowley, "Afghans See Pakistan Role in Karzai Plot," *New York Times,* June 26, 2008.

6. See, e.g., Gall and Rohde, "Pakistan Struggles;" and Mark Mazzetti and Eric Schmitt, "C.I.A. Outlines Pakistan Links With Militants," *New York Times,* July 30, 2008.

7. One of the most puzzling failures of U.S. public diplomacy and information operations in Pakistan has been its inability to counter these powerful narratives about Pashtun disenfranchisement in Afghanistan.

8. The Cold Start doctrine, even in nascent form, provides an unfortunate excuse for the Pakistani

military to retain an Indo-centric threat orientation. For more on Cold Start, see Walter C. Ladwig III, "A Cold Start for Hot Wars? The Indian Army's New Limited War Doctrine," *International Security* 32, no. 3 (Winter 2007/08).

9 As Robert Kaplan has argued, "Given these realities, you would think that the Bush administration would be coaching the Karzai government not to antagonize Pakistan unnecessarily by cozying up to India. Whatever coaching did happen has failed. The Karzai government has openly and brazenly strengthened its ties with India, and allowed Indian consulates in Jalalabad, Kandahar, Herat, and Mazar-e-Sharif. It has kept alive the possibility of inviting India to help train the new Afghan army, and to help in dam construction in the northeastern Afghan province of Kunar, abutting Pakistan." Robert D. Kaplan, "Behind the Indian Embassy Bombing," *Atlantic* online, August 1, 2008, http://www.theatlantic.com/doc/200808u/kaplan-pakistan.

10 Suggesting that the U.S. should account for Pakistani concerns over Indian influence in Afghanistan is not to side with Pakistan against India in any moral sense. (India's foreign policy in Afghanistan is entirely rational.) It is, rather, simply a realist calculus: the military-bureaucratic elite in Pakistan has, since the earliest days of the state, justified its predominance in large part based on the imminent threat from India. So long as this elite can point to a continuing Indian threat on both of its borders, whether real or imagined, it is unlikely to cede significant powers to a civilian regime. Many observers have also argued that American efforts to resolve the Kashmir dispute would substantially help to shift Pakistan's strategic focus away from India. See, e.g., Stephen Cohen, testimony before the Senate Committee on Foreign Relations, July 25, 2007; and Bruce Riedel, "Pakistan and Terror: The Eye of the Storm," *Annals of the American Academy of Political and Social Science* 618, no. 1 (July 2008): 40ff.

11 Carlotta Gall, "NATO Chief in Afghanistan Says Pakistan's Tack on Militants Is Not as Expected," *New York Times*, May 30, 2008.

12 An increase in state legitimacy also brings important tactical gains: "The lessons offered by the army's engagements since 2002 are stark and clear: unless the tribal populations that reside in the FATA are sympathetic to the government and are willing to warn the army of the militants' presence in their midst or desist from alerting the terrorists to the military's anticipated arrival in their hamlets, counterterrorism missions will fail or be condemned to rely on even greater applications of brute force for their success." Ashley J. Tellis, "Pakistan's Record on Terrorism: Conflicted Goals, Compromised Performance," *Washington Quarterly* 31, no. 2 (Spring 2008): 20.

13 Senate bill 3263, the "Enhanced Partnership with Pakistan Act of 2008," is available at http://frwebgate.access.gpo.gov/cgi-bin/getdoc.cgi?dbname=110_cong_bills&docid=f:s3263is.txt.pdf (accessed October 1, 2008).

14 See Eric Schmitt, "U.S.-Pakistani Brainstorming on Border Violence," *New York Times*, August 28, 2008.

15 This view has been widely held by U.S. diplomats working in Pakistan. Author interviews, 2005–8.

16 The JUI-F has taken a relatively moderate position on Pakistan's relations with India. Even the *Daily Times* editorial board — no friend of the religious parties — could not help but compliment Fazlur Rehman on his 2003 visit to Deoband and Delhi: "Last year when Mr Rehman went to India with a Jamiat Ulema-e-Islam delegation, his statements took the Indians by surprise. He was logical, rational, mild, eloquent and very convincing." "Editorial: Fazlur Rehman's deft political moves," *Daily Times*, June 21, 2004. Fazlur Rehman was appointed Chairman of the Kashmir Committee of the National Assembly in September 2008.

17 Markey, *Securing Pakistan's Tribal Belt*, 48.

18   Since Pakistan is an unaccompanied post (i.e., spouses and dependents are not allowed), such a proposal would probably not be welcomed by the Foreign Service.

19   The White House fact sheet for the visit, while not failing to mention the "Global War On Terror," ably framed U.S. policy in terms resonant with Pakistani values: "The United States will continue to work with the democratically elected government of Pakistan as we pursue extremists who are trying to kill innocent Pakistanis and weaken the government that is working to improve the economy, create jobs, and provide education and healthcare to Pakistani citizens. We support the Pakistani government as it moves forward with reforms that will deliver the benefits of democracy to the Pakistani people." The White House, "Fact Sheet: President Bush Meets with Pakistani Prime Minister Yousaf Raza Gillani," July 28, 2008, http://www.whitehouse.gov/news/releases/2008/07/20080728-8.html.

20   Quoted in "Bush advises Asif to ignore public opinion," *Dawn,* September 10, 2008.

21   See Anwar Iqbal, "US official makes public demand for reforming ISI," *Dawn,* September 17, 2008.

22   Congressman Tom Tancredo's statement in 2007 in which he threatened to attack Mecca and Medina in retaliation for any future attack on the United States received extensive press coverage in Pakistan. See, e.g., "Bombing Islamic sites an option: US presidential hopeful," *The News,* August 3, 2007.

23   National Counterterrorism Center, *Words that Work and Words that Don't: A Guide for Counterterrorism Communication,* March 14, 2008.

24   All three of these terms have widely-accepted pejorative translations in Urdu. Note also that the term "insurgents," while analytically descriptive, does not always translate well in the Pakistani context; some military officers tend to associate the term with groups which are pursuing formal independence from the state. For more on the public diplomacy challenges faced by the United States in Pakistan, see Peter Nasuti, Philip J. Reiner, and Joshua T. White, "A Strategy for Hearts and Minds in South and Central Asia," *Review of Faith & International Affairs* 6, no. 3 (Autumn 2008): 57–62.

25   For a sophisticated examination of religious education in Pakistan, see Matthew J. Nelson, "Dealing with Difference: Religious Education and the Challenge of Democracy in Pakistan," *Modern Asian Studies* (forthcoming).

26   H.R. 1, as passed by the House. http://frwebgate.access.gpo.gov/cgi-bin/getdoc.cgi?dbname=110_cong_bills&docid=f:h1eh.txt.pdf.

27   Author's observations, 2005–7, Peshawar.

28   Radio is widely acknowledged to be the most important means of communication and messaging in the FATA. See, e.g., Shinwari, *Understanding FATA,* 34.

29   Maulana Fazlullah of Swat, also known as "Maulana Radio," was the most prominent radio *mullah*; district Swabi also appears to have been a center of religious radio activity. See, e.g., Ghafar Ali, "90 illegal FM radio stations in NWFP," *Daily Times,* December 8, 2005; and Amir Mohammad Khan, "Radio Venom," *Newsline,* August 2006.

30   Author interview with a U.S. official, Peshawar, 2005.

31   A nationwide survey conducted in September 2007 found that 86% of respondents believed that it was a goal of the United States to "weaken and divide the Islamic world." It is reasonable to believe that the numbers would be even higher in the NWFP. Fair et al, "Pakistani Public Opinion," January 7, 2008.

32   In general, of course, the reverse tends to be true: America is unusually religious for a country of its wealth, but the U.S. bureaucracy is less religious than the general population.

33   Anna Simons, "Making Enemies, Part Two," *The American Interest,* Autumn 2006: 42.
34   Author's observations, 2005–7, Peshawar.
35   This public space can also be facilitated by scholarly exchanges, many of which were suspended after September 11, 2001.
36   Author's observations, 2005–7, Peshawar.
37   These dialogues might be most effective as a "track 1½" initiative. The next U.S. president should, Chris Seiple argues, "use his Office of Faith-Based Initiatives to convene different religious groups in the U.S. for intra-faith conversations about how they might work for peace with their co-religionists in the Middle East, and with other faiths who share the same values. Such an approach might inspire the president to consider even more creative options, such as commissioning an 'Abrahamic Corps' of young Jews, Christians, and Muslims to work on practical issues of social justice while demonstrating to the region and the world that the Abrahamic traditions respect each other so much that they will serve one other." Chris Seiple, "Seizing the Middle East Moment," *Review of Faith & International Affairs* 6, no. 3 (Autumn 2008): 53–6.
38   Peter Mandaville speaks for a growing number of scholars in lamenting that "the default assumption still appears to be that Islamism of any kind is more likely to be part of the problem rather than a potential component of counter-terrorism solutions. It is precisely this dogma that is in serious need of reexamination." Peter Mandaville, "Engaging Islamists in the West," *CTC Sentinel,* June 2008: 5–7.
39   Simons, "Making Enemies, Part Two," 42.
40   See, e.g., Husain Haqqani and Kenneth Ballen, "Sentiment Shifts In the Muslim World," *Wall Street Journal,* December 19, 2005. The most sophisticated analysis of the U.S. efforts can be found in Andrew Wilder, *Perceptions of the Pakistan Earthquake Response* (Feinstein International Center, February 2008). The International Crisis Group also released a report, which was more critical of U.S. accommodation toward Islamist groups during the relief efforts. International Crisis Group, *Pakistan: Political Impact of the Earthquake,* March 15, 2006.
41   The White House, "Fact Sheet."
42   This first provision of emergency assistance was only $50,000, but is expected to increase. U.S. Embassy Islamabad, "USAID Provides Emergency Assistance to the Displaced People of Bajour and Mohmand Agencies," August 20, 2008; and Richard Boucher, press conference, October 20, 2008, Islamabad, available at http://islamabad.usembassy.gov/pr-08102001.html (accessed October 25, 2008).
43   In October 2008 the U.S. announced a $30 million program in support of Pakistan's energy sector.
44   Jane Perlez, "Ex-Pakistani Official Says Policy on Taliban is Failing," *New York Times,* January 27, 2008.
45   See, e.g., "Elite Force to combat terrorism, says IGP," Frontier Post, March 18, 2008; Mohammed Riaz, "Violence to be curbed through jirga: Hoti," *Dawn,* April 11, 2008; and Afrasiab Khattak, "Fata's growing disconnect," *Dawn,* July 31, 2008.
46   Iqbal Khattak, "NWFP advised to raise elite police strike force," *Daily Times,* March 12, 2008.
47   "Kidnapping for ransom — source of income for militants, says IGP," *Frontier Post,* July 24, 2008.
48   In late 2007, the U.S. announced a modest increase in its program to support Pakistani law enforcement. The assistance, much of which focused on the NWFP, intended to "strengthen Pakistani law enforcement agencies' ability to implement effective border control regimes, build investigative capabilities of Pakistani police and sustain counter-narcotics efforts...." U.S. Em-

49   bassy Islamabad, "U.S. Provides Additional $20.4 Million In Assistance To Law Enforcement Agencies," September 27, 2007. Other commentators have also urged the U.S. to focus greater attention on policing. See, e.g., Husain Haqqani, testimony before the House Armed Services Committee, October 10, 2007.

49   See "NWFP govt forms special force to counter terrorism," *Daily Times*, June 21, 2008; and "Kidnapping for ransom," *Frontier Post*.

50   For more details on need for police reforms, see International Crisis Group, *Reforming Pakistan's Police*, July 14, 2008.

51   Author interviews, Peshawar, August 2008. See, e.g., "Tribesmen will counter Taliban activities in Dir," *Daily Times*, September 22, 2008; Anwarullah Khan, "Two tribes join drive against Taliban," *Dawn*, September 24, 2008; and "More tribesmen take up arms against Taliban," *Daily Times*, October 7, 2008.

52   See, e.g., Zahid Hussain, "Pakistan Turns to Tribal Militias," *Wall Street Journal*, September 31, 2008; Zulfiqar Ali, "Lashkars fail to subdue militants," *Dawn*, October 21, 2008; and Jane Perlez and Pir Zubair Shah, "Pakistan Uses Tribal Militias in Taliban War," *New York Times*, October 24, 2008.

53   Some civil cases, such as land disputes, can take *decades* to resolve. Author interviews with students and local officials, Bannu district, 2006.

54   Akhtar Amin, "Taliban set up illegal courts in FATA, NWFP," *Daily Times*, June 29, 2008.

55   See Muhammad Amir Rana, "A Court of One's Own," *Herald*, May 2007. While a princely state, Swat was reputed to have had a relatively efficient system of justice.

56   As Chris Seiple notes, "...freedom absent the context of the community can come across as licentious to the Muslim world, with no respect for tradition and honor.... Instead, we must try to honor the Muslim worldview through the use and understanding of words important to them as found in their sacred texts. These words include justice, mercy, and compassion...." Chris Seiple, "Seizing the Middle East Moment."

57   The government's extension of *qazi* courts into Swat, Dir, and Chitral is a welcome development insofar as it recognizes the importance of judicial discontent in facilitating insurgent activity, and puts civil officers (with the new title of *qazis*) at the forefront of the new process; but nonetheless problematic in that it is not narrowly targeted, and does not address the underlying problems of the civilian judicial system. See, e.g., I.A. Rehman, "Playing with fire: Plan for Qazi courts," *Dawn*, January 23, 2008.

58   It is widely believed that the Pakistan army negotiated a deal by which the TTP would not disrupt the February elections. Author interviews with U.S. officials, March 2008, Washington. See also Rahimullah Yusufzai, "Pakistan's Taliban Negotiating Peace, Preparing for War," *Jamestown Terrorism Focus*, May 6, 2008.

59   Typically skeptical views can be found in Daveed Gartenstein-Ross and Bill Roggio, "Descent into Appeasement," *Weekly Standard*, June 9, 2008; and Mitchell Shivers, testimony before the Senate Foreign Relations Committee, June 25, 2008.

60   See Khalid Aziz, "Risks in peace agreements in NWFP and FATA," *The News*, May 4, 2008.

61   Author interviews, Islamabad and Peshawar, August 2008.

62   For more on this "tenuous balancing act," see Daniel J. Simons, "A US attack on Pakistan?" *New Statesman*, July 29, 2008; and Lisa Curtis, "U.S. Strategy Must Address Afghan-Pakistan Tension," Heritage WebMemo, September 26, 2008, available at http://www.heritage.org/research/AsiaandthePacific/wm2087.cfm (accessed October 1, 2008).

63   This point was raised repeatedly in author interviews in the NWFP, 2006–7.

64 The strike unsuccessfully targeted al Qaeda leader Ayman Zawahiri. Bajaur is known as the tribal agency with perhaps the most eclectic set of Islamist militant organizations, including TNSM, al Qaeda, and Wahhabi groups. See Khaled Ahmed, "A profile of Bajaur," *Friday Times,* March 10, 2006; and Sami Yousafzai and Ron Moreau, "Where 'The Land Is on Fire'," *Newsweek,* June 7, 2008.

65 See Alok Bansal, "Did US bomb Pak madrassa?" *Rediff News*, November 6, 2006, http://in.rediff.com/news/2006/nov/06guest.htm (accessed October 1, 2008).

66 Eric Schmitt and David E. Sanger, "Pakistan Shift Could Curtail Drone Strikes," *New York Times,* February 22, 2008.

67 An individual strike which kills prominent civilians or a large number of innocents could still, of course, serve as a catalyzing event.

68 See, e.g., Eric Schmitt, "Pakistani and American Troops Exchange Fire," *New York Times,* September 26, 2008.

69 Many experts believe that U.S. officials were genuinely taken by surprise by the strong official Pakistani opposition to the incursion. See, e.g., Mark Mazzetti and Eric Schmitt, "U.S. Takes to Air to Hit Militants Inside Pakistan," *New York Times,* October 27, 2008.

70 The sections which follow draw on a recent article by the author which examines in detail the governance challenges in the Frontier; their relation to local security issues; and paths-forward for reform in both the settled areas and the FATA. See White, "The Shape of Frontier Rule."

71 For an overview of the Devolution plan's impact, see Saeed Shafqat and Saeed Wahlah, "Experimenting with Democratic Governance: The Impact of the 2001 Local Government Ordinance on Pakistan's Bureaucracy" in *Pakistan 2005*, ed. Charles H. Kennedy and Cynthia A. Botteron (Karachi: Oxford University Press, 2006); and Social Policy and Development Centre, *Social Development in Pakistan Annual Review 2006–7: Devolution and Human Development in Pakistan* (Karachi: SPDC, 2007).

72 A more detailed presentation on this subject was made by the author in "Governance, Islamic Contestation, and Political Stability in Pakistan's Frontier," Political Transformations in Pakistan conference, March 29, 2008, Washington, DC. (Sponsored by the American Institute of Pakistan Studies and Johns Hopkins SAIS.)

73 See, e.g., Raja Asghar, "NA runs out of steam as debate on local govts divides house," *Dawn,* June 7, 2008; and Mohammad Ali Khan, "Nazims' executive powers clipped: NWFP governor amends ordinance," *Dawn,* April 3, 2008. Note also the revealing comment by an anonymous district *nazim* (mayor), expressing relief at being relieved of certain law and order responsibilities: "Being a political person[,] it was difficult for me to ban processions usually organised by political parties. Now that these powers have been taken away, we would not be required to take difficult administrative decisions."

74 See White, "The Shape of Frontier Rule:" 235ff.

75 Politics aside, the problems inherent in bifurcating administration of the settled and tribal areas constitute a compelling rationale for gradually integrating the FATA into the adjacent Frontier province, rather than preserving its status as a region administered under a separate channel of federal oversight. Olaf Caroe, who served as the last governor of the Indian NWFP, reflected years later on the challenge of administering this boundary: "The juxtaposition of the two societies, the settled and the tribal, posed in acute form the problem of securing the surrender of criminals. … It was a problem which was never solved." Olaf Caroe, *The Pathans*, pp. 350–51. As a corollary, it would be logical to gradually integrate the PATA into the settled regions as well. See, e.g., Khalid Aziz, *Extending Stability to Pakistani Tribal Areas* (Peshawar: RIPORT, 2008), 9.

76. In addition to the Bannu region, Darra Adam Khel has proved to be a problematic point of interface between settled and tribal systems.
77. See "Coordination offices for tribal areas, settled districts," *Dawn,* January 19, 2008; and Riaz Khan Daudzai, "RCOs to cope with law, order in Fata, NWFP," *The News,* February 5, 2008.
78. "NWFP govt approves revival of DC office," *Daily Times,* October 23, 2008.
79. See I.A. Rehman, "Playing with fire: Plan for Qazi courts," *Dawn,* January 23, 2008; Asif Nisar, "'Govt overstepping its authority,'" *Statesman,* January 24, 2008; Ali Waqar, "CII seeks explanation on Shariah draft," *Daily Times,* January 26, 2008; "Against any parallel judicial system," *Daily Times,* February 3, 2008; Raza Khan, "Another judicial crisis," *The News,* February 3, 2008; Akhtar Amin, "Revised draft of Shari Nizam-e-Adl Regulation 2008 sent to president," *Daily Times,* May 9, 2008; and Ghulam Dastageer, "Pata lawmakers weighing Sharai Nizam-e-Adl: Minister," *The News,* May 12, 2008.
80. See, e.g., "Govt approves appointment of 100 Qazis in Malakand," *Frontier Post,* September 25, 2008; Daud Khattak, "NWFP govt finalises draft Nizam-e-Adl Regulations 2008," *Daily Times,* September 28, 2008; and "NWFP governor signs Shariah bill for Malakand," *Daily Times,* October 7, 2008.
81. The first FCR, which was quite modest in scope, was promulgated in 1873, and was subject to minor amendments over the subsequent three decades. The 1901 regulation was considerably more comprehensive, and forms the basis for the current system of governance in the FATA. For the updated text of the 1901 regulation, see *The Frontier Crimes Regulation, 1901: Regulation III of 1901, as modified up to 31st October, 1971* (Peshawar: Government Stationery and Print. Dept., 1973).
82. See, e.g., Peter Chalk, "Case Study: The Pakistani-Afghan Border Region," in *Ungoverned Territories: Understanding and Reducing Terrorism Risks* (Santa Monica, CA: RAND, 2007), 49–76; and Robert D. Lamb, *Ungoverned Areas and Threats from Safe Havens* (U.S. Office of the Under Secretary of Defense for Policy, January 2008).
83. By bypassing the authority of the political agent when conducting armed operations in the FATA, the military inadvertently disempowered its traditional conduit of influence in the tribal areas. The number of *maliks* killed in Waziristan over the last several years is estimated by some local observers to constitute less than three percent of the total. Even so, the targeted killings have dissuaded tribal elders from cooperating with the government. Author interview with an NGO leader working in the FATA, February 2008, Islamabad. See also Khalid Aziz, *Extending Stability,* 7ff.
84. The FCR has been criticized by the Human Rights Commission of Pakistan, the legal community, and civil society groups. See, e.g., International Crisis Group, *Appeasing the Militants,* pp. 7–9; Masood Rehman, "FSC seeks NWFP govt's comments on FCR petitions," *Daily Times,* January 30, 2008; and Asad Jamal, "A law that must go," *The News,* April 6, 2008.
85. For examples of the state's use of FCR collective punishment provisions, see Human Rights Watch, *Pakistan: Protect Civilians From Fighting in North Waziristan,* March 6, 2006. For a discussion of the financial aspects of the political agent system, see Humayun Khan, "The Role of the Federal Government and the Political Agent," in *Tribal Areas of Pakistan: Challenges and Responses,* ed. P.I. Cheema and M.H. Nuri (Islamabad: IPRI, 2005), 109–11.
86. See especially the work of Khalid Aziz at the Regional Institute of Policy Research and Training (RIPORT) in Peshawar, available at http://riport.org; and Shinwari, *Understanding FATA.*

87 As late as July 2007, a senior USAID official in Islamabad argued that "Politically, it's not the right time for changing the FCR.... We have to start a basis for dialogue" on political reforms. By the spring of 2008, a senior U.S. official acknowledged that FATA reforms constituted "a huge gap in our policy." Author interviews.

88 See, e.g., "FATA Council demanded for Tribal Areas," *Daily Times,* July 18, 2008.

89 In their otherwise insightful review of the Pak-Afghan border areas, Thomas Johnson and Chris Mason present a contradictory set of views on Pashtunwali, at first labeling it "flexible and dynamic," only to conclude that the "unbending nature" of the Pashtuns' "compulsory social code" makes it uniquely resistant to external governance. This conclusion informs their central recommendation to "strengthen and rebuild the tribal structures from the inside" rather than attempting to extend the reach of the central government. While it is true that there is an identifiable difference in political cultures between lowland and highland Pashtuns, and between those who have historically lived in settled and tribal areas, the authors are overly pessimistic about the potential for tribal communities to adopt new forms of local governance which blend state institutions and tribal norms. Thomas H. Johnson and M. Chris Mason, "No Sign until the Burst of Fire: Understanding the Pakistan-Afghanistan Frontier," *International Security* 32, no. 4 (Spring 2008): 41–77.

90 See Shinwari, *Understanding FATA.*

91 See "Epilogue: Frontier 2010."

92 See White, "The Shape of Frontier Rule:" 230ff.

93 See "PM decision on FCR attracts mixed reaction," *The News,* March 30, 2008; Ismail Khan, "Implications of repealing FCR," *Dawn,* March 30, 2008; and "Wazirs say Shariah only acceptable alternative to FCR," *Daily Times,* April 1, 2008.

94 The Minister for States and Frontier Regions assured a *jirga* that the new system would be "in conformity with local customs and traditions" and would not be against Islam. Syed Irfan Raza, "Jirga help sought to restore Fata peace," *Dawn,* May 6, 2008.

95 See http://www.usaid.gov/pk/mission/news/fata.htm (accessed October 1, 2008).

96 "USAID reopens office in Peshawar," *Dawn,* July 12, 2006.

97 Author interview with Governor Orakzai and other officials in the NWFP and FATA Secretariats, August 2007.

98 The largest component of the plan, a $300 million livelihoods program, was awarded to the Cooperative Housing Foundation and the Academy for Educational Development. Education and health grantees include American Institutes of Research, Associates in Development, UNICEF, John Snow Incorporated, Save The Children, Abt Associates, WHO, Research Triangle Institute, and J.E. Austin & Nathan Associates.

99 The FATA Capacity Building Program ($43 million), contracted to DAI Inc., focuses on the FATA Secretariat. The USAID Office of Transition Initiatives (OTI) also runs a capacity building program ($45 million) that focuses on small community development programs, but does not build institutional capacity in a traditional sense. See also Mark Ward, testimony before the Subcommittee on the Middle East and South Asia of the House Committee on Foreign Affairs, May 14, 2008.

100 Section 5(e) of S. 3263 (Enhanced Partnership with Pakistan Act of 2008, as introduced in the Senate) encourages the President "to utilize Pakistani firms and community and local nongovernmental organizations in Pakistan to provide assistance…"

101 See Anwar Iqbal and Masood Haider, "'Friends' unveil initiative to avert collapse: Over $15bn needed: media," *Dawn,* September 27, 2008.

102 This subject has garnered much more significant attention with respect to the settled areas. See e.g., World Bank and Government of NWFP, *Accelerating Growth;* and Social Policy and Development Centre, *Social Development in Pakistan.*

103 Civil Secretariat (FATA), *FATA Sustainable Development Plan (2006–2015).*

104 For a helpful discussion of the relationship between aid and security, see Kimberly Marten, "The Effects of External Economic Stimuli on Ungoverned Areas: The Pashtun Tribal Areas of Pakistan," presented at the annual meeting of the International Studies Association, San Francisco, California, March 26, 2008, available at http://www.allacademic.com/meta/p254657_index.html (accessed October 1, 2008).

105 Author interview with a USAID project subcontractor operating throughout the FATA, August 2008, Islamabad.

106 There are indications that USAID is considering implementing FATA-oriented projects in the nearby settled areas. The Request for Application for the Livelihood Development Program (LDP) noted that "public works activities" designed to create jobs will be "focused in FATA and to a certain extent in the Frontier Regions (FRs) and the adjoining four cities i.e. Peshawar, Kohat, Bannu, and Dera Ismail Khan." USAID/Pakistan, *FATA Livelihood Development Program (LDP) Request for Application (RFA 391-2007-030),* September 19, 2007.

107 The ROZ legislation was introduced in the Senate in March 2008 as S. 2776 (Afghanistan and Pakistan Reconstruction Opportunity Zones Act of 2008) and in the House in June 2008 as H.R. 6387 (Afghanistan-Pakistan Security and Prosperity Enhancement Act).

108 A preliminary study on the ROZs conducted for USAID in 2006 suggested that placement of the zones in the FATA would be unwise. An "Area Assessment Matrix" which ranked security factors at potential ROZ sites on a scale from 0 to 9 assigned the FATA (Khyber and Mohmand agencies) a score of "–3." BearingPoint, *Reconstruction Opportunity Zones: Pakistan and Afghanistan Assessment of Possible Locations and Products,* Draft Report for Internal USG Review, October 2006.

109 USAID hopes to expand programming into Swat in the near future. Mark Ward, testimony before the Senate Committee on Foreign Relations, June 25, 2008.

110 On the one hand, this charge is belied by USAID's coordination with DFID and other donors after 2002 to divide up areas of emphasis by province. On the other hand, the agency's handling of the FATA program has occasionally reinforced the perception that USAID operates on its own terms. When asked about coordination with other international donors, a USAID official in the summer of 2007 noted curtly, "We should hope the international players get on board with what we're doing." Author interview, Islamabad, 2007.

111 This program, contracted to DAI Inc., covered the national and provincial legislatures, and built upon a similar USAID program in Pakistan from the mid-1990s.

112 Virtually all hydroelectric projects require the province to consult closely with the central government. World Bank and Government of NWFP, *Accelerating Growth,* 13.

113 When transfers and royalties from the central government increased during the MMA's tenure, the provincial government allocated the majority of these funds toward development programs. Author review of provincial development documents, and interviews with provincial officials, July 2007, Peshawar.

114 This program, though small, can serve an important niche in facilitating low-volume, high-impact entrepreneurship on both sides of the border. See Austin Bay, "Synergy crisis diplomacy," *Washington Times,* June 27, 2008.

115 A recent study examining how terrorist groups end concluded that politicization and policing were the two most important reasons, accounting for 43% and 40% of the cases, respectively.

"Victory" and military force accounted for a combined total of only 17%. Seth G. Jones and Martin C. Libicki, *How Terrorist Groups End: Lessons for Countering al Qa'ida* (Santa Monica, CA: RAND, 2008), 18ff.

116 Recently, the state has also worked to separate local groups from foreign influences. See, e.g., Sadia Sulaiman, "Empowering 'Soft' Taliban Over 'Hard' Taliban: Pakistan's Counter-Terrorism Strategy," *Jamestown Terrorism Monitor*, July 25, 2008; and Rahimullah Yusufzai, "A Who's Who of the Insurgency in Pakistan's North-West Frontier Province: Part One – North and South Waziristan," *Jamestown Terrorism Monitor*, September 22, 2008.

117 The historical dimension of conflict in the FATA is often overlooked in journalistic accounts. As Joshua Foust has noted, "Missing from the excited calls for another 'Awakening' movement is an understanding of Pakistan's history before it was Pakistan. Tribal unrest, even Islamist-fueled tribal unrest, is a regular and cyclical occurrence." Joshua Foust, "Did We Just Invade Pakistan?" *Columbia Journalism Review*, September 26, 2008, available at http://www.cjr.org/behind_the_news/did_we_just_invade_pakistan.php (accessed October 1, 2008).

EPILOGUE: FRONTIER 2010

What follows is fiction. It is a narrative answer to the question, "What could the U.S. do in partnership with the government of Pakistan over the next two years to deny space to neo-Taliban insurgent groups in the Frontier?" The account is intentionally optimistic, and brackets substantial questions about the situation in Afghanistan, the nature of interagency coordination within the U.S., the stability of the Pakistani coalition government, and the state of U.S.-Pakistani bilateral relations. All the same, the picture it paints is not far-fetched.

In fact, it presents but one of many possible policy approaches to the Frontier, the particulars of which are far less important than the overall strategic framework which attempts to integrate governance, development, and security initiatives in a geographically focused and politically coordinated manner. The narrative first addresses the NWFP region of the Frontier, and then the FATA. Although these two areas are increasingly interconnected, they nonetheless require somewhat different strategies, particularly in the near-term.

ADDRESSING THE NWFP: NEW SECURITY COOPERATION

It is 2010. Two years ago, the situation in NWFP was nearly intolerable. Tehrik-e-Taliban-e-Pakistan militants were clashing with Pakistan army forces in Swat, insurgents were threatening Peshawar from nearby Khyber agency, the spill-over from military operations in Bajaur had brought hundreds of thousands of residents from the FATA into the settled areas, and NWFP provincial government officials were regularly being targeted by militant groups.

In spite of stepped-up military action by the Pakistan army, the United States remained worried that the insurgency was metastasizing and that its spread to the settled areas of the Frontier had the potential to seriously destabilize the new coalition government in Islamabad. A review of the U.S. policy portfolio by the new administration revealed that Washington had traditionally focused relatively little attention on the NWFP itself — with most of the programs oriented around anti-narcotics, and a few modest development and civil society initiatives.

In early 2009, U.S. officials, in consultation with the provincial government and Islamabad, identified two major factors facilitating the insurgency in the settled areas: frustration with the local justice system (which Taliban groups exploited by establishing *qazi* courts), and profoundly low expectations by the public of a timely government response to insurgent advances (which caused local populations to bandwagon with the militants).

Seeking to assist in addressing the first problem, the U.S. began a needs-assessment on local NWFP justice issues, carried out in cooperation with the provincial government and managed under USAID's Democracy and Governance programming. Field surveys identified four high-risk districts in which discontent threatened to create openings for the neo-Taliban. The research also underscored that while most local communities wanted *shariah,* they did not want to be governed by clerics or subjected to harsh and arbitrary punishments in the style of the Afghan Taliban. In a second phase of the project, building on this research, the U.S. funded provincial government programs aimed at speeding the caseload at the district court level and also initiatives which helped to set up alternative dispute resolution mechanisms consistent with local norms and traditions.

Attempts to deal with the "bandwagoning" problem in the settled areas focused on the critical role of police forces operating in vulnerable areas. Here the problem was fairly clear: local police were the first line of defense, but had insufficient resources or incentives to push back against insurgent advances; the Pakistani military, meanwhile, had the capabilities, but was often unwelcome in these areas. Local security officials argued that the province needed to develop a rapid-response police force that could deploy quickly to build confidence in the government and encourage local populations to side with the state — acting both in response to insurgent activities, and preemptively to shore up areas which were coming under increased threat.

Although it recognized the need, the U.S. bureaucracy was not well organized to support police programs in the Frontier. Resources, expertise, and authorities were spread out among the departments of State, Justice, and Defense. Eventually, however, the U.S. Embassy coordinated a joint plan to assist the Pakistani government in equipping, funding, and training the force on a three year trial basis, and the program was rolled out in five high-risk districts bordering conflict zones: Buner, Lower Dir, Kohat, Mardan, and Peshawar. A joint U.S.-Pakistani working group was set up to monitor the program and conduct regular needs-assessments.

Operationally, this rapid-response force was overseen by a special committee led by the NWFP chief minister along with the inspector general of the Frontier Corps, inspector general of police, and a representative from the army's XI corps in Peshawar. The goal of the program was to do more than simply add one additional type of security force. It was, rather, to facilitate robust security coordination at the provincial level, and provide capacity for the state to implement a *graduated* response to new threats rather than waiting until situations required full-scale military intervention.

One critical aspect of the program was that each Regional Coordination Officer (RCO) was given the authority to deploy subsets of the force in his area on short notice without going up the chain of command. Provincial police officials, recognizing that the objectives of this new force were 80% "optical" (designed to shift perceptions) and only 20% "kinetic" (designed to physically displace insurgents), also mapped out an outreach plan to local politicians, bureaucrats, police officers, and religious leaders to assure them that the rapid-response force would provide ground support within 24 hours, and could be called upon in support of local community *lashkars* raised against the insurgents.

The program got off to a slow start. It took nearly a year for the provincial government to induct personnel (most of whom were recruited from areas outside of the five focus districts), set up the new coordination mechanisms, and determine the best way to divide the force within the districts. The first training programs, moreover, were only barely adequate to prepare the force for its new duties.

By early 2010, however, the program was beginning to have noticeable impact. Local communities dissatisfied with Taliban influence in their areas were increasingly calling on the rapid-response force for assistance. And the provision by CENTCOM of several helicopters to facilitate the insertion of police forces into remote areas further strengthened perceptions that the provincial government was committed to standing with local communities. The special police force also took on another important role in mid-2010 when, at the request of the Pakistan army, it was expanded to "backfill" stability operations in the Swat valley following the military's formal departure. By late 2010 the force's area of operations had been expanded to 10 of the NWFP's 24 districts, and had contributed to a significant diminution of insurgent influence in the settled areas.

Concomitant with these programs focused on justice and policing, the U.S. State Department had in early 2009 initiated a more broad-based strategy of engagement at both the federal and provincial levels with right-of-center and religious parties. While these parties' rhetoric about American involvement in the region continued to be just as heated as ever, behind the scenes U.S. officials found the party leaders to be quite pragmatic, and interested — for their own reasons — in seeing the neo-Taliban insurgency wane in the Frontier, and in finding new vocational avenues for their *madrassah* graduates.

By the time that the PML-N engineered a surprise return to power in mid-2010, bringing with it greater participation by the religious parties in the NWFP, the U.S. had built a measure of trust with these groups. Working together with officials from the British, German, Saudi, and Emirati governments, American diplomats had begun a dialogue with *madrassah* leaders about practical ways to support programs that would drain support from the most extreme neo-Taliban activities, and provide new vocational training opportunities for their graduates.

ADDRESSING THE FATA: COUNTERINSURGENCY AND MRZS

It is 2010. Two years ago, it was clear that the security situation in the FATA was rapidly deteriorating. Localized insurgencies — from Bajaur to South Waziristan, and practically everywhere in between — were increasingly inter-connected. American security officials were consumed with targeting not only TTP, but also the Haqqanis' cross-border network based in Waziristan. Distrust between the U.S. and Pakistani governments had increased steadily over the years, and had come to a flash point following the American ground incursions from across the border in Afghanistan in September 2008.

As part of then-President Bush's $750 million aid pledge, USAID had begun implementing development programs in the FATA. A number of these projects were seen as innovative, but the collapsing security situation and the lack of any real governance framework in the tribal areas through which to implement meaningful political and economic change produced a growing skepticism in Washington that the funds would contribute to U.S. security objectives. The new government in Islamabad appeared at first to be open to substantive FATA reforms which might begin to integrate the tribal areas with the Pakistani mainstream, but, lacking political will, eventually fell back on plans which implemented reforms only at the margins.

U.S. military officials were similarly at a crossroads. Focus on the insurgency in Afghanistan was intensifying, and policy reviews of the situation in the Pakistani tribal areas made it clear that the lack of access — and, more fundamentally, the lack of a real government in the tribal areas — made any kind of "Anbar model" from Iraq almost impossible in the FATA. The egalitarian tribal structure of the Pashtuns also made it difficult to imagine sustaining *ad hoc* alliances in the absence of a broader political framework.

Realizing that the security, development, and governance challenges were increasingly inter-connected, U.S. officials settled on a new approach which adapted existing counterinsurgency models to the unique circumstances of the tribal areas: they would focus aid and stability efforts on a select number of Model Reform Zones (MRZs) in the FATA, each of which would also be given a new system of local governance and representation. Sponsored by an international consortium which grew out of the Friends of Pakistan initiative (and which was given strong public backing by Saudi Arabia, Turkey, and the United Arab Emirates), these zones would concentrate the effects of Pakistani development efforts, plant the seeds for political activity and sustainable governance frameworks, and create a demonstration effect throughout the tribal areas.

The MRZ effort required sustained negotiations and buy-in at the highest levels. The PPP-led government in Islamabad, although initially skeptical, eventually realized that the political gains from targeted, highly visible development efforts could be substantial; they also welcomed the excuse to put off major FATA-wide reforms which might be politically unpalatable. The ANP leadership in Peshawar saw the plan as a first step toward integrating the FATA with the NWFP, an idea that they had long called for. The religious parties saw opportunities for expanding their political presence in the tribal areas. And the Pakistan military agreed to the plan in exchange for U.S. commitments to provide special equipment for use in the MRZ areas in addition to increased access for Pakistani military officials to U.S. military training abroad. (The army leadership was somewhat ambivalent about undertaking counterinsurgency programs in the FATA, even in relatively peaceful areas. But pressure from the new CENTCOM commander, along with a deteriorating security situation which put nearly all of the $750 million in USAID projects at risk, convinced the military that the MRZ program was worth supporting.)

The program began with five MRZs, one in each of the five tribal agencies outside of Waziristan. Each zone encompassed approximately one *tehsil* (sub-agency administrative unit). The program was essentially "opt-in." Tribal communities in a particular area were presented with a deal: if they agreed to the establishment of an MRZ in their area, they would benefit from a windfall of development projects, as well as increased security assistance from the Frontier Corps. In return they would come under a redesigned governance framework which, while respecting local customs and traditions, would establish new institutions and rules for political competition.

The details of this plan contained a number of compelling political incentives. The government and the international consortium focused development projects in the MRZs and fielded extra personnel and resources, respectively, for the FC units who operated there. The military agreed not to operate regular army troops in the zones except under narrowly defined conditions. The office of the political agent retained its robust discretionary powers, but was stripped of the authorities granted under the antiquated Frontier Crimes Regulation to exact collective punishment. The government agreed to preserve *riwaj* (custom); to extend a right of judicial appeal to the Peshawar High Court; and to allow *qazi* courts under the oversight of the political agent. The government also set up a new wing within the Frontier Corps which, under the direction of the RCOs, acted analogously to the rapid-response police force in the settled areas.

The MRZ framework also established, for the first time, a substantive system of local governance in the FATA. Elected councils were set up at the *tehsil* and union council (sub-*tehsil*) levels, and elections were held on a party basis. A parallel structure of youth councils was also established in each *tehsil* in order to encourage political participation by the younger generation. These councils were given broad authority to propose local development initiatives — though the final approval rested with the bureaucracy in Peshawar — and each council member was given discretionary funds for development in his own constituency. The framework also provided for an interface between elected councils and local *jirgas*, with the latter being given a formal role in proposing development projects, handling complaints, and resolving disputes under the oversight of the political agent.

The plan included an array of efforts to obtain and sustain buy-in by local leaders. *Tehsil*-level elected leaders were granted observer status in the NWFP provincial assembly in Peshawar, and were afforded some of the privileges formerly retained by the *maliks,* such as the ability to distribute foreign work permits. Local *maliks,* who had long been the recipients of generous subventions by the state, were for the most part co-opted into the new system by the prospect of participating in the new (and lucrative) elected councils, of directing development projects to tribal clients, and of taking advantage of a special "transition fund" which continued to provide subventions at current levels for five years.

The political objective of the MRZs was to gradually incentivize an expansion of the state's writ in the tribal areas and institutionalize that expansion by cultivating new forms of political legitimacy. The reality, at least initially, proved to be more complicated. There were disputes and legal hurdles over the new administrative frameworks. It took time to raise new Frontier Corps levies which would operate in the MRZ areas. The first set of elections was marred by neo-Taliban attacks. And U.S. officials became concerned when some of the religious parties came to hold a sizeable number of seats in the governing councils.

Taliban groups targeted several of the reform zones during the first year, but only twice did the government have to bring in the regular army to clear the area and drive out insurgents. By late 2009, however, the dynamic was beginning to change. It had become clear that the state was committed to securing these areas, and to undertaking visible and community-driven development work. USAID capacity-building efforts were being extended to include training for NGOs and recent university graduates from nearby areas such as Peshawar, Kohat, Bannu, and Dera Ismail Khan. Once the security situation in the MRZs stabilized, the zones became a draw for NGOs, construction companies, and young people seeking work. There was even talk of situating a tariff-free Reconstruction Opportunity Zone (ROZ) in the area with support from a Punjabi textile magnate.

At the outset, the MRZs were criticized for simply displacing insurgent activity into other areas of the FATA, and indeed that was the short-term effect. But by the middle of 2010, it was increasingly obvious that the MRZs were having a broader impact: other tribal leaders were clamoring to see the program expanded to their regions; the government of Pakistan was able to point to tangible progress in local livelihoods, development indicators, and job creation; the state had learned, by trial and error, a great deal about coordinating security and development activities at the local level; new leaders were beginning to emerge in the MRZs who had a stake in local institutions and development; the religious parties were competing fiercely with the Pashtun nationalist politicians to demonstrate who could build the greatest number of basic health units; and, perhaps most importantly, the program had introduced a much-needed change dynamic to the FATA.

The MRZ elected leaders, meanwhile, had begun insisting that their observer status in the NWFP provincial assembly be converted into full membership, and there was a growing sense in the FATA that some kind of gradual administrative integration of the tribal areas into the NWFP would not necessarily come at the expense of *riwaj* or the special privileges which the tribes historically enjoyed. The debate over FATA reform had noticeably shifted, and although the situation in Waziristan was still very poor, there appeared to be a growing consensus about the need to bring institution-oriented reform to the tribal areas at large. From a security perspective, the MRZ experiment had done little to directly disrupt the hard-core neo-Taliban networks in the FATA. But combined with counterinsurgency-oriented programs in the NWFP, U.S. and Pakistani officials were cautiously optimistic that the MRZs had begun to isolate the insurgents to smaller and smaller areas of the FATA, create momentum for key structural reforms, and increase the reach and credibility of the state into areas which had previously been all but ungoverned.